CROSSCURRENTS

CROSSCURRENTS

West Indian Immigrants and Race

Milton Vickerman
University of Virginia

New York • Oxford
OXFORD UNIVERSITY PRESS
1999

Oxford University Press

Oxford   New York
Athens   Auckland   Bangkok   Bogotá   Buenos Aires   Calcutta
Cape Town   Chennai   Dar es Salaam   Delhi   Florence   Hong Kong   Istanbul
Karachi   Kuala Lumpur   Madrid   Melbourne   Mexico City   Mumbai
Nairobi   Paris   São Paulo   Singapore   Taipei   Tokyo   Toronto   Warsaw

and associated companies in
Berlin   Ibadan

Published by Oxford University Press, Inc.,
198 Madison Avenue, New York, New York 10016
http://www.oup-usa.org

Oxford is a registered trademark of Oxford University Press

Library of Congress Cataloging-in-Publication Data

Vickerman, Milton.
   Crosscurrents: West Indian immigrants and race / Milton Vickerman.
      p.   cm.
   Includes bibliographical references (p.   ).
   ISBN 0-19-511744-1 (cloth : alk. paper). — ISBN 0-19-511745-X
(pbk. : alk. paper)
   1. West Indian Americans—Race identity.   2. United States—Race
relations.   I. Title.
E184.W54V53 1999
305.896'9729—dc21   97-36958
                                                               CIP

9 8 7 6 5 4 3 2 1

Printed in the United States of America
on acid-free paper

For Hilary and Jessica

CONTENTS

PREFACE ix

INTRODUCTION 1

■ Adapting to American Society: Problems and Contradictions 3
■ Ethnic Identity 6
■ Constructing "West Indians" 9
■ Conclusion 12
■ A Note on Methodology 13
   Notes 14

CHAPTER 1 RACE IN JAMAICA 23

■ Race Relations in Jamaica: A Brief Overview of the Classic Model 27
■ Explaining Change in Jamaican Society 29
   Cultural Pluralism 29
   Adam Kuper's Analysis 31
   Carl Stone's Analysis 32
■ Factors Muting Racial Consciousness in Jamaica:
   Demography and Ideology 35
   The Role of Ideology 37
■ Race in Jamaica and the United States: A Brief Comparison 40
■ Conclusion 43
   Notes 45

CHAPTER 2 ECONOMICS AND MIGRATION 59

■ The Tradition of Immigration 59
   Immigration to the United States 61
■ West Indians in the Economy 63
   Ethnic Niches 66
   Ethnic Niches and Racial Issues 72
■ Conclusion 81
   Notes 82

CHAPTER 3   ENCOUNTERING RACE IN AMERICA   91

■ Apprehending the Salience of Race   92
■ Racial Encounters and Coping Strategies   96
   Confrontation   98
   Assertion   103
   Resignation   106
   Pragmatism   109
■ Racial Consciousness   112
■ Generalizing the West Indian Experience   120
■ Conclusion   126
   Notes   127

CHAPTER 4   ATTITUDES TOWARD AFRICAN AMERICANS   137

■ Social Distancing   139
   Southern Exceptionalism   144
■ The Pull of Race   147
   Political Responses   152
■ Role Modeling   155
■ Conclusion   159
   Notes   160

CHAPTER 5   IDENTITY IN A CHANGING SOCIETY   165

■ West Indians' Identity Options   167
   Opting for a "West Indian" Identity   169
   Continuing a Tradition: Distancing and Identification   172
■ The Second and Later Generations   173
■ Conclusion   177
   Notes   178

REFERENCES   183
INDEX   203

PREFACE

As more West Indians have entered the United States in recent years, the long-standing question of what they illustrate about race has only become more pressing. This focus on the issue of race reflects the fact that gaps, ranging from the economic to the perceptual, have persisted between blacks and whites, even as the society has diversified. The country's history has led to the presumption that these gaps result from antiblack attitudes and discrimination. While discrimination demonstrably existed in the first half of the present century, increasingly the argument is made that factors other than race determine the place of blacks in American society. West Indians seem to confirm this thesis, because though largely of the same ancestry as African Americans, viewed from the perspective of statistical indicators such as poverty rates and rates of welfare dependency, they outperform the latter group. Since such indicators appear to negate the effects of race, the question arises as to what other factors could help West Indians outperform African Americans. The answer has been advanced that the most important of these other factors is culture; that such attributes as possessing entrepreneurial skills, practicing alternative forms of capital accumulation (i.e., through rotating credit associations), and valuing higher education have enabled West Indians to achieve where African Americans have not.

The truth is that not just scholars, but West Indians themselves, often agree with the assessment that culture significantly affects the level of West Indian achievement. A few would even assert that race is not important at all. However, examining West Indians' perspective on American society shows that the sharp dividing line that has been drawn between race and other factors affecting achievement is fictional. This perspective stresses that multiple factors—especially culture, class, and race—intertwine to determine levels of achievement. The latter factor, ironically, is particularly important. This irony stems from a certain tendency to view West Indians as being oblivious to race; as examplars who are helping to point the way to a color-blind America. In truth, because of their history and culture, many West Indians would wish it so. They tend to be profoundly uncomfortable dealing with race, because, despite a history of colonialism, their societies socialize them to ignore it. Overt racism often surprises them. A few years ago, for instance, a friend of the writer's, visiting from Jamaica, responded with what can only be described as astonishment when told of the racial incidents which peppered New York in the 1980s. He found it unbelievable that at this late stage in the twentieth century, blatant racial violence still occurred. However, to those socialized in the West Indies—as this writer was—such attitudes are understandable. In many West Indian societies, the postindependence period of West Indian history has magnified a preexisting tendency to downplay racial issues, while emphasizing achievement through merit. This does not mean that racial issues are absent in the West Indians. Rather, these are so submerged that, often, West Indians hardly notice them. Just as important is the fact that, objectively speaking, racial tensions in most West Indian countries are at a much lower level than is the case in the United States. These realities mean that West Indians, for all their focus on achievement, view the United States as being intensely color-conscious, rather than color-blind.

The everyday lives of West Indian immigrants reveal to them that "blackness" carries a more severe stigma in the United States than in the West Indies. It takes them a long time to get used to this. In fact, the process of getting used to it tends to be quite painful—all the more so because, as Roy Bryce-Laporte has pointed out, West Indians have often been "invisible." Their invisibility is one reason why their attitudes toward race and their racial experiences deserve to be examined more closely: Where race is concerned, West Indians are dealing with the reality of everyday life, rather than with abstract notions of a "race issue" affecting the society. However, there is another reason why the West Indian encounter with race in America deserves closer attention: From a larger social and theoretical perspective, this encounter illustrates the social nature of race, shows West Indians to occupy an ambivalent position in the society, and illustrates that race remains a crucially important factor in the lives of all blacks. Despite their distinctive culture, West Indians find that where race is concerned their fate often merges with that of African Americans. Nevertheless, this distinctive culture is important, since it causes them to see race in America from a peculiarly West Indian point of view. What follows is a reporting and analysis of these immigrants' experiences and subjective viewpoints regarding race.

In writing this book, I have benefited greatly from discussions with, and comments from, friends and colleagues such as Donovan Dawes, Anthony Ferriera, Philip Kasinitz, Beverley Kerr, Paul Kingston, Edward Lehman, Murray Milner, Steve Nock, and Jan Rosenberg. Special thanks must also go to the many people who were patient enough to sit through hours of interviews and give me the benefit of their insight. In this respect, I am particularly thankful to Hyacinth Vickerman and her many close friends who helped me to gather my sample. Finally, I must add that my argument in this book has been shaped by the many researchers—especially Roy Bryce-

Laporte, Nancy Foner, Suzanne Model, Ransford Palmer, Orlando Patterson, Carl Stone, Constance Sutton, Roger Waldinger, and Mary Waters—who have written insightfully about West Indians.

Charlottesville, Virginia
June 1997

Introduction

In the curious[1] 1984 film, *The Adventures of Buckaroo Banzai Across the 8th Dimension*, an alien race attempts to conquer Earth but finds itself being opposed, and finally defeated, by a renegade[2] from within its own ranks. In positing such a storyline, *Buckaroo Banzai* presents typical science fiction melodrama and hardly seems to stand out in any way. However, apart from its unusual blending of science fiction, "action," and comedy, *Buckaroo Banzai* is unique among science fiction films because the renegade alien "hero" who helps to save Earth is a Rastafarian whose accent marks him as being unmistakably West Indian. This very unusual use of a West Indian character in a science fiction film is significant because it illustrates, well, that West Indians have started to register as a distinct presence on the American cultural landscape.

While, at first glance, the presence of a Rastafarian West Indian in a film of this genre appears very odd, in fact *The Adventures of Buckaroo Banzai* is only the most extreme example of several recent films, set in the United States, that have featured West Indian characters.[3] These include *Modern Problems* (1981), *Trading Places* (1983), *Clara's Heart* (1988), *Married to the Mob* (1988), *Marked for Death* (1990), *Predator II* (1990), *Thelma and Louise* (1991), *Whore* (1991), *Cool Runnings* (1993), and *Joey Breaker* (1993). Despite the diversity of themes represented by these films, they have in common a recognition that West Indians are a recognizable presence in the United States. This is not to argue that these films necessarily present West Indians in a positive light—they usually do not.[4] Rather, it is to make the important point that the culture has begun to reflect certain social realities.

One of these social realities is that large numbers of nonwhite immigrants have poured into the country over the past three decades. Data on immigration show a distinct decline in the numbers of Europeans migrating to the United States and a marked increase in immigration from Asia, Central and South America, and the West Indies. Where, for instance, about 92 percent of immigrants in the first decade of this century were Europeans; in the decade 1980 through 1990 they composed only about 13 percent. At the same time, the percentage of Asians climbed from 4 to approximately 37 percent and Latin Americans from 2 to 47 percent (Table I.1). West Indians, often defined as non-Hispanic individuals from countries in the Caribbean Sea, along with those from mainland territories—such as Guyana and Belize—with historical and cultural links,[5] have also migrated to the United States in large numbers over the past three decades. For instance, Jamaica, long the main source of West Indian immigrants, sent 79, 670 people between 1951 and 1970 but 357,959 between 1971 and 1993. During the same two periods, Guyana sent 8,582 and 147,946 immigrants; while Trinidad and Tobago sent 26,493 and 104,972 immigrants.[6] In 1995, Jamaica ranked ninth on the list of countries sending the most immigrants to this country.[7]

While the specific reasons for this large influx from the West Indies range from 1965 changes in American immigration law to favor the reunification of families, to the attainment of political independence by several West Indian countries, the effects in this country are clear enough. Distinct West Indian neighborhoods are to be found in the New York City core area of concentration, where estimates place West Indians at approximately 25 percent of the city's black population.[8] In neighborhoods such as Flatbush and Crown

TABLE I.1 Legal Immigration to the U.S., by Region of the World, 1901–1990

Decade	Total Number	Percentage of Total			
		Europe Total	Asia	Africa	Latin America[a]
1901–1910	8,795,386	91.6	3.7	0.1	2.1
1911–1920	5,735,811	75.3	4.3	0.1	7.0
1921–1930	4,107,209	60.0	2.7	0.2	14.4
1931–1940	528,431	65.8	3.0	0.3	9.7
1941–1950	1,035,039	60.0	3.1	0.7	14.9
1951–1960	2,515,479	52.7	6.1	0.6	22.2
1961–1970	3,321,677	33.8	12.9	0.9	38.6
1971–1979	4,493,314	17.8	35.3	1.8	40.3
1980–1990	7,388,000	12.5	37.3	3.1	47.1

Source: Adapted from Silvia Pedraza, "Origins and Destinies: Immigration, Race, and Ethnicity in American History," in *Origins and Destinies,* ed. Silvia Pedraza and Ruben Rumbaut (Belmont: Wadsworth, 1996), Table 1, p.4.

[a]Includes Mexico, Caribbean, Central America, and South America.

Heights in Brooklyn, St. Albans and Cambria Heights in Queens, and in portions of the North Bronx, reggae, calypso, and soca music mix with island accents and signs advertising such dishes as beef patties and roti to declare that these areas are West Indian. Symbolically, the clearest sign that West Indians form a distinct ethnic group is the annual Labor Day parade that wends it way along Eastern Parkway in Brooklyn. An all-day affair, the music, food, floats, and colorful costumes dotting the parade recall the annual carnival for which Trinidad has become famous. But if, as Kasinitz has argued, the Labor Day parade is the premier example of West Indians creating ethnicity from the ground up, it has also become a primary venue for a "top down" construction of ethnicity through political jockeying. The West Indian Labor Day parade is a choice venue for politicians seeking votes and "ethnic entrepreneurs" seeking to push particular agendas.[9]

ADAPTING TO AMERICAN SOCIETY: PROBLEMS AND CONTRADICTIONS

Although the West Indian presence in New York City and surrounding areas is, today, more obvious, it is not new. Several writers[10] have noted that this presence stretches back many decades. Perhaps the most well known has been Ira De A. Reid's seminal study, *The Negro Immigrant* (1939), which chronicled West Indian immigration to the United States in the first three decades of this century. In this work, Reid showed how racial discrimination combined with cultural differences between West Indians and African Americans to produce conflict in Harlem. This conflict stemmed, primarily, from the fact that West Indians, as demographic majorities in their home countries, had developed a self-confidence that was rooted in superior numbers. This demographic fact tended to offset the real racial discrimination, directed at blacks, existing in those societies. Moreover, West Indians, in contrast to Americans, had long interpreted race broadly: Being "black" or "white" or "colored" was subject to a degree of interpretation and did not predestine individuals to particular outcomes. Over time, these realities had formed attitudes in West Indians that made adjusting to more rigid American racial definitions and barriers very difficult. The difficulties of adjustment often manifested itself as chauvinism, while African Americans, for their part, resented the foreignness of West Indians and the economic threat they represented in the job market.

The issue of the economic adaptation of West Indian immigrants has, for practical and theoretical reasons, taken on great significance. Reid noted that while, as a general rule, West Indians struggled to adjust to the American economy, migration impacted these immigrants differently, depending on their occupational skills prior to migration. Unskilled workers made use of relatively greater opportunities existing in this country for training, but those with skills often faced downward mobility. One result, he argued, was that West Indians turned aggressively to self-employment in small businesses. This mode of adaptation, combined with the fact that a disproportionately large percentage of professionals in Harlem were West Indian (Reid estimated this at one-third), gave rise to the notion that West Indians have a particular predilection for starting and operating businesses. Picking up on this thread, later writers—e.g., Glazer and Moynihan in *Beyond the Melting Pot*[11] and Thomas Sowell in several publications[12]—have advanced the notion that cultural factors, and not racial discrimination, are the primary determinants of how much upward mobility blacks achieve in the United States. This literature has implied that West Indians can serve as models for the advancement of African Americans.

However, other aspects of the literature on West Indian immigrants have shown that the situation is more problematic than the modeling notion would suggest. For instance, Reid's discussion of the economic aspects of the adaptation of West Indians shows that more than culture was involved in the relative success of early immigrants: prior to migration, many had been afforded the opportunity—often denied to African Americans living under Jim Crow segregation—to attain advanced skills. More generally, West Indians' insertion into America's ethnic[13] hierarchy has always been very problematic; for while, in some respects, their presence seems to deny the potency of discriminatory barriers directed at blacks in particular, in other respects they match the African American population closely. Thus, for instance, West Indians tend to have higher median family incomes than African Americans, but they often live in segregated neighborhoods; they emphasize values favoring law and order, but find themselves subjected to police harassment; and they often self-consciously wish to be viewed as a distinct, hard-working ethnic group, but must contend with the reality that powerful mainstream agents such as the media often present a uniformly negative portrayal of blacks.

Contradictions such as these are an inherent part of the West Indian experience in the United States. In an insightful discussion of this fact, Bryce-Laporte has argued that, "Black immigrants operate—as blacks and immigrants—in the United States under more levels of cross-pressures, multiple affiliations, and inequalities than either native blacks or European immigrants."[14] He attributes this to such factors as their origin in racially discriminatory societies with long histories of colonialism that have nevertheless successfully downplayed the notion that race is important to social advancement; their foreignness, which affords a modicum of exoticness in the United States, even while they are being discriminated against as blacks; and their being torn between the desire to return to their homelands and the realization that economic, social, and (sometimes) political conditions make such a return unfeasible.[15]

The fact that the West Indian experience in the United States involves inherent contradictions is the central thesis of this book. It seeks to examine, using primary and a variety of secondary data, the attitudes of present-day West Indian immigrants toward race, by placing these within the framework of cross-pressures. As noted by Bryce-Laporte and elsewhere in the literature[16] on West Indian immigrants, the concept of cross-pressures provides a useful tool for explaining the situation of these immigrants, because it conjures up the notion of contending forces pulling at a group. As has been shown in the social sciences literature, the existence of these forces tends to lessen the ability to predict the behavior of individuals. For instance, cross-pressures have been found to cause voters to procrastinate, to exhibit unstable voting behavior, and to withdraw from the political process altogether.[17] With respect to religion, individuals subject to cross-pressures have been found to exhibit discrepancies between their stated religious preference and actual participation in religious organizations espousing doctrines consistent with these preferences.[18] In ethnic relations, cross-pressures have been found to splinter intragroup unity in situations where ethnic groups are engaging in conflict with other groups.[19]

In the case of West Indians, the primary forces producing cross-pressures are, on the one hand, conservative[20] socialization in societies in which they form majorities and which urge them to downplay race while emphasizing merit; and, on the other, immersion into a host-society (the United States) which provides greatly expanded opportunities for upward mobility but which also views race as being a key organizing principle. In other words, generally speaking, the attitudes exhibited by West Indian immigrants in this country derive from the conflict between the strong desire for upward mobility that is implied in the immigrant ethos, and the existence of an entrenched ethnic hierarchy which tends to tightly constrain individuals of African ancestry. One "story" about which I write is of the structural conditions generating these cross-pressures and how West Indians cope with them. In the process, I describe the factors in their societies that cause West Indians to downplay race and how this impacts the racial problems which they encounter in America. With respect to all this, a very important subtheme centers on the role African Americans play in helping West Indians define their identity in America. As it turns out, African Americans are the focal point at which contending views of race meet.

Concretely, these contending views are about the relationship between race and achievement and West Indians have become entangled in this debate because they are mostly of African ancestry but display fairly high socioeconomic indicators. However, there has been a tendency to highlight only those aspects of the West Indian immigrant experience that show them emulating other ethnic groups who have achieved material success; a tendency to portray them as individuals who effortlessly overcome the constraints of race to achieve the "American dream." The reality is more complex than this. The experience of West Indians illustrates an important truth about race in present-day America: Despite significant changes over the past few decades, permitting blacks greater upward mobility, race continues to profoundly affect their quality of life. Hence, discussions of the latter—the real reason why conceptions of race matter—cannot properly be formulated in an either/or manner. Instead, on the contemporary scene, we find the existence of a counterintuitive reality: opportunities for upward mobility for blacks mixed with continuing high levels of discrimination. This contradictory situation, rather than social advancement in the absence of racial barriers, is the norm for many West Indians and upwardly mobile African Americans. Thus, in the process of describing how West Indians manage their cross-pressures, I also show how they highlight the contradictions facing blacks in present-day America.

■ ETHNIC IDENTITY

This juxtaposition of West Indians and African Americans is not accidental. It is well known that the question of who is black, the mechanisms involved in the construction of notions of "blackness," and the consequences of being defined as such are issues that have long resided at the heart of racial problems in the United States.[21] The voluminous literature on race and ethnicity in this country has pointed to the fact that blacks are the exception to many of the assumptions undergirding "America" and what it means to be "American." For instance, the idea that America is a "melting pot" is true only of individuals defined as "whites," some Asians, and some Hispanics.[22] Those defined as "black," on the other hand, have always been seen as inferior, a component of the population that has been excluded, confined, and restricted. And if America is a "land of opportunity," then blacks have been able to appropriate this opportunity only very slowly. Even West Indians, who like other immigrants are—in the words of Bryce-Laporte—"ardent practitioners" of the Protestant work ethic,[23] find that skin color, though only one factor affecting upward mobility, is a powerful hindrance which cannot be discounted.

American definitions of who is black are consequential because of the continued salience of race in this country and because, being very strict, they also implicate black immigrants. To use the term *definitions*, however, is to imply that ideas of "blackness," like ideas of ethnicity, in general, are socially constructed rather than being "primordial." The former conceptualization, rather than the latter, is the perspective which guides my argument in this book. From the perspective of primordialist theory, ethnic groups derive from inborn ineffable sentiments that tie together members of such groups. These sentiments are viewed as being a priori and belonging to members of ethnic groups by virtue of being born into such groups. In this sense, ethnic sentiments are a natural endowment for such individuals. Isaacs, for instance, defines ethnicity as, "the ready-made set of endowments and identifications which every individual shares with others from the moment of birth by the chance of the family into which he is born at that given time in that given place."[24]

These endowments consist, most importantly, of an individual's physical appearance, name, culture, nationality, religion, and an internalization of the geographical characteristics typical of the place in which the individual is born. Similarly, van den Berghe has posited that ethnic sentiments are rooted in genetics. He argues that human beings desire to maximize their reproductive success and, therefore, tend to favor kin to nonkin and close kin over those who are more distant. Ethnic groups are an extension of the principle of kinship, since these groups help to maximize reproductive success. Just as kin can be expected to favor each other over nonkin, so individuals belonging to ethnic groups can be expected to favor each other over individuals who are perceived as being nongroup members. Thus, ethnic group bonds are inherent and functional for the continued existence of such groups.[25]

In contrast to the primordialist perspective, the social constructionist view of ethnicity holds that ethnic sentiments derive from social interaction occurring within specific economic, political, and historical contexts. Therefore, rather than being inherent, mysterious,[26] and fixed, these sentiments are variable and often serve rational purposes. Ethnic identity derives from a combination of social processes that are internal to a group and external societal definitions that amount to a form of labeling.[27] This interaction causes both the contents of ethnic groups (i.e., the internal practices defining ethnicity) and group boundaries to be variable. For instance, Nagel and Snipp have shown how some Native American tribes have undertaken ethnic reorganization as a means of surviving outside pressures. This reorganization has taken such forms as changing the rules defining membership to make these rules more exclusionary, in some cases, and in others, more inclusionary; changing the norms regulating marriage; reorganizing the tribes' political structure; and adopting new economic activities to ensure the survival of groups.[28] Similarly, Verkuyten, De Jong, and Masson have shown how native-born Dutch whites, through discourse, construct notions of what it means to be "Dutch" by varying conceptions of "we" and "they" to exclude foreigners, regardless of their legal status.[29]

The variability pertaining to ethnic groups affects not only their internal culture and boundaries but also the existence, or not, of these groups. That is, ethnic groups may emerge where none existed before, or groups that were once identifiable may become dormant and then reemerge at a later date. Nagel has referred to the former as emergent ethnic groups and the latter as resurgent ethnic groups.[30] Both types often result as a rational response to particular societal conditions, but this is not to argue that affective bonds are unimportant.[31] Also, it needs to be remembered that powerful outside agencies, notably the state, fashion the overall parameters of responses undertaken by ethnic groups.[32] Bearing this in mind, it could be argued that "African Americans" are an emergent group in the sense that they have creatively utilized a history of oppression to fashion a distinctive culture from the several African tribes that were forcibly intermingled under slavery.[33] Patterson has also given a good example of emergent ethnicity that derives from the desire to consolidate material wealth. He has shown that Chinese immigrants in Jamaica and Guyana incorporated into those two societies very differently, even though both groups of Chinese originated in approximately the same location and came to the West Indies around the same time. In Jamaica, the Chinese managed to gain control over the grocery business and, having done so, set about the construction of affective bonds in an effort to consolidate their lock on that business. That is, the development of the Chinese as an ethnic group in Jamaica took place after, and in response to, their having carved out a particular economic niche. Moreover, the early wave of Jamaican Chinese, in the construction of their ethnicity, incorporated as fully "Chinese," mixed race children who had resulted from relationships between Chinese men and black women. While the construction of this ethnicity slowed, for several decades, the assimilation of the Chinese into Jamaican society, in Guyana they quickly and fully assimilated as Guyanese. This was a response to the fact that in the latter society they could not dominate any particular economic niche and concluded that the path to success lay in becoming a part of the larger society.[34] A good example of resurgent ethnicity would be the revival of such sentiments among white Americans in the 1960s and 1970s. This resurgence is noteworthy because, after an initial period of discrimination, white ethnics had very successfully assimilated into American society. However, in the climate of heightened group awareness accompanying the Civil Rights movement, many whites found it appropriate to assert, through emphasizing their particular national backgrounds, their own sense of distinctiveness.[35]

The point made earlier, with respect to the role of outside forces in limiting expressions of ethnic identity, has special relevance for individuals who are defined as "black." As writers such as Gans, Waters, and Alba[36] have shown, ethnic identity in the United States occurs on something of a continuum, with whites having the greatest freedom to manipulate it and blacks, the least. In the case of the former, successful assimilation has reduced the costs of being "ethnic." Consequently, for many white Americans, ethnicity has become "symbolic"—an aspect of life which, if expressed, adds "spice" but does not seriously affect quality of life. Because of intermarriage, whites may choose from a wide range of ethnicities (reflecting the background of their ancestors); or choose not to be ethnic at all but simply unhypenated

Americans.[37] Blacks, on the other hand, being defined primarily by skin color and African ancestry, find the expression of any identity other than "black" very difficult.[38] While whites may choose to be "Irish Americans," "Italian Americans," or "Hungarian Americans," the society tends to look askance at claims, among blacks, of being—for instance—"Nigerian American" or "Kenyan American."[39]

These limitations are of special consequence to West Indians, since they form the largest body of black immigrants to the United States. Much of my discussion in this book revolves around how West Indians attempt to deal with the societally imposed restraints on individuals of African ancestry. Despite a history of racial discrimination and continuing color consciousness in many West Indian societies, powerful forces suppress the overt expression of racialism in those societies. However, this century has also seen the development of racial pride—notably through the growth of Rastafarianism—among the black majorities in many of these societies. These facts result in the apparent paradox of many West Indians, at one and the same time, attempting to be raceless through an emphasis on merit and expressing pride in African ancestry. This contradiction is only apparent, since, from the viewpoint of West Indians, being of African ancestry and emphasizing merit are not contradictory.[40] Their whole socialization constantly exposes them to daily experiences in which blacks hold a wide range of occupations. As immigrants, they capture these experiences and characteristics in the identity "West Indian," which combines the aforementioned pride in African ancestry and focus on merit with somewhat conservative social values. In terms of the social construction of ethnicity, they attempt, through viewing themselves as "West Indians" to overcome, altogether, the imposed and confining American racial category "black," through redefining this concept (i.e., the "contents" of "blackness") to reflect the more positive West Indian view. Whether or not West Indian immigrants can successfully accomplish this is an open question, since, as noted before, the social pressure to conform to this society's conceptualization of what it means to be "black" is very strong. In fact, as I show in what follows, and as shown by Waters in her work among second-generation West Indians,[41] these immigrants are to be found at different stages in the assimilation process. Most immigrants, it would seem, strongly hold to the identity "West Indian," while the second and later generations exhibit a stronger tendency to accept the American definition of "blackness."

■ CONSTRUCTING "WEST INDIANS"

In the United States, the very concept "West Indian" is, itself, socially constructed. In areas with high concentrations of these immigrants—especially in New York City—the West Indian community consists of individuals from many different islands. A sojourn in the Flatbush area of Brooklyn, for instance, will show Jamaicans, Trinidadians, Barbadians, Anguillans, Grenadans, and Haitians (just to name a few) living side by side, often in the same buildings.[42] As a Jamaican immigrant, myself, this writer has long had personal experience of this geographic and social commingling.

Yet, given the uncertainties surrounding the definition of the term "West Indian," the interaction between various immigrants from the Caribbean is, in some ways, unexpected. The "West Indies" has been defined in various ways by different writers and agencies. Some adopt a wider view, seeing the term as being coterminous with the word "Caribbean." This perspective tends to concatenate the islands in the Caribbean Sea, Central American countries, and countries on the South American mainland that border the Caribbean Sea. American foreign policy toward the region has tended to adopt this perspective. For instance, the list of countries intended as targets for the Caribbean Basin Initiative shows that the Reagan administration adopted a unified view of the whole region. These countries included Anguilla, The Bahamas, Jamaica, The Dominican Republic, El Salvador, Suriname, Panama, and Guyana.[43] On the other hand, some writers adopt a very narrow view of the "West Indies." For instance, historian Gordon Lewis has defined it as including the English-speaking territories in the Caribbean Sea, in Central America, and on the South American mainland.[44] Intermediate between these two views is the one which keeps the broad definition but excludes the Spanish-speaking territories of Cuba, Puerto Rico, and Santo Domingo, viewing these as being more similar to Central and South America because of language and culture.[45] From this perspective, the "West Indies" incorporates the British, French, and Dutch islands in the Caribbean Sea; and mainland societies—British Guyana, French Guyana, and Suriname in South America, and Belize in Central America—with strong cultural and historical ties to these islands.[46] In this book, I adopt the intermediate position although, like Lewis, I am primarily concerned with immigrants from the Anglophone territories.

Focusing on the Anglophone Caribbean will show that this region has exhibited basic cultural similarities because of the existence of a common language, educational system, pastimes—especially cricket—political institutions, and, under colonialism, policies originating in London and directed toward the region as a whole. Despite these important underlying similarities, however, unity among the various territories that constitute the Anglophone Caribbean has, historically, been problematic. One basic problem has been geographic—for instance, Jamaica is 1100 miles from Trinidad. This geographic spread has tended to combine with nationalistic proclivities to thwart political unity. The best known example of this obstacle was the failure, in 1962, to create a Caribbean federation; a failure that has been attributed to, among other things, rivalry between Jamaica and Trinidad as to which country would lead the new political entity, fears in the larger islands that they would bear a disproportionate burden in carrying the lesser developed islands of the Eastern Caribbean,[47] and opposition, in an era of intense nationalism, to the federation as representing the class interests of the old colonial order.[48] In contrast, attempts at economic unity have been somewhat more successful, with the formation, in 1968, of CARIFTA and CARICOM, in 1973. However, even these entities have encountered difficulties bringing about true regional economic integration, because of the conflicting interests of the various countries and the overall dependent status of the Caribbean. For instance, while population distribution is skewed in favor of Jamaica, Trinidad and Barbados have healthier economies; and when faced with economic recessions, individual island governments tend to react by closing their borders to imports from other CARICOM countries.[49]

Considering, together, the underlying similarities and strains existing in the Anglophone Caribbean, it could be said that, at most, people in the region exhibit a sort of proto-ethnicity. That is, only the preconditions for ethnicity, rather than a real regionwide sense of ethnicity, exist within the region. It takes settlement in metropolitan centers such as London and New York City to fully form this sense of ethnicity. In these and other cities abroad, Anglophone West Indians confront the difficulties of adjusting to new societies, as manifested in such factors as dealing regularly with people of other nationalities, obtaining employment, and finding places to live.[50] Due to previous patterns of settlement and racial discrimination, these immigrants find themselves living in particular areas. Over time, these interactions and structural impositions magnify the underlying similarities between Anglophone West Indians and erode the differences. The strength of this magnification is seen in the fact that the category "West Indian" has extended to embrace individuals—notably Haitians and other French speakers—from the other culture areas in the Caribbean. This process of ethnic construction is not "natural" in the sense of being primordial. Rather, as those who have written about West Indian immigrants have shown, these immigrants, through a combination of social interaction—such as the Labor Day Carnival—and deliberate political mobilization have striven to create a distinct sense of themselves as "West Indians." The process whereby they have done this recalls Lopez and Espiritu's theory of panethnicity, in which ethnic subgroups develop bridging organizations and feelings of solidarity to form a larger and stronger ethnic group.[51] These writers' suggestion that this process is facilitated by structural similarities, and can be observed on both the organizational and interpersonal levels (through intramarriage), applies well to West Indians. For instance, with respect to the first point, West Indians tend to occupy a similar niche in the economy (e.g., low level service work) and display similar levels of income;[52] with respect to the latter point, it has been found that West Indian immigrants express a preference for marrying other West Indians rather than non-West Indians.[53]

In this book, I take the attitudes of Jamaican immigrants to be typical of those of other West Indian immigrants. This is not to discount the existence of cultural variations that are peculiar to immigrants from other territories in the region. Rather, it is to argue—as I stated earlier—that the similarities between West Indian immigrants outweigh their differences.[54] For instance, Stafford has shown that on a variety of issues, Haitians exhibit responses that are very similar to those of Anglophone West Indians.[55] Yet, another reason for viewing Jamaicans as being representative of other West Indian immigrants is that the former make up the largest segment of that immigrant community. Moreover, from a subjective point of view, Jamaican immigrants tend to see few differences between themselves and other immigrants from the West Indies—especially those from the Anglophone territories. For instance, in drawing in-group/out-group lines, the Jamaicans whom I interviewed tended to make distinctions between "West Indians" (non-Hispanic immigrants and their descendants from the Caribbean—especially the Anglophone territories) and non-West Indians (e.g., whites and African Americans), rather than between immigrants from individual West Indian territories. The argument that Jamaicans are representative of other West Indians might possibly be weaker in the case of Trinidadian and Guyanese immigrants, since those two societies, unlike many others in the West Indies, tend to see overt conflict between individuals of African and East Indian descent. However, in interacting with individuals from those territories, this writer has not discerned any noticeable difference between these immigrants and those from other parts of the West Indies.

■ CONCLUSION

West Indians form a significant component of the "new immigration" that was ushered in by the 1965 Immigration Act. This is especially true in their core area of settlement, New York City, where approximately one-half of West Indian immigrants live.[56] These immigrants originate in a variety of culture areas in the Caribbean but a combination of structural constraints—primarily racial—, previous settlement patterns, and social processes that are internal to these immigrants combine to strengthen underlying similarities between them. They are in the process of becoming a distinct ethnic group.

The processes shaping this sense of ethnicity are best understood as being social rather than primordial in nature. That is, they can be traced to distinct historical and social factors and their sense of "West Indianness" is not inherent or mysterious. That this is the case is shown by the fact that in the West Indies, group identification tends to revolve primarily around national origin, while, in this country, national origin tends to becomes a factor of secondary importance. What becomes primarily important is the reality that immigrants from the West Indies encounter social conditions that impress on them their basic similarities, as compared to the Americans with whom they deal on a daily basis. Of these social conditions, the most significant is that they enter a society with a distinct ethnic hierarchy, in which individuals who are defined as "black" tend to occupy the bottom rungs. Race, therefore, looms as a very significant factor in the adjustment of West Indians to American society, because most of them are of African ancestry. However, despite a history of colonialism and continuing color consciousness, West Indian societies tend to downplay race and emphasize merit as the basis for upward mobility. West Indians are socialized to minimize race and are inculcated with conservative values; moreover, their primary impetus for migrating is economic. These contending forces set up cross-pressures that tend to shape how West Indians react to race and other issues in the United States. Their responses reflect their racial identification as "black"—but defined in a West Indian, rather than American sense—their conservative social values, and their focus on attaining economic success in America.

In chapter 1, using Jamaica as an example and contrasting it with the United States, I describe how the cross-pressures affecting West Indians originate. In chapter 2, I describe the West Indians' focus on "making it" in America, and in chapter 3, I show the difficulties they have dealing with American racism. I conclude the chapter by drawing parallels between West Indians and African Americans, arguing as others have done that opportunities for upward mobility exist for blacks but these are in the face of continuing racism. In chapter 4, I discuss West Indians' attitudes toward African Americans, making the point that it is here that one sees most clearly how cross-pressures affect West Indians. Chapter 5 concludes the book by reviewing the structural reasons for the cross-pressures that affect West Indians and showing how these cross-pressures interact with West Indians' problem of defining ethnic identity in a society that still maintains strict rules for blacks, even while it is becoming more heterogeneous.

■ A NOTE ON METHODOLOGY

The discussion I put forth in this book is based on a combination of primary data, census data, and insights derived from being an insider in the West Indian community. The primary data consist of 106 interviews I conducted with Jamaican immigrants between 1988 and 1990, using a "snowball" sample. To do this, I initially contacted individual Jamaicans with whom I was acquainted. These referred me to acquaintances and so on. In this manner, I was able to interview immigrants across the New York City area.[57]

Most interviews were conducted at the immigrants' homes, some at their workplaces, and some at my home. The interviews were open-ended, tape-recorded, and took approximately one hour and a half. I attempted to interview Jamaicans performing a variety of occupations and who had resided in the United States varying lengths of time. Eventually, I interviewed sixty men who were in white collar occupations (e.g., accountants and college professors) and forty-six in blue collar occupations (e.g., mechanics and metal fabricators). The average age of the men was forty-one years and they had resided in the United States an average of 11.5 years.

One obvious disadvantage of this methodology is that it often presents a male point of view. However, in this book I augment this standpoint with informal discussions, on various aspects of West Indian immigrant life, which I have had with immigrant female acquaintances over an extended period of time. A second disadvantage of the methodology is that, in a strict statistical sense, it is not representative. Also, in my formal interviews, as an insider, I ran the risk of biasing the immigrants' responses. However, to minimize that risk I tried to inject myself into the discussion as little as possible and allowed the respondents to speak at length on various issues. For me, being an insider was an advantage, since it allowed the Jamaicans to reveal more of themselves than would, perhaps, otherwise be the case. After conducting many interviews, I noticed that certain themes kept recurring and, more, the Jamaicans' responses corresponded with each other. This served as a very rough check of internal validity. Being an insider also helped in that respect, since it helped me to understand whether what was being said made intuitive sense. However, the strongest evidence that the Jamaicans' responses in this particular study resonate with the concerns of the larger West Indian community is the fact that these responses correspond with those of other researchers in the field. In the end, my observations compose only a small part of ongoing research that is being conducted by many researchers in a fairly understudied area.

Notes

1. Reviewers of the film have termed it "curiously appealing," "offbeat," and "silly." See Steven Goldman, "The Adventures of Buckaroo Banzai Across the 8th Dimension," in *The Time Out Film Guide*, ed. Tom Milne (London: Penguin Books, 1991), p. 6; *Video Hound's Golden Movie Retriever* (Detroit: Visible Ink Press, 1994), p. 84; and Mick Martin and Marsha Porter, *Video Movie Guide 1994* (New York: Ballantine Books, 1993), p. 998.
2. He is aided by a team of Earth adventurers led by the eponymous, Buckaroo Banzai.
3. Usually, the films clearly announce the entrance of a West Indian character by

playing a reggae or calypso soundtrack and (often) show a dreadlocked individual.

4. For instance, *Marked for Death* presents stereotypes of Jamaicans that are so extreme that the film has been termed racist. See, for example, Carolyn Cooper, *Noises in the Blood* (Durham: Duke University Press, 1995), p. 97.

5. See below for a discussion of definitions of the term *West Indies*.

6. Immigration and Naturalization Service, *1991 Statistical Yearbook*.

7. Immigration and Naturalization Service, *1995 Statistical Yearbook*.

8. The 1990 census records, for the various locations, the percentage of the black population that is foreign-born. If New York City is defined as including The Bronx, Brooklyn, Manhattan, Queens, and Staten Island, the percentage of that city's population that is foreign-born comes to approximately 27 percent. The bulk of these immigrants are known to be of West Indian origin. If Africans, the next largest group of black immigrants, are subtracted from this overall figure, one arrives at approximately 25 percent (about 517,552 immigrants) of the city's black population being foreign-born (i.e., West Indians). However, individual boroughs can exhibit even higher percentages. For instance, Brooklyn records a figure of approximately 32 percent foreign-born (31 percent if African are subtracted).

9. Philip Kasinitz, *Caribbean New York* (Ithaca: Cornell University Press, 1992); Philip Kasinitz and Judith Freidenberg-Herbstein, "The Puerto Rican Parade and West Indian Carnival: Public Celebrations in New York City," in *Caribbean Life In New York: Sociocultural Dimensions*, ed. Constance R. Sutton and Elsa M. Chaney (New York: Center for Migration Studies, 1987), pp. 327–350; "The Caribbean American Labor Day Parade." *Focus*, Vol. 1, No. 3 (October, 1988): 1–9. As the West Indian Labor Day parade has attained a higher profile in recent years, it has drawn greater interest from the media. See, for instance, the *New York Times* editorial entitled, "Caribbean New York" (*New York Times*, September 7, 1994): A22; Matthew Purdy, "Parade Shows off West Indian Political Clout" (*New York Times*, September 7, 1994): A1; and Charisse Jones, "West Indian Parade Returns to Fill Streets of Brooklyn" (*New York Times*, September 1, 1996): B41.

10. See, for example, Gilbert Osofsky, *Harlem: The Making of a Ghetto* (New York: Harper Torchbooks, 1965); Harold Cruse, *The Crisis of the Negro Intellectual* (New York: William Morrow and Company, 1967); Roi Ottley and William J. Weatherby, *The Negro in New York: An Informal Social History* (New York: Praeger Publishers, 1967); Dennis Forsythe, "West Indian Radicalism in America: An Assessment of Ideologies," in *Ethnicity in the Americas*, ed. Frances Henry (The Hague: Mouton Publishers, 1976); Keith S. Henry, "Caribbean Migrants in New York: The Passage from Political Quiescence to Radicalism," *Afro-Americans in New York Life and History*, Vol. II, No. 2, (July 1978): 29–41; Reed Ueda, "West Indians," in *Harvard Encyclopedia of American Ethnic Groups*, ed. Stephan Thernstrom, Ann Orlov, and Oscar Handlin (Cambridge: Harvard University Press, 1980), pp. 1020–1027; Roy S. Bryce-Laporte, "Introduction," in *Caribbean Immigration to the United States*, ed. Roy S. Bryce-Laporte and Delores Mortimer (Washington, D.C.: Research Institute on Immigration and

Ethnic Studies, 1983), pp. v–x; Kasinitz, *Caribbean New York*; Irma Watkins-Owens, *Blood Relations* (Bloomington: University of Indiana Press, 1996).

11. In a later work, *Ethnicity: Theory and Experience*, Glazer and Moynihan also clearly outline the argument that groups differ in status according to how closely their norms match those of a dominant culture. See, "Introduction," in *Ethnicity: Theory and Experience*, ed. Nathan Glazer and Daniel Patrick Moynihan (Cambridge: Harvard University Press, 1975), pp. 1–26.

12. See, for example, *Ethnic America: A History* (New York: Basic Books, 1981); *Markets and Minorities* (New York: Basic Books, 1981); *The Economics and Politics of Race* (New York: Quill, 1983).

13. Here, I am using the term *ethnic* in a broad sense to refer to a wide variety of groups that demonstrate a subjective sense of belonging together and/or have an identity imposed on them. Although these processes differ from each other, they are closely related, since the process of labeling a group often serves as a catalyst for members of that group to develop a subjective sense of identification, around the label or other criteria. A race, as a type of ethnic group, is particularly important in this respect, since races are often defined by powerful outsiders (e.g., the state) using physical criteria that are peculiar to particular groups. With respect to this, the important point is that the physical criteria do not have intrinsic meaning but, rather, derive meaning from the particular society in which they are embedded. This means that individuals with similar features can be defined differently in different societies. For instance, West Indians have long recognized the existence of a distinct "colored" or mixed race category intermediate between "blacks" and "whites." However, in the United States, such individuals have been considered "black." Another important aspect of the social definition of race is that once a group is labeled a "race," it becomes very difficult for individuals in such a group to change their identity. Indeed, the "racial" designation tends to facilitate discriminatory treatment. In the United States, this appears to be more true of "racial" groups than of other types of ethnic groups. The evidence seems to be more in favor of those (e.g., Hacker, 1991) who argue that being defined as "black" carries a special stigma, rather than those (e.g., Kristol, 1966) who argue that such a designation does not place special impediments in the path of individuals carrying the label. See, for example, F. James Davis, *Who Is Black? One Nation's Definition* (University Park: The University of Pennsylvania Press, 1991); Andrew Hacker, *Two Nations: Black and White, Separate, Hostile, and Unequal* (New York: Charles Scribner's Sons, 1992); Sharon Lee, "U.S. Census Racial Classifications: 1890–1990," *Ethnic and Racial Studies*, Vol. 16, No.1 (January 1993): 75–94; Richard Jenkins, "Rethinking Ethnicity: Identity, Categorization and Power," *Ethnic and Racial Studies*, Vol. 17, No. 2 (April 1994): 197–223; Jonathan Marks, *Human Biodiversity* (New York: Aldine de Gruyter, 1995); Irving Kristol, "The Negro Today Is Like the Immigrant of Yesterday," in *Nation of Nations: The Ethnic Experience and the Racial Crisis*, ed. Peter I. Rose (New York: Random House, 1972 [1966]), pp. 197–210; Ronald Takaki, "Reflections on Racial Patterns in America," in *From Different Shores*, ed. Ronald Takaki (New York: Oxford University Press, 1987), pp. 26–37; Gregory Howard Williams, *Life on the Color Line* (New York: Dutton, 1995).

14. "Black Immigrants: The Experience of Invisibility and Inequality," *Journal of Black Studies* (September 1972): 29–56.
15. "Caribbean Migration to the United States: Some Tentative Conclusions," in *Caribbean Immigration to the United States*, ed. Roy S. Bryce-Laporte and Delores Mortimer (Washington, D.C.: Research Institute on Immigration and Ethnic Studies, 1983), pp. 193–204.
16. That this concept is implicit or explicit in much of the literature can be seen in discussions as widely spaced as Reid's, *The Negro Immigrant* and Linda Basch's, "The Politics of Caribbeanization: Vincentians and Grenadians in New York," in *Caribbean Life in New York: Sociocultural Dimensions*, ed. Constance R. Sutton and Elsa M. Chaney (New York: Center for Migration Studies, 1987), pp. 160–181.
17. Bernard R. Berelson, Paul F. Lazarsfeld, and William N. McPhee, *Voting* (Chicago: The University of Chicago Press, 1954).
18. Wade Clark Roof, "The Ambiguities of 'Religious Preference' in Survey Research—A Methodological Note," *Public Opinion Quarterly* 44 (3) (1980): 403–407.
19. Stephen S. Fugita, and David J. O'Brien, "Economics, Ideology, and Ethnicity: The Struggle between the United Farm Workers Union and the Nisei Farmers League," *Social Problems*, Vol. 5 (1977): 146–156.
20. By this, I mean that they often subscribe to values and norms of behavior which, in this country, would be labeled "traditional." Journalist Larry Rohter, commenting on the differences between foreigners' expectations and the realities of life in the West Indies, captured this conservative bent when he wrote: "As visitors are often surprised to discover, the Caribbean is full of morally conservative societies often appalled by what they see as the licentiousness of their visitors and the complicity of their rulers. Barbados, the most prosperous and content of the eastern tourist islands, is probably the best example of that sort of rectitude. But other islands . . . forbid topless or nude bathing as well, and their residents seethe when moneyed tourists blithely ignore those regulations . . ." ["The Real Caribbean: Paradise Stops at the Beach's Edge" (*New York Times*, February 16, 1997), Section 4: 1]. Similarly, Rohter has argued that West Indians favor capital punishment and, because of this, have expressed popular dissatisfaction with the Privy Council (the British-based court of final appeal) for its perceived "softness" on the issue. See "Death-Row Rule Sours Caribbean on Britain" (*New York Times*, July 7, 1997): A1. In the United States, West Indian social conservatism manifests itself, for instance, in a clash between their belief in corporal punishment and the reluctance of many Americans to physically punish children. See Celia Dugger, "A Cultural Reluctance to Spare the Rod" (*New York Times*, February 29, 1996): B1. It should also be noted, however, that despite their social conservatism, West Indians have often played leading roles in various far-left political organizations. Moreover, like African Americans, West Indians tend to vote Democratic. See, for instance, Cruse, *The Crisis of the Negro Intellectual;* Henry, "Caribbean Migrants in New York: The Passage from Political Quiescence to Radicalism"; and Kasinitz, *Caribbean New York*.
21. See, for example, F. James Davis, *Who Is Black?: One Nation's Definition*.
22. The usage of these terms recognizes that they are problematic, since they mask

wide variation between groups exhibiting different cultures and enjoying different levels of socioeconomic success.

23. Bryce-Laporte, "Black Immigrants," p. 44.

24. Harold Isaacs, "Basic Group Identity: The Idols of the Tribe," in *Ethnicity: Theory and Experience*, ed. Nathan Glazer and Daniel Patrick Moynihan (Cambridge: Harvard University Press, 1975), pp. 30–52.

25. Pierre van den Berghe, "Race and Ethnicity: A Sociobiological Perspective," *Ethnic and Racial Studies*, Vol. 1, No. 4 (October 1978): 401–411; "Ethnicity and the Sociobiology Debate," in *Theories of Race and Ethnic Relations*, ed. John Rex and David Mason (New York: Cambridge University Press, 1988), pp. 246–263.

26. One criticism of the primordial perspective has been that it posits an almost mystical view of ethnicity and, therefore, is unsociological. See, for example, Jack David Eller and Reed M. Coughlan, "The Poverty of Primordialism: The Demystification of Ethnic Attachments," *Ethnic and Racial Studies*, Vol. 16, No. 2 (April 1993): 183–202.

27. Fredrik Barth, "Introduction," *Ethnic Groups and Boundaries*, ed. Fredrik Barth (Boston: Little, Brown and Company , 1970), pp. 9–38; Stanley Lieberson, "A New Ethnic Group in the United States," in *Majority and Minority: The Dynamics of Race and Ethnicity in American Life*, ed. Norman Yetman (Boston: Allyn and Bacon, 1991), pp. 444–457; Paul Brass, "Ethnic Groups and the State," in *Ethnic Groups and the State*, ed. Paul Brass (London: Croom Helm, 1985); Joane Nagel and C. Matthew Snipp, "American Indian Social, Economic, Political and Cultural Strategies for Survival," *Ethnic and Racial Studies*, Vol. 16, No. 2 (April 1993): 203–235; Richard Jenkins, "Rethinking Ethnicity: Identity, Categorization and Power"; Joane Nagel, *American Indian Ethnic Renewal* (New York: Oxford University Press, 1996).

28. Nagel and Snipp, "American Indian Social, Economic, Political and Cultural Strategies for Survival."

29. M. Verkuyten, W. De Jong, and C. N. Masson, "The Construction of Ethnic Categories: Discourses of Ethnicity in the Netherlands," *Ethnic and Racial Studies*, Vol. 18, No. 2 (April 1995): 251–276.

30. Joane Nagel, "The Political Construction of Ethnicity," in *Competitive Ethnic Relations*, ed. Susan Olzark and Joane Nagel (Orlando: Academic Press, 1986).

31. The clearest example of this "rationalism" occurs in cases of ethnic group formation for the pursuit of materialistic objectives. However, ethnicity cannot be reduced only to the pursuit of such objectives, since affective bonds (as emphasized in the primordialist perspective) remain quite important. Nagel, for instance, has argued that the symbolic ethnicity characterizing white Americans is an example of the significance of such bonds, since mobilization, by whites, for material purposes yields few benefits. See Nagel, *American Indian Ethnic Renewal* and Brass, *Ethnic Groups and the State*.

32. Jenkins, for instance, has made the distinction between categories and groups; the one, being a definition imposed on certain individuals by powerful agencies such as the state, and the other, consisting of the lived day-to-day experiences and culture developed by these individuals within the constraints imposed by the categorizers. See Jenkins, "Rethinking Ethnicity: Identity, Categorization, and Power."

33. On this point see, for instance, James E. Blackwell, *The Black Community: Diversity and Unity* (New York: HarperCollins Publishers, 1991) and F. James Davis, *Who Is Black?* In the latter work, Davis has shown that though the "one-drop-rule" designating all individuals of even remote African ancestry as "black" originated as a means of oppression, individuals so-designated have now thoroughly embraced this definition of "blackness."

34. Orlando Patterson, "Context and Choice in Ethnic Allegiance: A Theoretical Framework and Caribbean Case Study," in *Ethnicity: Theory and Experience*, ed. Nathan Glazer and Daniel Patrick Moynihan (Cambridge: Harvard University Press, 1975), pp. 305–349.

35. See, for example, Orlando Patterson, *Ethnic Chauvinism: The Reactionary Impulse* (New York: Stein and Day, 1977); Michael Omi and Howard Winant, *Racial Formation in the United States* (New York: Routledge, 1986); Stephen Steinberg, *The Ethnic Myth* (Boston: Beacon Press, 1989); Peter I. Rose, *They and We* (New York: McGraw Hill Publishing Company, 1990); Richard Alba, "Italian-Americans: A Century of Ethnic Change," in *Origins and Destinies*, ed. Silvia Pedraza and Ruben Rumbaut (Belmont: Wadsworth, 1996); Nagel, *American Ethnic Renewal*.

36. Herbert Gans, "Symbolic Ethnicity: The Future of Ethnic Groups and Cultures in America," *Ethnic and Racial Studies*, Vol. 2, No. 1 (January 1979); Mary C. Waters, *Ethnic Options: Choosing Identities in America* (Berkeley: University of California Press, 1990); "Optional Ethnicities: For Whites Only?" in *Origins and Destinies*, ed. Silvia Pedraza and Ruben Rumbaut (Belmont: Wadsworth, 1996), pp. 444–454; Alba, "Italian-Americans: A Century of Ethnic Change."

37. Lieberson, "A New Ethnic Group in the United States"; Waters, "Optional Ethnicities: For Whites Only?"

38. Davis, "*Who Is Black?*"; Waters, *Ethnic Options*.

39. Kasinitz, *Caribbean New York*.

40. This is in contrast to the United States where some young African Americans, for instance, have developed an "oppositional identity" which derives from the internalization of societal elements that they view as "nonwhite." In this formulation performing well in school, for instance, is perceived as being "white" and, by implication, not doing well (or at least appearing not to do well) is perceived as "black." See, Signithia Fordham, "Racelessness as a Factor in Black Students' School Success: Pragmatic Strategy or Pyrrhic Victory?" *Harvard Educational Review* Vol. 58, No. 1 (1988): 54–84., Signithia Fordham and John Ogbu, "Black Students' School Success: Coping with the 'Burden of Acting White,' " *Urban Review*, Vol. 18, No. 3 (1986): 176–206.

41. Mary C. Waters, "Ethnic and Racial Identities of Second-Generation Black Immigrants in New York City," *International Migration Review*, Vol. xxviii, No. 4 (1994): 795–820.

42. Conway and Bigby's analysis of the spatial distribution of West Indians in New York City confirms that black Caribbean immigrant groups (i.e., those from the non-Hispanic regions) tend to cluster together. See, Dennis Conway and Ulathan Bigby, "Where Caribbean Peoples Live in New York City," in *Caribbean Life in New York: Sociocultural Dimensions*, ed. Constance R. Sutton and Elsa M. chaney (New York: Center for Migration Studies, 1987), pp. 74–83.

43. Bakan, Cox, and Leys have argued that the policy was intended to maintain American economic hegemony in the Caribbean area through the use of bilateral aid, tax incentives for American businesses to invest in the region, and concessionary trade arrangements. It targeted twenty-seven countries in all: Anguilla, Antigua-Barbuda, The Bahamas, Barbados, Belize, Dominica, the Dominican Republic, El Salvador, Grenada, Guatemala, Guyana, Haiti, Honduras, Jamaica, Nicaragua, Panama, St. Lucia, St. Vincent and the Grenadines, Suriname, Trinidad and Tobago, the Cayman Islands, Montserrat, the Netherlands Antilles, St. Kitts-Nevis, the Turks and Caicos islands, and the British Virgin islands. See Abigail B. Bakan, David Cox, and Colin Leys, *Imperial Power and Regional Trade* (Waterloo, Ontario: Wilfrid Laurier University Press, 1993).

44. Gordon K. Lewis, *The Growth of the Modern West Indies* (New York: Modern Reader Paperbacks, 1968), p. 9; "The Contemporary Caribbean," in *Caribbean Contours*, ed. Sidney Mintz and Sally Price (Baltimore: Johns Hopkins University Press, 1985), pp. 219–252.

45. This is not to deny that these islands share similar histories of slavery, political domination by outside forces, and problems of economic development with the British, Dutch, and French territories. However, Hispanic and non-Hispanic peoples from the Caribbean often view each other as having little in common. Their settlement patterns, as demonstrated by Conway and Bigby (see above) for New York City, show this, since they tend to segregate themselves from each other.

46. See David Lowenthal, *West Indian Societies.* (London: Oxford University Press, 1972) and Sidney Mintz, "The Caribbean Region" *Daedalus*, Vol. 103, No. 2 (1974): 45–71.

47. Lewis, *The Making of the Modern West Indies;* Clive Y. Thomas, *The Poor and the Powerless: Economic Policy and Change in the Caribbean* (London: Latin American Bureau, 1988), p. 305.

48. Thomas, *The Poor and the Powerless.*

49. Thomas, *The Poor and the Powerless;* "The Caribbean: Columbus's Islands," *The Economist* (August 6, 1988): 1–18.

50. See, for example, Lowenthal, *West Indian Societies,* and Mel. E Thompson, "Forty-and-One Years On: An Overview of Afro-Caribbean Migration to the United Kingdom," in *In Search of a Better Life: Perspectives on Migration from the Caribbean,* ed. Ransford Palmer (New York: Praeger, 1990), pp. 39–70.

51. David Lopez and Yen Espiritu, "Panethnicity in the United States: A Theoretical Framework," *Ethnic and Racial Studies*, Vol. 13, No. 2 (April 1990): 198–224.

52. For instance, according to the 1990 census, the median family income of Guyanese immigrants was $36,278, Jamaicans, $34,018, and Trinidadians, $33,206.

53. See, for instance, Milton Vickerman, "The Responses of West Indians towards African Americans: Distancing and Identification, " in *Research in Race and Ethnic Relations*, Vol. 7, ed. Rutledge Dennis (Greenwich: JAI Press, 1994): 83–128.

54. See, for example, Mary Waters, "The Role of Lineage in Identity Formation among Black Americans," *Qualitative Sociology*, Vol. 14, No. 1 (1991): 57–76.

55. Susan Buchannan Stafford, "The Haitians: The Cultural Meaning of Race and

Ethnicity," in *New Immigrants in New York,* ed. Nancy Foner (New York: Columbia University Press, 1987), pp. 131–158.

56. Ellen Percy Kraly, "U.S. Immigration Policy and the Immigrant Populations of New York," in *New Immigrants in New York,* ed. Nancy Foner (New York: Columbia University Press, 1987), pp. 35–78.

57. Staten Island was the exception, although I did interview at least one individual who lived in that borough.

C H A P T E R
1
Race in Jamaica

A discussion of conceptions of race as they relate to Jamaica might best begin by considering one of the paradoxes that is inherent in these conceptions. Over the years, foreign observers of the Jamaican scene have often perceived, in that society, more consciousness of race than have Jamaicans themselves.[1] Historian Nyamayaro Mufuka, for instance, in his analysis of the social turmoil that affected Jamaica in the 1970s, wrote that, "Jamaica . . . suffers from a malignant racism, of a variety almost unknown in Africa or the United States. . . . The African heritage, common to 85 percent of the population, for a long time remained the laughing stock of most Jamaicans, black, white, or brown."[2] Similarly, journalist Mark Kurlansky has written,

> In 1968 the Reverend Martin Luther King, Jr., went to Jamaica and said, "I am a Jamaican and in Jamaica I really feel like a human being." The poor blacks of Kingston's slums, the masses Jamaicans sometimes call "the sufferers," had trouble understanding why being black in Jamaica should feel so good to this man.[3]

In the same vein, Ronald Segal, discussing Jamaica as part of his broader project of analyzing the Black Diaspora, has argued that though racial discrimination is not widespread on that island, consciousness of race is the most palpable of any society belonging to the Diaspora:

> Nowhere else in the Black Diaspora did I have such a sense of the slave past as in Jamaica. . . . In Jamaica, along with a social order that seems to bear the tracks of the slave past, as fossilized rocks retain the prints of some extinct species in its passage, there is the counterculture of consciousness that reaches back to an old resistance and in doing so, accepts the experience of the slave, not as servile but as defiant.[4]

These sentiments contrast sharply with those expressed by a Jamaican in a recent letter to the *Gleaner*.[5]

"I'm Jamaican," I say. To which the response is, "But ... aren't you Chinese? Well, yes, but what has that got to do with being Jamaican? Jamaicans have a rich heritage, with ancestors of many nations, including Europe, China, Africa and India. But we have mixed and integrated in such a way that no matter what our color, our primary identity is Jamaican. . . . There exists here (in Jamaica), such a variety of skin tones that when people refer to "that red skin girl," the "browning," or "that chiney boy," it is not meant with the least bit of disrespect. Neither do those descriptions carry with them any of the connotations of color or race that are so pervasive in North America. . . . In fact, most Caribbean people are hardly even aware of racism in their everyday lives. As one Caribbean woman put it, "Imagine, I had to come all the way to Canada to discover I was Black!"[6]

Or take a recent controversy reported on by the same newspaper. As part of the process of applying for nonimmigrant visas to the United States, Jamaican immigrants are required to answer a question stating their "complexion." Although, among themselves, Jamaicans commonly make note of shade differences, this process is often subconscious and very rarely are they required to formally indicate such categories as complexion or race. Indeed, to do so would be to breach strongly held norms regarding the discussion of race in public. Therefore, in mandating that such a question be answered, the American embassy has contravened one of the society's strongest taboos; and this fact is not lessened by the claim that the "complexion" question is standard, throughout the world, for all individuals seeking visitors' visas to the United States. The suspicion among Jamaicans—as pointed out by Barry Chevannes, sociologist at the University of the West Indies—is that the question is trying to measure the numbers of potential dark skinned visitors to the country. He has argued that a question soliciting information on race or, especially, complexion is likely to have more salience to individuals defined as "black," since they, more than other populations, demonstrate a wide variation in skin shade. The article reports that potential Jamaican visitors to the United States who have faced having to answer the "complexion" question have been very perplexed as to how to respond. Some have checked "brown." Others, interpreting the question to refer to race, have written "black." And some, unsure of what to put, have left the question unanswered.[7]

The perplexity that has been raised by a question such as the one required by the American embassy is a genuine one. Here, the last point raised by the letter writer to the *Gleaner* becomes important because researchers studying West Indian immigrants in the United States have found that many of these immigrants claim to have discovered what it means to be black only after they have migrated to this country.[8] On its face, this claim seems to contradict common sense, given the history and demographic composition of the West Indies. Taking Jamaica, for instance, Table 1.1 shows the clear

TABLE 1.1 Racial and Ethnic Composition of the Jamaican Population, 1844-1982

Year	Black		Mixed Race		White		Chinese		Indians		Others	
	No.	%	No.	%	No.	%	No.	%	No.	%	No.	%
1844	293,128	77.7	68,529	18.1	15,776	4.2	—	—	—	—	—	—
1861	346,374	78.5	81,065	18.4	13,816	3.1	—	—	—	—	9	0.0
1871	392,707	77.6	100,346	19.8	13,101	2.6	—	—	—	—	—	—
1881	444,186	76.5	109,946	18.9	14,432	2.4	99	0.0	11,016	1.9	1,125	0.2
1891	488,624	76.4	121,955	19.1	14,692	2.3	481	0.1	10,116	1.6	3,623	0.6
1911	630,181	75.8	163,201	19.6	15,605	1.9	2,111	0.3	17,380	2.1	2,905	0.3
1921	660,420	77.0	157,223	18.3	14,476	1.7	3,696	0.4	18,610	2.2	3,693	0.4
1943	965,960	78.1	216,348	17.5	13,809	1.1	12,394	1.0	26,507	2.1	2,045	0.2
1960	1,236,337	76.8	272,059	16.9[a]	14,498	0.9[b]	9,658	0.6	27,366	1.7	49,904	3.1
1970	1,663,560	90.0	107,207	5.8	12,938	0.7	12,938	0.7	31,422	1.7	3,697	0.2[c]
1982	1,636,289	74.4	280,271	12.8	6,571	0.3	4,380	0.2	28,475	1.3	234,377	10.7[c]

Source: G. W. Roberts, *The Population of Jamaica* (London: Cambridge University Press, 1957), Table 14, p. 65; Colin Clarke, *Kingston, Jamaica* (Berkeley: University of California Press, 1975), Table 28, p. 152, Copyright © 1975 Regents; The Statistical Institute of Jamaica, *Pocketbook of Statistics* (Kingston: The Statistical Institute of Jamaica, 1989), Table 12, p. 27.

[a]Includes the following categories: "Afro-European," "Afro-East Indian," and "Afro-Chinese."

[b]Includes Syrians.

[c]Includes individuals who did not state their race.

demographic dominance of individuals of African descent. In fact, this dominance is even greater than the Table indicates, given the social nature of racial definitions and the imprecision accompanying such definitions.[9] For instance, the significant dip in 1970 among individuals identifying themselves as mixed race and the accompanying rise in those claiming a black identity probably results from the fact that, in the late 1960s, the American Black Power movement exerted a notable influence on Jamaican society.[10] Many Jamaicans of African descent publicly affirmed that ancestry and downplayed their mixed heritage, but even given the evident decline in such sentiments by 1982 it is clear that the majority of the Jamaican population would be counted as black.[11]

Given this reality, the fact that Jamaicans and other West Indians would claim to have discovered their "blackness" only after migrating to America appears puzzling, but only until it is realized that they are referring to the social meanings attributed to skin color, rather than to skin color itself. These social meanings differ significantly between the West Indies and the United States. In America, "blackness" signifies a whole continuum of negative attributes, ranging from low intelligence to criminality. In the West Indies, negative attributes have also long attached to black skin, but, significantly, these have tended to be less all pervading and have not acted as an absolute bar to upward mobility. Because of this relative difference, black West Indian immigrants can, in migrating, discover the full implications of antiblack stereotyping. They learn what it means to be "black," because in the transition from one country to another, the social expectations of those having African ancestry and/or black skin become much more constrained.

Clearly, a large gap exists between how some foreign observers view Jamaica and how many Jamaicans view themselves. This difference stems from the fact that the historical, social, and political forces that have shaped issues of race in Jamaica have given rise to inherent contradictions. Jamaica is, at one and the same time, a country that has traditionally denigrated African ancestry, but not so much that it has prevented upward mobility for some of these individuals; confined the mass of the black population to poverty, but historical changes in the society have loosened the traditional correlation between skin color and social class; exhibited a "white bias,"[12] but the society has defined race so broadly that the exact meaning of racial designations is subject to a good deal of negotiation; and, overall, has been quite racially conscious, yet strong social norms prohibiting race thinking have effectively convinced many in the population that race is not a factor in Jamaican society.

In showing how these contradictions have played out, I proceed in this chapter by first giving a brief overview of the historical development of race relations in Jamaica, showing how ideas of race have intertwined closely with social class.[13] Then I argue that, from a theoretical point of view, present-day Jamaican society is best explained by perspectives which recognize that the society is not what it once was, but neither has it reached the point where race and class are nonissues. Thus, a perspective such as the one put forward by political scientist Carl Stone is probably a more accurate reflection of the current state of race relations in Jamaica than is cultural pluralist theory or the perspective put forward by someone like Adam Kuper; the one presents a picture of a static social structure, while the other argues that race and class are now irrelevant in Jamaican society. I end the chapter by drawing some parallels between race in Jamaica and in the United States.

■ RACE RELATIONS IN JAMAICA: A BRIEF OVERVIEW OF THE CLASSIC MODEL

Although Jamaica's association with various European powers began in 1494 when Columbus encountered it, the century and a half of Spanish occupation left so little impression that most modern histories emphasize the period of English domination from 1655 onward.[14] Under the British, Jamaica developed into the sugar cane dominated plantation society that became typical of the whole Caribbean. Jamaica's social structure reflected its economic underpinnings. Typically characterized as a pyramid, this structure consisted of three primary segments. At its apex, a small white elite exercised economic, political, and social domination over the whole society; at the base, a large mass of black slaves served as the engine of the economy but suffered brutal subjugation.[15] Intermediate between these two extremes lay a mixed-raced "colored" segment—the product of miscegenation between dominant whites and slaves . A close correlation developed between skin color and privilege: To be white was to enjoy privilege in all its forms; to be black, by definition, meant degradation; while coloreds experienced an uncomfortable melding of privilege (vis-à-vis blacks) and disenfranchisement (vis-à-vis) whites.[16]

In reality, the social system was more complicated than this: internal differentiation based on occupation and race characterized each segment, and the society afforded individuals some latitude for defining the latter. With respect to differentiation, it happened that the most powerful whites were the wealthy owners of large plantations or their representatives, and the governor. Falling below them were a variety of whites employed as—among other things—overseers, craftsmen, soldiers, and teachers.[17] The intermediate colored segment also exhibited internal differentiation according to color and economic function. Those with the lightest skin and owning the largest plantations constituted the topmost layer of the colored population. The bottommost layer of the colored community consisted of those with dark skin and with occupations barely differentiating them from those performed by free blacks—e.g., servants. These freed blacks, though often lumped with the colored population, were a distinct and subordinated segment of that population by virtue of their slave origins. Typically, they were sailors or mechanics. Slaves constituted the most debased layer in the social hierarchy of plantation society. However, even this layer exhibited a differentiation between relatively privileged house slaves (often light skinned), skilled workers, and the hard-pressed field slaves.[18] Indeed, house slaves (especially women) sometimes managed, through their relationship with their slave masters, to obtain their freedom, thereby undergoing upward mobility of sorts into the freed black population.[19]

Internal differentiation within each segment of the three-tiered social structure accompanied not only occupation but color as well. The result, especially among coloreds and black slaves, was a gradual lightening of complexion as one went from less to more prestigious occupations.[20] But since the society afforded individuals some latitude for defining their race, the correlation between color and occupation was imperfect, with some degree of overlap existing between the segments. The ability to negotiate racial identity was least evident among field slaves, and their status was virtually fixed. Coloreds, on the other hand, ranged in complexion from dark to very fair skinned; and since the society defined race to include not only biological features (i.e., skin color, hair type, size and shape of lips and nose) but also wealth, whites sometimes accepted the wealthiest and fairest coloreds as "white."[21] Thus, at the upper levels of the intermediate stratum, coloreds achieved "whiteness" through a combination of biological and socioeconomic criteria and merged into the dominant white segment.

The existence of other, smaller, groups rendered the three-tiered model even more complex. Historically, Jews have been the most important of these groups. In the past, their position in the society included a variety of contradictory indicators that rendered them marginal for long periods of Jamaican history. Economically, they tended to be well-off, having acquired in the eighteenth and nineteenth centuries defunct sugar estates from their indebted English and Scottish owners. However, most of their wealth was centered in the capital, Kingston, where they dominated the retail trade.[22] As Caucasians, Jews enjoyed an advantage over blacks and coloreds in a society operating on the principle that the closer an individual approximated the British elite, the greater the probability of upward mobility. However, as Jews, they suffered from a variety of obstacles (e.g., the inability to vote or serve as jurors), which reminded them of their tentative acceptance by the elite. Thus, until 1831, when these obstacles were removed, Jews were— to use Thomas August's phrase—"off white."[23]

After 1831, Jews achieved upward mobility by replacing British plantation owners who quit the island as the sugar industry declined. By the 1930s, they had shed their marginal position in the society and had consolidated themselves as the new elite.[24] Similarly, Syrian merchants, though entering the society only in 1891, have become an integral part of this new elite. And in the last forty years or so, these have also been joined by some individuals of Chinese extraction. Because of the mobility of these various groups, the pyramidal model of race relations which developed during slavery emerged into the twentieth century basically intact, but with some reordering of its constituent parts. Jews, Syrians, coloreds, a few whites, and some Chinese individuals have come to constitute a light skinned elite. Blacks, the largest portion of the population, and long relegated to the bottom, have largely been excluded from this elite. Nevertheless, in the last fifty years, they have also experienced substantial upward mobility into the middle and even upper classes (though not into the elite).[25]

■ EXPLAINING CHANGE IN JAMAICAN SOCIETY

Although the changes outlined previously are empirically verifiable, their exact meaning is subject to interpretation. The basic question is whether present-day Jamaican society differs fundamentally from what it was in previous centuries and the role that race has played in its change or lack of it. On the one hand, the cultural pluralist model, positing a static society, argues that present-day Jamaican society is essentially similar to its past manifestations. In this model, conceptions of race and culture are crucial in preventing significant change. Conversely, other analyses have argued that race and class are so irrelevant in present-day Jamaica that the contemporary social scene is quite different than it used to be. Between these two are to be found analyses arguing that though race and class are still important in Jamaica, they no longer correlate as closely as they once did. Consequently, social change is not only possible but has, in fact, occurred. Comparing three representative perspectives on Jamaican society—cultural pluralism, Adam Kuper's analysis, and that of Carl Stone—helps to illustrate the middle path between a static and a completely changed society, which I believe characterizes present-day Jamaica.

Cultural Pluralism

Because it has been rooted in the historical realities of what I have described as the classic model, cultural pluralism has proven to be very influential as a tool for analyzing race relations in Jamaica. This can be seen in works as widely spaced as M. G. Smith's, *The Plural Society in the British West Indies* (1965) and Segal's, *The Black Diaspora* (1995). Perhaps because it looks back at Jamaican history, the theory tends to project that history into the present, offering in effect a picture of a static society. As social analyst David Lowenthal has put it:

> The century following emancipation bore witness to great changes, to be sure. . . . Yet these changes fundamentally altered neither the structure of society nor most relationships between ruler and ruled, white and black, landowner and laborer. West Indian ways of life, social circumstances, and prevalent viewpoints remained substantially those of a hundred years before. . . . In other countries travelers look assiduously for traces of the past; in the Caribbean the past is a living presence.[26]

In taking this perspective, Lowenthal has followed anthropologist M. G. Smith, the primary exponent of cultural pluralism in West Indian societies.[27] In Smith's view, a direct connection exists between the tripartite social structure originating in slavery and the present social structure. Outlining the theory, Smith has argued that the most important feature of West Indian societies is the fact that they are culturally heterogeneous; by which he means that within particular societies are to be found distinct populations practicing different cultural traditions. The core of a culture is its institutional system, because this system "defines and sanctions the persistent forms of social life."[28] The basic institutions are marriage, the family, religion, and property; and a society is plural because groups within it practice different forms of each of these institutions—as opposed to a homogeneous society, in which there would be less variation in the practice of each institution. For instance, in the case of the family one might, in a plural society, find some groups adhering to the nuclear family model, while other groups would adhere to some other form—say, the extended family model. In contrast, a homogeneous society would see most individuals practicing one or the other form of marriage.[29]

Smith argues that present-day pluralism in Jamaican society means the existence of a hierarchical differentiation between three primary segments— "white," "brown," and "black"—corresponding to the segments originating in slave society: "white," "colored," and "slave." Significantly, he argues that culture, and not biological race, is the primary criterion distinguishing between the three segments. For instance, even though the dominant "white" segment consists primarily of light skinned individuals (Europeans, Syrians, Jews, etc.), the predominance of this phenotype does not define it. Rather, it is the fact that this segment practices "European" cultural forms. Thus defined, an individual of African ancestry could, theoretically, belong to the "white" segment if that individual adheres to these cultural forms. However, most such individuals belong to the "black" segment which practices "a folk culture containing numerous elements reminiscent of African societies and Caribbean slavery."[30] The colored segment practices cultural forms derived from both the "European" and "black" segments and, therefore, its cultural practices reflect its structural intermediacy. With this diversity in basic institutions, social order becomes very problematic. The central question becomes how to meld into a single society, groups with widely differing practices. Smith suggests that force provides this vital glue, for each plural society is "a political unit simply because it has a single government. But the task of government can only be discharged consistently within culturally diverse populations if one or other of these sections dominates the political structure."[31] Thus, a plural society maintains itself over the long run through coercion.

Adam Kuper's Analysis

Smith's viewpoint, in focusing on the role of cultural differences in a color-coded society, implies that Jamaicans define race socially—for example, individuals from the lower reaches of the social hierarchy who practice "higher" culture forms become progressively "whiter." This insight helps explain the flexibility of Jamaican views of race. However, the overall inflexibility of the theory, in viewing present-day Jamaica as closely resembling its nineteenth-century predecessor, has come in for much criticism.[32] Adam Kuper, for one, has argued that the theory, though basing its propositions on folk concepts, has transformed these ambiguous concepts into "timeless models."[33] Focusing especially on race and class, he tries to show the variability and overlap inherent in folk conceptions of these two key factors. Kuper is particularly struck by sociologist Ferdinand Henriques's discussion of race in Jamaica, since the latter has argued that, in assessing this variable, multiple criteria—i.e., color, skin texture, facial features, hair form, and socioeconomic status—must be considered together.[34]

Kuper argues that the use of such multiple factors in constructing race and, in general, social status is evidence that, contrary to what sociological models predict, ordinary Jamaicans possess no clear-cut way of ranking individuals.[35] The resulting ambiguity has lessened the amount of conflict one would expect to find in a highly inegalitarian society with a history of racial discrimination. Where conflict occurs it centers primarily on the entrenched two-party system.[36] Overall, concludes Kuper, Jamaican folk conceptions of race and class are so ambiguous, one can say definitively that clearly defined strata do not exist in Jamaica. Such strata only seem to exist because academics impose definitive criteria on a situation which is inherently fluid.[37]

The usefulness of Kuper's analysis lies in his underlying assumption that social relations in Jamaica are dynamic. Far from being a society ossified since the end of slavery, the picture is one of social change—especially in the twentieth century—tending toward the undermining of preslavery social relations. He cites the following as being the most important changes: (1) the domination of the island's political structure by individuals of African ancestry; (2) the inclusion of the masses in the political process because of the need of both main political parties for their votes; (3) the rise of black racial consciousness through the Garvey and Rastafarian movements; (4) and massive immigration.[38] Together, these changes have led to a society that differs in fundamental ways from society before the present century.

The problem is that Kuper exaggerates the degree of social change that has occurred in Jamaican society; in reality, modern-day Jamaica is neither quite what is used to be, nor has it become egalitarian. For instance, race and class no longer correlate as closely as the classic tripartite model posits but this does not mean, as Kuper argues, that Jamaica exhibits no fixed racial or socioeconomic strata. Indeed, Kuper's analysis of a small rural village in Jamaica reveals the existence of such strata. His study shows that: (1) folk views in Jamaica, though indeed ambiguous, are not infinitely variable; (2) real divisions exist within the society and these stem primarily from the ownership/nonownership of property and occupation. The village exhibited four primary groups: big landowners, small landowners, laborers, and a "middle class" deriving its position from such service occupations as teaching and shopkeeping. These material criteria correlated only loosely with socially defined race. Locals esteemed "whiteness" over "blackness," but these designations embraced not just color, but occupation, social status, and lifestyle. Generally speaking, big landowners were "white," but this group also included dark skinned individuals who, having acquired property, made a living by renting it to others. Moreover, most of these landowners avoided exclusivity, since they had married dark skinned women. Similarly, Kuper found large color variation among the local middle class, with no clear correlation between phenotype and social status.[39]

Carl Stone's Analysis

Unlike the cultural pluralist view or that of Kuper, Carl Stone takes a middle path in analyzing Jamaican society.[40] In his view, Jamaican society is to be analyzed primarily in terms of social class, but race remains a potent though deliberately suppressed variable. Stone's analysis falls midway between the pluralists' and Kuper's, since he stresses the importance of change over time, but he also recognizes that class and race remain salient variables. Stone's analysis of changes taking place in Jamaica's social structure distinguishes between four periods: (1) from the emancipation of slavery in 1834 to the great depression in the 1930s; (2) the 1930s to the 1960s; (3) the decade of the 1970s; and (4) the decade of the 1980s.[41] Period one, which has already been discussed, saw the decline of the plantation economy, the consequent decline of the old British elite, and the rise to power of Jews and Syrians. Essentially, ethnic succession took place in the upper reaches of the society. The second period entrenched the influence of the new elite;

but perhaps more importantly, it saw the rise of black political power through a gradual process of decolonization, culminating in the granting of independence from Britain in 1962. This was a fundamental change, since, for most of its history, the Jamaican elite had wielded both economic and political power. Independence in 1962 marked the official recognition of the division of these two spheres of influence between competing racial/ethnic groups. During the period leading up to independence in 1962 and after, the elite was forced to deal with a newly assertive black population. Balancing the economic interests of this elite and the political and material demands of the black poor became the primary goal of public policy.[42] The fulcrum of this balancing act has been a democratic political system dominated by two multiracial, multiclass political parties—the People's National Party and the Jamaican Labour Party—which alternate in holding political power.[43]

The shift to black political power in Jamaican society created new opportunities for blacks in the civil service and has led to upward mobility for many. Moreover, changes in the economy[44] created economic growth and other opportunities for upward mobility.[45] These changes have significantly affected the composition of the middle class, traditionally a bastion of fair skinned Jamaicans. For instance, analysis by sociologist Derek Gordon has shown that between 1943 and 1984, the percentage of blacks who qualify as middle class increased from approximately 3 percent to 25 percent; and because they constitute the majority of the Jamaican population, in absolute terms, most members of the middle class are now black.[46] However, it is also important to note that relatively speaking, other groups have benefited even more than did blacks, since proportionally more of the others are middle class. For instance, in 1984, 47 percent of Indians were middle class, even though they makeup a little over 1 percent of the population.[47]

The decade of the 1970s—the third period discussed by Stone— impacted black upward mobility significantly. Characterized by economic depression, political conflict, crime (especially against the rich), and black militancy, this period resulted in blacks moving beyond their traditional power base in politics into the business world. The catalyst for the change was the socialist People's National Party. Advocating policies meant to empower the poor, this party (especially through its leader, Michael Manley) created rising expectations among blacks but fear among members of the elite. Perceiving a rejection of their economic hegemony many members of the elite migrated, along with their capital, to North America. Blacks filled the resulting economic vacuum. They moved in large numbers into high level private sector jobs from which they had been previously excluded. The means through which blacks achieved this differed. Some ethnically (i.e., Chinese, Indians, etc.)[48] owned enterprises, afraid of criticism, promoted blacks to high level positions. Other blacks bought out firms that were being sold by departing members of ethnic groups. Yet others started new firms. More controversially, Stone has suggested that drug smuggling provided new sources of capital for blacks (along with some nonblacks), thereby enabling them to bypass the elite's lock on startup capital.[49] At lower levels in the economy, thousands of enterprising lower class women (higglers) bypassed established retail stores and began a flourishing (sometimes illegal) trade supplying scarce goods.[50]

If the 1970s Jamaica saw widespread social changes in favor of blacks, the 1980s witnessed a reaction against such changes. More than anything else, the defeat, in the 1980 general elections, of the People's National Party by the more conservative Jamaica Labour Party symbolized this shift. Among the multifaceted reasons for this backlash were the 1970s surge in violent crime; the depressed state of the economy; and concerted attacks by entrenched members of the elite against the PNP's leftist policies.[51] Equally important, the elite consolidated its hegemony over the Jamaican economy by buying out smaller companies. Through such means, they not only profited disproportionately from the turmoil of the 1970s, but managed to blunt black upward mobility. By increasing corporate and financial ownership in their hands they enhanced their role as gatekeepers to the elite. At present, blacks still experience difficulties obtaining the capital to start companies that would move them beyond the middle class in large numbers.[52] The political, economic, and social changes that have affected Jamaica over the past few decades have resulted in a situation where blacks now constitute the majority of the middle class, but the poor in Jamaica are also disproportionately black. The country still exhibits a very skewed income distribution.

Table 1.2 compares income distribution in Jamaica and a select group of underdeveloped countries (and, for purposes of comparison, two developed countries). As can be seen, Jamaica compares unfavorably. In 1958, the bottom 20 percent of the country enjoyed only 2.2 percent of the total income, while the top 20 percent enjoyed 61.5 percent. By 1972, the situation had worsened, as the bottom 20 percent fell to 2 percent of total income, while the top 20 percent rose to 64 percent of income. Only Brazil had a (slightly) worse income distribution; while a much richer country such the United States exhibited notably milder income inequality. In fact, these data understate the full extent of income inequality, since much of total income in Jamaica is concentrated among the not more than twenty-three elite families which dominate the economy through intermarriage and control of the island's largest corporations.[53]

Given the correlation between wealth and skin shade (if not actual color),[54] one would expect surging racial tension. However, these sentiments are very muted (although ever present). Instead, as shown by writers such as Nettleford, Foner, Kuper, Austin, and Stone,[55] Jamaicans tend to conceive of conflict between groups as revolving around social class, rather than race.[56] The post–World War II empowerment of blacks accounts for some

TABLE 1.2 Income Distribution of Household Income in Selected Countries by Percentile Groups

Country	Year	Lowest 20%	Second 20%	Third 20%	Fourth 20%	Highest 20%
Jamaica	1958	2.2	6.0	10.8	19.5	61.5
Jamaica	1971/72	2.0	5.0	10.5	18.5	64.0
Trinidad	1975/76	4.2	9.1	13.9	22.8	50.0
Brazil	1972	2.0	5.0	9.4	17.0	66.6
India	1975/76	7.0	9.2	13.9	20.5	49.4
United Kingdom	1979	7.0	11.5	17.5	24.8	39.7
United States	1970	5.5	12.0	17.4	23.5	41.6

Source: Adapted from Derick A. C. Boyd, *Economic Management, Income Distribution, and Poverty in Jamaica* (New York: Praeger, 1988), p. 85, Table 6.1. Copyright 1988 by Praeger. Reproduced with permission of Greenwood Publishing Group, Inc., Westport, CT.

of this. As the dominant political force in the island, Jamaican blacks share a widespread (though, in some respects, questionable)[57] sense of being in control of their lives. They reason that though the ethnic minorities may enjoy disproportionate wealth, blacks' political power somewhat offsets this. One would not want to push this reasoning too far, however, since to the poor black individual living in the slums of Trench Town, such reasoning would appear as so much abstract nonsense. For such individuals, the material expression of black power—i.e., patronage—is what matters; while, for educated blacks, it is the observation that over the past few decades, blacks have come to dominate the middle class. And for the thousands who find their aspirations blocked, for whatever reason, immigration has always acted as a safety valve. For the present generation of Jamaicans, America is still the land of opportunity. But as important as all of these factors are in shaping perceptions of race, they do not tell the whole story. To do this, we need to focus attention on two aspects of Jamaican life that especially mute racial feeling: demographics and the ideology guiding postwar Jamaican politics.

■ FACTORS MUTING RACIAL CONSCIOUSNESS IN JAMAICA: DEMOGRAPHY AND IDEOLOGY

Demographics has been a major factor counteracting the weighty historical role of race in Jamaica. Black numerical preponderance has created self-confidence among people of African ancestry by ensuring that ordinary Jamaicans, in their everyday lives, routinely encounter blacks in a wide variety of roles: from social failures to supreme court justices. The fact of blacks occupying high status roles is commonplace and unremarkable. Race has become detached from notions of success and failure, because, within the same race,[58] one can observe many individuals covering the full spectrum of social possibilities. Unlike the United States, a correlation is not routinely made between race and success: failure is not viewed as "black" nor is success viewed as "white."

We can say, therefore, that black preponderance in the population tends to reduce the salience of race in the everyday lives of Jamaicans. Their daily interactions, positive and negative, are largely independent of race. Consequently, race has taken on the aspect of a background variable—important, but largely distant. In this, Jamaica contrasts quite sharply with the United States, where West Indian immigrants come, over a period of time, to understand that race is an integral aspect of the everyday lives of blacks (see chapter 3). Moving beyond day-to-day interactions to long-term goals, Jamaicans, generally, have black role models whom they view as emulatable.[59] So, for instance, other things being equal, they know that it is possible for an ordinary individual to become prime minister.[60] If being a member of a minority group[61] involves feelings of powerlessness because of ascribed characteristics, and a member of a majority group the reverse, then Jamaicans would have to be placed in the latter category.[62] Some writers have argued that despite the subjugation of black people for long periods of Jamaican history, this numerical preponderance has imparted to them a psychological edge: they know that numbers mean power—actual[63] or potential—and these numbers are on their side. The reverse side of this coin is that the elites who have dominated the society feared these numbers. During slavery, whites—especially plantation owners—expressed this fear as a pervasive worry about being surrounded by blacks. One gets a palpable sense of this by reading, for instance, the diary of Maria Nugent, wife of the official who served as the island's lieutenant governor from 1799 to 1806. Worrying about the reaction of her Jamaican slaves to news of a successful slave uprising in Haiti, she wrote (in 1803):

> People here are so imprudent in their conversation. The splendor of the black chiefs of St. Domingo, their superior strength, their firmness of character . . . are the common topics at dinner; and the blackies in attendance seem so much interested, that they hardly change a plate, or do anything but listen . . . what must it all lead to![64]

Something of this fear still remains because of Jamaica's unequal distribution of wealth. Some writers[65] have suggested that it is a primary reason for the development of ideologies positing race as a nonissue in Jamaican society.

The Role of Ideology

Over the past three decades, the numerical preponderance that allows blacks to sidestep race as an issue in their everyday lives has been very effectively bolstered by a strong belief that race should *not* be an issue. Manifested most potently in the national motto, "Out of Many, One People,"[66] this belief argues that Jamaica is a multiracial society in which a variety of groups co-exist so amicably that the society is effectively *non-racial*.[67] Thus, ironically, the ideology of multiracialism easily verges into one of nonracialism. Consequently, Jamaicans view public discussions of race as, at best, impolite and, at worst, troublemaking; the injection, into public discourse, of an emotionally charged but irrelevant factor.[68] Since a relationship exists between economic deprivation and racial consciousness, this broad generalization must be qualified. Generally speaking, the poorer the individual, the more likely that individual is to exhibit racial consciousness. In practical terms, this means that impoverished blacks are most likely to view their social status from a racial perspective. On the other hand, members of the upper classes, regardless of race or ethnicity, tend to deny the relevance of race as a factor in Jamaican society.[69] Despite these class differences, a general perception exists that the key to social advancement is not race but individual effort. Even poor Jamaicans, more likely than most to exhibit racial consciousness, tend to advance these individualistic factors over racial explanations in accounting for their social status.[70] Thus, the ideology of nonracialism has penetrated Jamaican society very deeply.

Given the historical institutionalization of notions of black inferiority and the provocative correlation between wealth and race/ethnicity, the irony of a nonracialist Jamaica is obvious. The society successfully perpetuates this misconception, because, as noted earlier, in most day-to-day situations Jamaicans do not need to think about race. Moreover, the idea of a nonracial society, far from being new, can be traced back at least into the last century. For instance, the historian Philip Curtin, writing of Jamaica in the immediate postemancipation (1834) period noted that:

> In Jamaica the race question was often hidden behind other issues, while in the American South other issues tended to hide behind racial conflict. Many Jamaicans took a certain pride in their lack of overt racial distinctions, and the racial equality of Jamaica was frequently stressed in immigration appeals.[71]

Therefore, even when the castelike social structure of slavery prevailed, some Jamaicans claimed that race was a relatively unimportant factor in their society.

Curtin indicates that the Jamaicans who downplayed race in the nineteenth century sought, because of fears centering on the availability of black

labor, to appeal to potential immigrants. In other words, they were attempting to put the best face on the island. In the twentieth century, one
finds the exact same rationale behind appeals to a nonracial Jamaica. The
idea is advanced to both promote and protect the status quo. Because of
Jamaica's sharp economic disparities, racial appeals focused specifically on
the fact of disproportionate black poverty would create widespread social
turmoil. To prevent this possibility, the frustrations of the Jamaican poor
have been deflected onto race neutral ideals—such as the national motto—
which exhort the supremacy of the nation, as a whole, over the partisan interests of any one group.[72] Not surprisingly, strong negative sanctions attach
to overt appeals to race. Influential Jamaicans deflect such appeals by either
attributing them to foreign agitators[73] or, if local, by branding the perpe-
trators as "racists"—a serious charge in a society that, supposedly, has moved
beyond such particularistic considerations.[74]

The ideology of nonracialism has achieved penetrating power through
institutionalization by the educational and political systems. The former has
tried to substitute alternative criteria for achieving upward mobility. They
have included the following core assumptions: (1) upward mobility is possible for all regardless of race; (2) education is the means for achieving this;
(3) because the system is meritocratic, whether individuals rise or fall depends on how hard they work; and (4) more than the mere acquisition of
knowledge, "education" means adhering to such values as law and order and
speaking "properly" (that is, standard English). Thus, to say that an individual is "educated" is to make positive assertions about—among other
things—the individual's learnedness, beliefs, behavior, speech, and groom-
ing.[75]

The educational system rests upon a profound contradiction' since
these values exist within a society which cannot provide equality of opportunity for all Jamaicans. In reality, quality of schooling correlates closely
with socioeconomic status.[76] Nevertheless, Jamaicans accept the system's
underlying assumptions—a reality that has led analysts such as Adam Kuper
to charge that education is "a functional alternative to 'race' in the ideological justification of Jamaican social inequality."[77] Nancy Foner's late
1960s/early 1970 study of a small rural Jamaican village illustrates this
very well. She found that among the overwhelmingly black population of
this village, race was, at best, a background variable. Instead, status striv-
ings centered around the desire to attain higher education. Most parents
accepted education as the legitimate means of attaining upward mobility
and endured great sacrifices to enable their children to attend good schools.
Successful children (measured in terms of passing exams) conferred pres-
tige on their families through their achievements. In contrast, families of
unsuccessful children felt shame, and their envy of more successful families often led to quarrels.[78]

In the past fifty-five years, the political system has rivaled education as a mechanism for institutionalizing the ideal of a nonracial Jamaica. This system, consisting as it does of two dominant parties which alternate in holding power, and resting on coalitions which cut across class lines, deliberately and effectively dampens appeals to race in Jamaican society. As noted previously, the system performs the vital function of balancing the economic interests of the dominant ethnic elites and the material demands of the black majority. Since most of the Jamaican poor are black (despite increasing opportunities for upward mobility in recent years), racial considerations intertwine with these demands. But to express material demands in openly racial terms is too dangerous.[79] Thus, in the modern development of Jamaica's political system, an "unstated pact" evolved whereby the dominant political parties would protect the interests of the elite, while dispensing benefits to the poor.[80] A crucial aspect of this pact was that the race issue should be kept off the political agenda; the other, more proactive side of the pact, was that the ideal of nonracialism would be promoted. Thus, race has become a virtual nonissue, and, in its place, have been elevated the aforementioned more neutral symbols of Jamaican nationalism—the flag, national heroes, and the national motto.[81]

One measure of the success of this policy is that questions of race have been raised explicitly in Jamaican politics only a few times since the 1940s when the movement toward self-government began. Most notable in this regard have been the Rastafarian movement, the pro-black People's Political Party of the early 1960s, the Black Power movement of the late part of the same decade and, to some extent, during the socialist period (under Michael Manley) from 1972 to 1980. Of these four, the Manley government has, arguably, had the most lasting impact on the social structure, for as Stone notes, the PNP broke the unstated pact between the elite and the black masses by attempting to level some of the inequalities inherent in Jamaican society. While the PNP did not systematically appeal to race, its incorporation of young radical blacks and attacks on the economic hegemony of the elites had an underlying racial appeal.[82] As mentioned before, these attacks helped create social turbulence, which resulted in upward mobility for blacks. However, this turbulence failed to dislodge the elite from its dominant position. As noted earlier, the society views overt appeals to race as being beyond the pale and sanctions them through public opinion. Moreover, members of the elite effectively circumvent the crystallization of such sentiments by co-opting some blacks into high level positions within their corporations. In so doing, they increase support among influential members of the black community and these, in turn, help to deflect appeals to race among the poor.[83] It would not be overstating to say that, ultimately, the ideology of a nonracial Jamaica stems from fear of the black poor and helps to maintain the status quo.

■ RACE IN JAMAICA AND THE UNITED STATES:
A BRIEF COMPARISON

The previous discussion has shown that while race remains a very sensitive issue in Jamaica, most people downplay it for experiential and ideological reasons. Beyond that, the concept of race, itself, has always been complex, well illustrating the idea of social construction. With respect to this, Jamaica resembles the United States but goes beyond it in possessing more flexible definitional criteria. The most obvious similarity between the two societies is that both assume the inferiority of African ancestry. This similarity stems from the fact of New World slavery. North America and the Caribbean constituted the western end of the triangular slave trade which linked the Americas, Europe, and Africa. The United States and the Caribbean derived slaves from a common source, for the same reasons, and developed similar ideologies justifying slavery. The core ideology was the argument that the "innate inferiority" of Africans made them fit to be slaves.[84]

Though similar, these ideologies were articulated in very different structural contexts. In the United States, Africans were a numerical minority in a society stressing egalitarian ideals. Ironically, this circumstance may have promoted greater repression, since such an obvious exception to the country's ideals had to be justified. North Americans achieved this justification by dichotomizing human beings into "civilized" people and "savages." The restricted (or *Herrenvolk*)[85] democracy thereby created represented a compromise between egalitarianism and a profitable slave system. West Indian societies—including Jamaica—also created restricted democracies. However, in most of these societies Africans vastly outnumbered Europeans. Moreover, slaveowners' routine exploitation of their female slaves produced a large colored population; but where such individuals in the United States struggled and failed to retain a separate identity, in the West Indies they became a valuable (albeit socially despised) buffer against the much larger slave population.[86] Thus, structural conditions have conspired to simplify racial complexity in the United States but to maintain them in Jamaica and other West Indian countries.[87]

Although both the United States and Jamaica institutionalized the idea of black inferiority, these ideas became much more entrenched in the former than in the latter. As a classic minority group, blacks in America have struggled to effectively challenge these stereotypes. Jamaican blacks, while also having to struggle, have enjoyed (through circumstance) certain advantages not available to American blacks. Most important, their numerical preponderance has imparted a degree of self-confidence that has helped them to cope with persistent subjugation. Socialization in a society made up mainly of blacks has made having black role models seem normal. At the same time, there has always been an awareness that the various elites who have dominated the society have felt a certain nervousness at being surrounded by a large number of blacks. As one Jamaican whom I interviewed put it:

> Black Americans . . . are under a pressure cooker of a system that we in Jamaica don't know what it is like. [Be]cause remember you know, these are people who for generations and generations have been surrounded by a hostile white majority. We were under slavery, yes! And we got the lash, yes!; but whites feared us on the broad general scale. We might have feared, individually, the whims and fancies of the individual master, but in terms of a collective psychology: they feared us rebelling because we outnumbered them 10 to 1. And even after the growth[88] of the country . . . you still have the situation where you are confident just by the simple fact that the numbers around you look like you. . . . It's a very important thing.

Historically, demographic majority status gave blacks potential power; and this potential became actualized in the early decades of this century as decolonization within the context of a democratic political system placed power in their hands.

In the United States, the reverse has been true. With power resting securely in the hands of a white majority, racial discrimination has been very penetrating—sanctioned by the state, rigidly enforced, and extensively affecting the everyday interaction of individuals. While the present post–Civil Rights period has witnessed a decline in monolithic Jim Crow–style racism, discrimination continues to afflict blacks widely, especially with respect to housing and their experience in public places.[89] Another indicator of the continued salience of race in America is the existence of hate groups such as the Ku Klux Klan, the Southern League, The Historic Preservation Association, and several neo-Nazi organizations.[90] In contrast to all this, racial discrimination in Jamaica has lacked state support since the abolition of slavery in 1834.[91] It nevertheless persisted, but with less intensity than has been the case in the United States. For instance, the fact that, traditionally, whites have constituted a tiny fraction of the Jamaican population has prevented the development of hate groups such as the ones mentioned above. Blacks in postemancipation Jamaica, unlike those in postemancipation America, have not had to face extreme and persistent efforts (e.g., lynchings and antiblack racial riots) to terrorize them into submission. Incidents of racial discrimination have been reported in the tourist areas of Jamaica and even in some private clubs in Kingston;[92] and debate continues as to whether concentration of corporate capital in the hands of ethnic minorities constitutes continuing antiblack discrimination or is a legacy of the past.[93] Nevertheless, it would be accurate to say that most Jamaicans—especially those of the postindependence generation—do not perceive daily, systematic, overt displays of racial discrimination. This, for instance, was the majority view of the Jamaican immigrants whom I interviewed. Only one of these immigrants alluded to an adverse experience, related to race, while living in Jamaica. In contrast, most argued that social conflict, stemming from inequalities in wealth, is endemic on the island.

Beyond the issue of racial discrimination, we also find that Jamaicans have traditionally defined race broadly enough to give the individual Jamaican some latitude for negotiating identity. This leeway is possible because in determining "race" the society weighs several factors. These include ancestry, skin color, hair type, facial features, and socioeconomic status. American society, relying on slight traces of African ancestry, adopts a very restrictive view of "blacks," including in that population individuals ranging from the very dark skinned to those who are very light skinned. However, Jamaicans' use of multiple criteria causes them to view these "blacks" as belonging to different groups. In effect, they disaggregate what Americans compress. Centuries of miscegenation between individuals from Africa, Asia (Indians and Chinese), Europe, and the Middle East (Syrians and Lebanese) have led to many combinations of types.[94] Thus, Jamaicans,[95] in distinguishing individuals, are more apt to rely on differences in shade than on rigid dichotomies such as are found in America.[96] The result is to add another layer of complexity on an already complex situation, since considering shade of skin implies continuous variation in racial designation. Such complexity means that, inevitably, the assignment of racial identity is a social process. For instance, Patterson has shown that early Chinese immigrants to Jamaica regarded the children of these immigrants and women of primarily African ancestry as "Chinese." Indeed, immigrants made made certain that this was the case by sending these children to China to become fully immersed into that culture.[97]

"Whiteness," no less than "blackness," or being "Chinese," or any other racial designation has been socially constructed in both Jamaica and the United States. American society has created "whiteness" by attempting to exclude from that category all individuals with even remote African ancestry. At the same time, the process has merged European immigrants from different national backgrounds ("ethnics")—especially those who, initially, may have felt a sense of exclusion from the mainstream society.[98] Also, judging by intermarriage rates, the "white" category is incorporating some Asians, Native Americans, and Hispanics.[99] A similar process occurs in Jamaica, but in that country the process of constructing "whiteness" might be even broader than it is in this country. For instance, as noted earlier, in Jamaica the category "white" embraces not only Anglo-Saxons, but also Jews, Syrians, some people of mixed race, and some Chinese individuals. However, there is also the notion that "money whitens," which means that, theoretically, as a dark skinned individual improves his or her ratings on such criteria as income, education, lifestyle, and overall wealth, that individual becomes progressively "whiter."[100] This concept points to the important role played by achieved criteria in considerations of race in Jamaica.

In practice, the "whitening" effect of upward social mobility has limits, since many Jamaicans extol pride in their African ancestry and reject any assertion that seeking upward mobility amounts to attempts to be "white." As noted previously, they tend not to associate success or failure with race; and those of the postindependence generation have the least incentive to do so, since they have been socialized in a society in which blacks are politically dominant . In fact, the present century has seen a trend toward increasing self-esteem among individuals of (primarily) African ancestry. For instance, in an analysis of social distance among groups in Jamaica, social scientist Mary Richardson has found that a sample of Jamaican college students ranked individuals of African ancestry as being the most acceptable group.[101] This finding suggests that, for many Jamaicans, the "payoff" with respect to upward mobility would come in the form of the intrinsic improvement to quality of life which it brings, rather than any "whitening" that may occur. Such would be even more true for Jamaicans who migrate to the United States. These immigrants tend to focus closely on improving themselves materially, educationally, and occupationally. However, they believe (see chapter 3) that antiblack racial discrimination is widespread and likely to continue into the foreseeable future—an attitude which they summarize by describing America as a "white man's country." Given such expectations, they do not expect to see anytime soon the full assimilation of blacks into American society. Even less than in Jamaica, do they expect to become "white." Nevertheless, they still argue that compared to Jamaica, America offers many opportunities for upward mobility for those who are willing to work hard. They may still face discrimination, but it is possible to improve quality of life by migrating.[102]

■ CONCLUSION

The issue of race in Jamaica is complex because of how it developed historically. During the period of slavery, skin shade became closely associated with wealth, political power, and social esteem: lighter skin color meant increasing command over these social desirables and darker skin color meant the reverse. These correlations stemmed from the racial slavery which lay at the foundation of the plantation system that characterized European settlement in the Caribbean. In Jamaica, as elsewhere, a tiny European elite exercised hegemony over a much larger mass of African slaves; and intermediate between these two groups lay a mixed-race group that derived its origins from sexual relations between the dominant Europeans and subordinated African slaves. Yet, even during slavery, the social system was more complex than these simple correlations would suggest. Each group—whites, mixed-race individuals, and blacks—displayed internal occupational differentiation. More importantly, from the viewpoint of group identity, racial definitions were, to some extent, plastic. This flexibility was seen in the very existence of a separate mixed-race group; and in the fact that the lighter skinned and more wealthy of these individuals could become "white." Thus, from the very beginning, racial designations in Jamaica have been more flexible than those in the United States. An individual's race has involved consideration of a host of factors, including ancestry, skin shade, wealth, occupation, and educational level. Moreover, race, while an important component in upward mobility, has been less of an absolute barrier than in this country.

Assessments of the issue of race as it affects contemporary Jamaica usually begin by considering the essential slave background. However, these assessments differ in the extent to which they see this background as intruding into the present. At one end of the spectrum, cultural pluralism sees contemporary Jamaica as closely replicating the slave past; while, at the other end, some social theorists, emphasizing the complex interpenetration of race and class, argue that Jamaica has no fixed racial or class hierarchies. A middling position might be better than either of these two extremes, since the process of decolonization and changes in the Jamaican economy have given the black majority political power and enabled upward mobility for many. At the same time, the majority of the poor are black and control of the island's key industries lies with a light skinned elite. Thus, in some respects, present-day Jamaica resembles the past but, in others, it is very different.

The paradox of race in Jamaica is that even though the distribution of wealth is highly skewed and correlates with shade of skin, Jamaicans tend not to view race as being a pressing issue in their everyday lives. This attitude occurs for several reasons. One key reason is black dominance of the population: Since people of a particular physical type are the norm, a black person becomes, essentially, just another face in the crowd. This sense of normalcy intertwines closely with a widely held belief—almost, in fact, a commonsense understanding—that higher education is *the* means of bettering quality of life. The reality that the education system cannot fully bear the weight of these expectations has not stopped the average Jamaican from having, as writer Carolyn Cooper puts it, a "persistent belief in the instrumentality of book learning as an engine of upward social mobility";[103] a belief that is continuously reinforced by the observation that, as the majority population, blacks are to be found at all levels in the society. In this respect, their control of the island's political apparatus is quite important, since it is the most tangible evidence of black influence. However, far from being merely a random occurrence, Jamaicans' belief in the utility of education is part of a consciously articulated ideology which seeks to downplay race as an issue in the society. Here, too, the political system has been very important, since it dampens appeals to race by basing party politics on cross-class coalitions. Ironically, another factor whose importance cannot be overlooked, is the strong appeal to the African heritage—as exemplified in the popularity of reggae music—that has become increasingly evident in the postindependence years. Thus, race in contemporary Jamaica remains a paradox—potentially a powerful issue but not systematically articulated. For Jamaican immigrants, the key fact, here, is that they perceive race to be a virtual nonissue in Jamaica and, in contrast, to be a very salient issue in the United States. This relative difference in perception, stemming from differences in experiences in both countries, leads to significant problems of adjustment for these immigrants, and also for other West Indians whose societies approximate the history and social structure of Jamaica.

Notes

1. This is not to argue that Jamaicans are unconscious of race. In fact, recognition of the integral role that race has played in that and other West Indian societies is a standard part of the analysis of those societies by local scholars. However, in their everyday lives, ordinary Jamaicans often adopt a very different point of view.
2. K. Nyamayaro Mufuka, "The Jamaican Experiment," *Current History*, Vol. 74, No. 434 (February 1978): 70–89.
3. Mark Kurlansky, *A Continent of Islands* (Reading: Addison-Wesley Publishing Company, 1992), p. 41.
4. Ronald Segal, *The Black Diaspora* (New York: Farrar, Straus & Giroux, 1995), p. 317.
5. The *Daily Gleaner* is Jamaica's leading newspaper.
6. *The Jamaican Weekly Gleaner* (October 20–26, 1995): 19.
7. Jenni Campbell, "US Demands J'cans Declare Complexion," *The Jamaican Weekly Gleaner* (March 15-21, 1996): 2. The use of physical, cultural, and socioeconomic criteria, by United States embassy officials, to judge eligibility for entrance into the United States has also sparked controversy in other countries and has been resisted by some of these officials. See Philip Shenon, "Judge Denounces U.S. Visa Policies Based on Race or Looks" (*New York Times*, January 23, 1998): A1.
8. For example, see Ira De A. Reid, *The Negro Immigrant* (New York: Columbia University Press, 1939), pp. 171–214; Nancy Foner, "The Jamaicans," in *New Immigrants in New York*, ed. Nancy Foner (New York: Columbia University Press, 1987), pp. 195–271; Vivienne Walt, "Caught Between Two Worlds," *New York Newsday* (April 15, 1988): 6; Milton Vickerman, "The Responses of West Indians towards African-Americans: Distancing and Identification, " in *Research in Race and Ethnic Relations*, Vol. 7, ed. Rutledge Dennis (Greenwich: JAI Press, 1994): 83–128.
9. The table also underestimates the black numerical advantage by not illustrating its historical length. Actually, this advantage became evident much earlier

in Jamaican history than the table indicates. For instance, Richard Dunn has shown that in 1661—six years after the British conquest of the island—whites accounted for 85 percent of Jamaica's population of 3470. By the following year, the population had increased 21 percent to 4205, and whites accounted for 87 percent of this number. However—illustrating the rapid growth of the slave trade—by 1673, whites accounted for only 45 percent of the population (17,272), with blacks accounting for the rest. Therefore, even from this early period, just eighteen years after its conquest, blacks already outnumbered whites in Jamaica. See Richard Dunn, *Sugar and Slaves: The Rise of the Planter Class in the English West Indies, 1624–1713* (New York: W.W. Norton and Company, 1972), p. 151.

10. See Rupert Lewis, "Black Nationalism in Jamaica in Recent Years," in *Essays on Power and Change in Jamaica*, ed. Carl Stone and Aggrey Brown (Kingston: Jamaica Publishing House, 1977), pp. 65–71; Aggrey Brown, *Color, Class and Politics in Jamaica* (New Brunswick: Transaction Books, 1979); Michael Kaufman, *Jamaica Under Manley* (London: Lawrence Hill and Company, 1975); Obika Gray, *Radicalism and Social Change in Jamaica, 1960–1972* (Knoxville: The University of Tennessee Press, 1991).

11. That is, defined as individuals who are primarily of African ancestry.

12. This is the term that is usually used in the literature to refer to a preference for Western, over African, culture. For instance, see Rex Nettleford, *Identity, Race and Protest in Jamaica* (New York: William Morrow and Company, Inc., 1972); Colin Clarke, "Social Patterns," in *Jamaica in Maps*, ed. Colin Clarke (London: Hodder and Stoughton, 1975), pp. 20–21; *Kingston, Jamaica* (Berkeley: University of California Press, 1975); Nancy Foner, *Jamaica Farewell* (Berkeley: University of California Press, 1978).

13. Analyses of West Indian societies inevitably point out that the close relationship between these two variables is the central dynamic in the social structure of these societies.

14. Jamaica received its independence from Britain in 1962.

15. Orlando Patterson, *The Sociology of Slavery* (London: Granada Publishing, 1973); Franklin Knight, *The Caribbean: The Genesis of a Fragmented Nationalism* (New York: Oxford University Press, 1978).

16. Philip Curtin, *Two Jamaicas: The Role of Ideas in a Tropical Colony, 1830–1865* (New York: Atheneum, 1970); Knight, *The Caribbean: The Genesis of a Fragmented Nationalism*, p. 95; Aggrey Brown, *Color, Class, and Politics in Jamaica*, pp. 44–55; George Beckford and Michael Witter, *Small Garden, Bitter Weed* (London: ZED Books, 1980). Philip Curtin's treatment of the colored population emphasizes their historically anomalous position in Jamaican society. Although he shows that whites subjugated them to various hindrances, he also views Jamaican society as consisting of two castes: European and African Jamaica. He includes coloreds in the first category because of their strong preference for European culture and, by the same token, aversion to the African side of their heritage.

17. Richard Dunn, *Sugar and Slaves: The Rise of the Planter Class in the English West Indies, 1624–1713*; Brown, *Color, Class, and Politics in Jamaica*, Ch. 2.

18. Patterson, *The Sociology of Slavery*, Ch. 2; Gad Heuman, *Between Black and*

White: Race, Politics, and the Free Coloreds in Jamaica, 1792–1865 (Westport: Greenwood Press, 1981), pp. 7–12; Knight, *The Caribbean: The Genesis of a Fragmented Nationalism,* pp. 104–106. With respect to this variation among slaves and between West Indian societies practicing slavery, Arthur Stinchcombe has argued that "freedom" should be likened to a continuous variable, rather than to a dichotomy consisting of two opposing legal statuses: "slave" and "free." Conceived of in this fashion, slaves enjoyed various degrees of autonomy depending on a slaveholder's need for a slave's consent and enthusiasm in performing particular jobs. Where this need was low—as in field labor on sugar plantations—slaves had the least autonomy; and where it was high—e.g., pearl diving—slaves had the most autonomy. Stinchcombe argues that, overall, three main factors determined the degree of slave autonomy and relative repressiveness of slave regimes: (1) the degree to which sugar cane cultivation dominated the economy, (2) the degree to which planters were internally organized, and (3) the degree of planter power within the empire government. A high ranking on these three criteria led to greater repressiveness and, therefore, lesser slave autonomy, while a low ranking led to the reverse. Based on these criteria, Stinchcombe argues that Barbados was the most "unfree" of all West Indian slave societies. However, it was closely followed by Jamaica, Surinam, the British Leewards, Martinique, and Guadeloupe. See Arthur Stinchcombe, "Freedom and Oppression of Slaves in the Eighteenth-Century Caribbean," *American Sociological Review,* Vol. 59 (December, 1994): 911–929.

19. Heuman, *Between Black and White: Race, Politics, and the Free Coloreds in Jamaica, 1792–1865.*
20. Knight, *The Caribbean: The Genesis of a Fragmented Nationalism,* p. 95.
21. Heuman, *Between Black and White: Race, Politics, and the Free Coloreds in Jamaica, 1792–1865,* p. 13.
22. Carol Holzberg, *Minorities and Power in a Black Society* (Lanham: The North South Publishing Company, 1987).
23. Thomas August, "Jewish Assimilation and Plural Society in Jamaica," *Social and Economic Studies,* Vol. 36, No. 2 (1987): 109–122.
24. Carl Stone, "Race and Economic Power in Jamaica," in *Garvey: His Work and Impact,* ed. Rupert Lewis and Patrick Bryan (Trenton: African World Press, 1991), pp. 243–264.
25. Derek Gordon, "Race, Class and Social Mobility in Jamaica," in *Garvey: His Work and Impact,* ed. Rupert Lewis and Patrick Bryan (Trenton: African World Press, 1991), pp. 265–282.
26. David Lowenthal, *West Indian Societies* (London: Oxford University Press, 1972), p. 68.
27. Smith, in turn, based his ideas on work done by J. S. Furnival in the Far East. See J. S. Furnival, *Colonial Policy and Practice* (London: Cambridge University Press, 1948).
28. M. G. Smith, *The Plural Society in the British West Indies* (Berkeley: The University of California Press, 1965), p. 766.
29. Ibid., p. 14.
30. Ibid., p. 163.

31. Ibid.

32. Much of this criticism concerns the theory's portrayal of a static society. For instance, Carl Stone has argued that cultural pluralism describes Jamaica as it was at the time of the abolition of slavery in 1834 rather than the present-day situation. Similarly, Susan Craig has argued that researchers need to "undertake empirical work in historical perspective" as a way of understanding social relations in particular historical periods. In addition to these criticisms, cultural pluralism has also been faulted for not clearly delineating the criteria for considering a society plural; misunderstanding the degree of normative value consensus existing between various groups in "plural" societies; assuming that heterogeneity necessarily implies conflict; and for being weak theoretically and methodologically. See Carl Stone, *Class, Race and Political Behavior in Urban Jamaica* (Kingston: ISER, 1973), p. 8; Susan Craig, "Sociology as Montage," *Social and Economic Studies*, Vol. 23, No. 1 (1974): 127–139; Vera Rubin, "Social and Cultural Pluralism by M. G. Smith," in *Social and Cultural Pluralism in the Caribbean*, ed. Vera Rubin (New York: Annals of New York Academy of Science, 1960), pp. 780–785; H. I. McKenzie, "The Plural Society Debate: Some Comments on a Recent Contribution," *Social and Economic Studies*, XV (March, 1966): 53–80; Lloyd Braithwaite, "Social Stratification and Cultural Pluralism," in *Social and Cultural Pluralism in the Caribbean*, ed. Vera Rubin (New York: Annals of New York Academy of Science, 1960), pp. 816–883; Malcolm Cross, "Cultural Pluralism and Sociological Theory: A Critique and Re-evaluation," *Social and Economic Studies*, XVII (1966): 381–397.

33. Adam Kuper, *Changing Jamaica* (London: Routledge and Kegan Paul, 1976), p. 10.

34. Fernando Henriques, *Jamaica: Land of Wood and Water* (London: Macgibbon and Kee, 1957), p. 42.

35. Kuper, p. 45.

36. Paradoxically, he views this most significant of Jamaican cleavages as tending toward social stability, since the two leading political parties—the Jamaica Labour Party and the People's National Party—consist of multiclass, multirace coalitions. See Kuper, p. 111.

37. Kuper, p. 60.

38. Ibid., pp. 103–104.

39. Ibid., p. 83. Kuper's findings jibe with those of Foner in her earlier study of another Jamaican village. Assessing the determinants of social stratification in this North Coast village, she found that the crucial factors were occupation, land ownership, income, and lifestyle. She characterized an additional set of factors—sex, leadership, color, residence, education, and age—as secondary in importance, since they operated only in conjunction with the first set. Like Kuper she found that social ranking stemmed primarily from material causes and, with respect to this, land ownership, occupation, and income were central. More than anything else, villagers valued "living independent," by which they meant a capacity to hire others to work for them and to dispense favors. As in the case of the village studied by Kuper, a cultural bias toward "whiteness" existed, since, as Foner states: "Many black wage laborers associate their

poverty with color and nearly all have an unquestioning acceptance of the superiority and beauty of white skin" (p. 27). Yet, light skin color, by itself, did not guarantee high social status. Indeed, villagers denied that this was the legitimate basis for deference, choosing instead to focus on "education" with its implications of esteemed occupations, high income, and prestigious lifestyles (such as speaking "proper" English and wearing fashionable clothes). See Nancy Foner, *Status and Power in Rural Jamaica: A Study of Educational and Political Change* (New York: Teachers College Press, 1973); "The Meaning of Education to Jamaicans at Home and in London," in *Adaptation of Migrants from the Caribbean in European and American Metropolis*, ed. Humphrey E. Lamur and John D. Speckmann (Leiden: University of Amsterdam and the Royal Institute of Linguistics and Anthropology, 1975), pp. 99–111.

40. However, Stone's methodology has been criticized. In *Class, Race, and Political Behaviour in Urban Jamaica*, Stone argues that though the Marxist emphasis on ownership/nonownership of the means of production captures a key aspect of class relationships in capitalist societies, this focus is too narrow. Instead, he urges a broader conceptualization which would focus on wealth and material dispossession. Operationalized, this would translate into an equation of class with occupations. Consequently, he derives a typology with the following categories: (1) big businessmen, (2) professionals, (3) small business men, (4) white collar, (5) self-employed artisans, (6) blue collar, and (7) lower class. These categories are subsequently used to analyze Kingstonians' views on various political issues, race, and class. While this methodology offers precision, it has been criticized for sometimes leading to muddled conclusions with respect to the intermediate categories. It has also been criticized for not fully dealing with the issue of class consciousness. For Stone's analysis see, *Class, Race, and Political Behaviour in Urban Jamaica* (Kingston: ISER, 1973); and for a critique of his work, see Kuper, *Changing Jamaica*, pp. 66–67 and Susan Craig, "Sociological Theorizing in the English-Speaking Caribbean: A Review" in *Contemporary Caribbean: A Sociological Reader, Vol.II*, ed. Susan Craig (Maracas: The College Press, 1982), pp. 143–180.

41. Carl Stone, "Race and Economic Power in Jamaica," 1991.

42. George Beckford and Michael Witter, *Small Garden, Bitter Weed*; Michael Kaufman, *Jamaica Under Manley*, EPICA Task Force, *Jamaica: Caribbean Challenge* (Washington, D.C.: EPICA Task Force, 1985), p. 36.

43. Twentieth-century Jamaican politics has been dominated by these two political parties, both of which emerged in the wake of islandwide riots by workers in 1938. This period set the pattern for subsequent Jamaican politics: twin political parties, each allied to powerful labor unions, and led by charismatic politicians. First to be formed (by Alexander Bustamante)—in 1938—was the Bustamante Industrial Trade Union. In the same year, Norman Manley formed the left-leaning People's National Party. In 1943 Bustamante formed the more conservative Jamaica Labour Party to contest elections made possible by the granting of Universal Adult Suffrage (by the British) in 1944. The Jamaica Labour Party won this election and the subsequent one in 1949. Perceiving its socialist orientation to be a major reason for its failures in the last two elections, the PNP purged itself—in 1952—of its leftist elements. This was ac-

companied by the formation of a new labor union allied to the PNP: the National Worker's Union. Perhaps because of its rightward drift, the PNP managed to win the next two general elections, in 1955 and 1959. However, the JLP won the 1962 and 1967 general elections. The People's National Party returned in 1972 and also won the 1976 general elections. In 1980 it lost to the JLP and because the PNP refused to contest the elections of 1983, the former party held office until 1989. In that year, Michael Manley and the PNP again returned to power and have held onto that power into the present. In December 1997, the PNP won a third consecutive term in office.

Apart from alternating in holding power, the two political parties are characterized by multiclass coalitions. Originally, the JLP derived most of its support from the working class via its affiliation with the Bustamante Industrial Trade Union. However, it gradually attracted support from the upper classes, especially after the PNP's declaration of its socialism after 1972. The latter party started out as a mainly middle class party but increasingly attracted working class support. Its affiliation with the National Worker's Union and especially the PNP's declaration of socialism after it took power in 1972 aided this process. This raised great expectations among poorer Jamaicans, many of whom came to see the JLP as the party of the privileged. Persistent economic decline in the 1970s, increasing crime, fear of communism, and a decline in the credibility of the PNP led to this party's defeat in the 1980 general elections. The literature on Jamaica's political history is voluminous. For examples, see Terry Lacey, *Violence and Politics in Jamaica, 1960–1970* (Bristol: Manchester University Press, 1977); Ken Post, *Arise Ye Starvelings: The Jamaican Labour Rebellion of 1938 and Its Aftermath* (The Hague: Martinus Nijhoff, 1978); Philip Sherlock, *Norman Manley: A Biography* (London: Macmillan, 1980); Michael Manley, *Jamaica: Struggle in the Periphery* (London: Writers and Readers Cooperative Society, Ltd., 1982); Monroe, *The Politics of Constitutional Decolonization: Jamaica, 1944–62;* Carl Stone, *Politics versus Economics: The 1989 Elections in Jamaica* (Kingston: Heinemann Publishers (Caribbean), 1989).

44. These changes, important because they shifted Jamaica's orientation away from Britain and toward North America, saw new American and Canadian investment in bauxite, tourism, and manufacturing. These investments caused a whole series of other changes in Jamaican society. Among the more important were the consolidation of Jews, Syrians, and coloreds as a new elite; the consequent shift of economic and political power from rural-based planters to the urban sector; and an upsurge in internal (to urban areas) and international migration (primarily to Britain) by poor rural blacks. See, EPICA Task Force, *Jamaica: Caribbean Challenge;* Carl Stone, "Race and Economic Power in Jamaica."

45. Omar Davies and Michael Witter, "The Development of the Jamaican Economy since Independence," in *Jamaica in Independence*, ed. Rex Nettleford (Kingston: Heinemann Publishers (Caribbean), 1989), pp. 75–101.

46. Derek Gordon, "Race, Class and Social Mobility in Jamaica," in *Garvey: His Work and Impact,* ed. Rupert Lewis and Patrick Bryan (Trenton: African World Press, 1991), pp. 265–282.

47. Ibid., p. 269.

48. In Jamaica, the term "ethnic" usually refers to individuals of East Indian, Chinese, or Middle Eastern descent.

49. Carl Stone, "Race and Economic Power in Jamaica."

50. Carl Stone, *The Political Opinions of the Jamaican People (1979–81)* (Kingston: Blackett Publishers, 1982); Elsie LeFranc, "Higglering in Kingston: Entrepreneurs or Traditional Small Scale Operators?" *Caribbean Review*, Vol. XVI, No. 1 (Spring, 1988): 15–35.

51. Kaufman, *Jamaica Under Manley*; Darrell Levi, *Michael Manley: The Making of a Leader* (Athens, Georgia: The University of Georgia Press, 1989); Stone, *Politics versus Economics: The 1989 Elections in Jamaica*; Stone, "Race and Economic Power in Jamaica."

52. Trevor Monroe, *The Politics of Constitutional Decolonization: Jamaica, 1944–62* (Kingston: ISER, 1983); Stone, "Race and Economic Power in Jamaica."

53. Analysis of the Jamaican corporate structure reveals a high degree of interlock. For instance, Tracey has shown that, in 1989, seventeen individuals from nine families served as directors or chairmen of thirty-one of Jamaica's leading companies. See Stanley Reid, "An Introductory Approach to the Concentration of Power in the Jamaican Corporate Economy and Notes on Its Origin," in *Essays on Power and Change in Jamaica*, ed. Carl Stone and Aggrey Brown (Kingston: Jamaica Publishing, 1977), pp. 15–44; Stone, "Race and Economic Power in Jamaica"; Lenworth Tracey, "Corporate Power Structure—The Stock Exchange," *The Jamaica Record* (March 19, 1989): 3A.

54. One factor that vastly complicates considerations of race in Jamaica, as compared to the United States, is that the former (as in most West Indian societies) has long taken notice of shades of color, where the latter has tended to make a sharper distinction between "blacks" and "whites." This attention implies that conceptions of race in the West Indies involve continuous variation instead of the existence of rigid categories. As noted below, this situation is made even more complex because color variation interweaves with social class such that the latter can offset the stigma associated with darker skin. As with other aspects of the social structure of West Indian societies, this topic has, historically, drawn much discussion and, therefore, the literature is very large. For a sampling of discussion on issues of color and class see Leonard Broom, "The Social Differentiation of Jamaica," *American Sociological Review*, Vol. 19, No. 2 (1954): 115–125; Kathleen Norris, *Jamaica, the Search for an Identity* (London: Oxford University Press, 1962); Gordon K. Lewis, *The Growth of the Modern West Indies* (New York: Modern Reader Paperbacks, 1968); "The Contemporary Caribbean," in *Caribbean Contours*, ed. Sidney Mintz and Sally Price (Baltimore: Johns Hopkins University Press, 1985), pp. 219–252; Douglas Hall, "The Ex-Colonial Society in Jamaica," in *Patterns of Foreign Influence in the Caribbean*, ed. Emannuel DeKadt (London: Oxford University Press, 1972), pp. 32–48; Rex Nettleford, *Identity, Race and Protest in Jamaica*; Kuper, *Changing Jamaica*; Foner, *Status and Power in Rural Jamaica: A Study of Educational and Political Change*.

55. Rex Nettleford, *Identity, Race and Protest in Jamaica*, p. 14; Kuper, *Changing Jamaica*; Diane Austin, *Urban Life in Kingston, Jamaica: The Culture and Class Ideology of Two Neighborhoods* (New York: Gordon and Breach, 1987);

Stone, *Class, Race and Political Behavior in Urban Jamaica;* "Race and Economic Power in Jamaica."

56. Although, as pointed out by—for instance—Kurlansky, poor blacks are more likely to see their impoverishment as having a racial component.

57. Most observers of the Jamaican scene note that the country's role as a small dependent country, inserted in a world capitalist system, significantly shapes its internal politics. This factor, for instance, helped undermine the rule of the left-ist People's Nationalist Party in the 1970s (whose policies championed the poor) and the conservative Jamaica Labour Party in the 1980s. The fact is that, regardless of ideology, Jamaican governments must deal with a number of basic economic problems: very high levels of debt to such international agencies as the IMF, the World Bank, and the Inter-American Development Bank; unfavorable rates of exchange with developed countries such as the United States; a dependence on imports; underproductivity in factories; the maldistribution of land; and high levels of unemployment. The literature on the interaction between dependency and internal Jamaican politics is voluminous. See, for example, Lloyd Best, "Size and Survival," in *Readings in the Political Economy of the Caribbean,* ed. Norman Girvan and Owen Jefferson (Kingston: ISER, 1977), pp. 29–36; Carl Stone, *Understanding Third World Politics and Economics* (Kingston: Earle Publishers, 1980); Manley, *Jamaica: Struggle in the Periphery;* Kaufman, *Jamaica Under Manley;* Edward Seaga, "Toward Resolving the Debt Crisis," *Caribbean Review,* Vol. XVI, No. 1 (1988): 1–30; Davies and Witter, "The Development of the Jamaican Economy since Independence"; Anthony Payne, "Liberal Economics versus Electoral Politics," in *Modern Caribbean Politics,* ed. Anthony Payne and Paul Sutton (Baltimore: The Johns Hopkins University Press, 1993), pp. 28–53.

58. It should be remembered that the term "race" is being viewed as being a socially constructed concept.

59. Orlando Patterson, "Toward a Future that Has No Past—Reflections on the Fate of Blacks in the Americas," *The Public Interest,* No. 27 (1972): 25–62.

60. Of course, the "other things being equal" involve the usual formidable organizational and interpersonal complexities inherent in attaining high status. However, the point is that in Jamaica race, though a potentially important factor in the political sphere, has become minimized. Consequently, even poor Jamaicans feel that they can aspire to such high status positions. See, for example, Stone, *Class, Race and Political Behavior in Urban Jamaica;* Foner, *Status and Power in Rural Jamaica: A Study of Educational and Political Change,* p. 61.

61. A potentially confusing point here is that the sociological meaning of the complementary terms, *majority group* and *minority group* emphasizes relative power. That is, sociologically speaking, a majority group is one exercising dominance over a society. Conversely, a minority group wields relatively little power. This emphasis cuts across the normal assumption that size is the defining characteristic. From this sociological point of view, therefore, a population constituting a numerical majority might, in fact, constitute a "minority group." The case of blacks under Apartheid in South Africa is the classic example of this situation. Nevertheless, size is an important criterion in discussions of majority

groups and minority groups. First, where small size overlaps with relative powerlessness (as in the case of blacks in the United States) the situation of the minority group might worsen. Second, where groups are relatively powerless but numerically large, sheer numbers can help to somewhat offset the power disadvantage. In the case of Jamaican blacks the situation becomes somewhat muddled because they tend to be disproportionately poor, the country's economic resources being controlled by a light skinned elite. On the other hand, blacks dominate the political system and constitute, by far, the largest proportion of the population. Apart from power and size, other criteria defining minority groups include endogamy, a subjective sense of fellow feeling, and the possession of distinctive physical and/or cultural traits. See Charles Wagley and Marvin Harris, *Minorities in the New World* (New York: Columbia University Press, 1958); Richard Schermerhorn, *Comparative Ethnic Relations* (New York: Random House, 1970).

62. This is not to deny the acceptance, by some Jamaicans, of notions of inferiority, for these sentiments have been documented. On the other hand, a number of writers have noted the aggressive self-confidence of Jamaican blacks. Gordon Lewis, especially, attributes this to population size. For examples of Jamaicans' internalization of feelings of inferiority see Madeline Kerr, *Personality and Conflict in Jamaica* (Liverpool: The University Press, 1952); Rex Nettleford, "The Matter of Melanin: Calling a Spade a Spade" (*The Jamaica Record*, March 19, 1989): 4. For examples of self-confidence in Jamaicans (and West Indians in general) see Ira De A. Reid, *The Negro Immigrant* (Columbia University Press, 1939); Lewis, *The Making of the Modern West Indies*; Carl Stone, "The Black Self-Concept," in *Carl Stone on Jamaican Politics and Society*, ed. Carl Stone (Kingston: The Gleaner Company, 1989), pp. 96–99; "Columbus's Isles: A Survey of the Caribbean" *The Economist* (August 6, 1988): 3–18.

63. The fact that the political system is dominated by blacks.

64. Frank Cundall, ed. *Lady Nugent's Journal* (London: The West India Committee, 1939), p. 254.

65. For example, see James A. Mau's, "The Threatening Masses: Myth or Reality?" in *Consequences of Class and Color: West Indian Perspectives*," ed. David Lowenthal and Lambros Comitas (New York: Anchor Books, 1973), pp. 57–78, Rex Nettleford, *Caribbean Cultural Identity: The Case of Jamaica* (Kingston: The Institute of Jamaica, 1978), pp. 5–6; "The Matter of Melanin: Calling a Spade a Spade"; Gray, *Radicalism and Social Change in Jamaica, 1960–1970;* Stone, *Class, Race and Political Behaviour in Urban Jamaica; Race and Economic Power in Jamaica.* See, also, Erna Brodber's discussion ("Socio-cultural Change in Jamaica," in *Jamaica in Independence*, ed. Rex Nettleford (Kingston: Heineman Publishers (Caribbean) Limited, 1989), pp. 55–74) in which she outlines a continuity between elite fears of the masses under colonialism and such fears, extended to include the black government, in contemporary Jamaica.

66. Jamaica's national motto is only one of several similar mottoes to be found in various West Indian countries. See Lowenthal, *West Indian Societies*, p. 18.

67. Norris, *Jamaica, the Search for an Identity*; Nettleford, *Identity, Race and*

Protest in Jamaica; Arnold Bertram, "The Light and the Dark" (*The Jamaica Record*, March 19, 1989): 5A; Bernard D. Headley, "Impressions of Mr. Seaga's Jamaica," *Freedomways* (Summer 1985): 95–100. Nettleford ("The Matter of Melanin: Calling a Spade a Spade") has argued that the Jamaican elite has more to gain from multiracialism rather than nonracialism, since the latter would force respect for all Jamaicans.

68. Henriques, *Jamaica: Land of Wood and Water*, p. 136; Bertram, "The Light and the Dark"; Gray, *Radicalism and Social Change in Jamaica, 1960–1970.*

69. Stone, *Class, Race and Political Behaviour in Urban Jamaica*; "A Look at Minority Economic Power," in *Carl Stone on Jamaican Politics and Society*, ed. Carl Stone (Kingston: The Gleaner Company, 1989), pp. 99–102; Kaufman, *Jamaica Under Manley*, p. 63. Ken Post has given a good example of this mind-set in his analysis of class struggle in early-twentieth-century Jamaica. He shows how the colonial establishment reacted negatively to the development of overt racial consciousness, through the Rastafarian movement, among the black poor in the 1930s. The embodiment of this growing racial consciousness was Haile Selassie, the self-styled "Light of the World." Criticizing this title, a November 4th, 1930, editorial in the establishment's main outlet, *The Daily Gleaner*, stated: "We respectfully submit that his light seems to be somewhat dark. We are not alluding to complexion: color questions are not permitted in these columns. But what has Abyssinia done to enlighten any of us, and how shall we be illuminated by the actions or dicta of this particular gentleman?" (Ken Post, *Arise Ye Starvelings: The Jamaican Labour Rebellion of 1938 and Its Aftermath*, p. 163). Similar sentiments are still to be found in present-day Jamaica. See, for example, Morris Cargill, "On Colonialism" (*The Jamaica Weekly Gleaner*, April 28–May 4, 1995), p. 7.

70. Foner, *Status and Power in Rural Jamaica: A Study of Educational and Political Change*; *Race and Political Behaviour in Urban Jamaica*; Stone, "The Black Self-Concept."

71. Curtin, *Two Jamaicas: The Role of Ideas in a Tropical Colony, 1830–1865*, p. 173.

72. Rex Nettleford (*Caribbean Cultural Identity: The Case of Jamaica*, p. 6) argues that this viewpoint stems from the ethnic minorities' realization that they constitute a tiny percentage of the Jamaican population.

73. See, for example, Nettleford, *Identity, Race and Protest in Jamaica*, p. 24; and Lowenthal, *West Indian Societies*, pp. 17–25.

74. See Bertram, "The Light and the Dark"; Nettleford, *Caribbean Cultural Identity: The Case of Jamaica*; Gray, *Radicalism and Social Change in Jamaica, 1960–1972;* Stone, "A Look at Minority Economic Power in Jamaica"; "Completing Garvey's Work," in *Carl Stone on Jamaican Politics, Economics and Society*, ed. Carl Stone (Kingston, The Gleaner Company, Ltd., 1989), pp. 102–105; "Race and Economic Power in Jamaica"; Monroe, "The Left and Questions of Race in Jamaica," in *Garvey: His Work and Impact*, ed. Rupert Lewis and Patrick Bryan (Trenton: African World Press, 1991), pp. 283–298.

75. Foner, *Status and Power in Rural Jamaica: A Study of Educational and Political Change*; Austin, *Urban Life in Kingston, Jamaica: The Culture and Class Ideology of Two Neighborhoods.*

76. Kuper, *Changing Jamaica*; Brown, *Color, Class, and Politics in Jamaica.*

77. Kuper, p. 75.
78. Foner, *Status and Power in Rural Jamaica: A Study of Educational and Political Change*; "The Meaning of Education to Jamaicans at Home and in London"; see, also, Smith, *The Plural Society in the British West Indies.*
79. Jamaica has occasionally seen incidents of racial violence (directed against, for example, the Chinese) stemming from a feeling, on the part of blacks, of economic deprivation. See, for example, Howard Johnson, "The Anti-Chinese Riots of 1918 in Jamaica," *Caribbean Quarterly*, Vol. 28, No. 3: (1982): 19–32; Brodber, "Socio-cultural Change in Jamaica."
80. Beckford and Witter, *Small Garden, Bitter Weed*, pp. 83–86; Kaufman, *Jamaica Under Manley*, pp. 51–53; Stone, "Race and Economic Power in Jamaica."
81. Kaufman, p. 215; Anthony Payne, "Jamaica's Approach to Independence," *Caribbean Review*, Vol. XVI, No. 1 (1988): 4–30; Stone, "Race and Economic Power in Jamaica."
82. Beckford and Witter, *Small Garden, Bitter Weed*; Kaufman, *Jamaica Under Manley.*
83. Stone, "Race and Economic Power in Jamaica."
84. See, for example, Sidney Mintz, "The Caribbean Region," *Daedalus*, Vol. 103, No. 2 (1974): 45–71; Winthrop Jordan, *The White Man's Burden* (New York: Oxford University Press, 1974); Barry Chevannes, "Race and Culture in Jamaica," *World Marxist Review*, Vol. 31, No. 5 (1988): 138–144. The question of whether Africans were enslaved because of preexisting racial biases against them, on the part of Europeans, or whether slavery resulted from the need of Europeans to find a stable source of labor is a controversial one. Examples of writers holding the former viewpoint include Jordon, *The White Man's Burden* and Carl N. Degler, "Slavery and the Genesis of American Race Prejudice," *Comparative Studies in Society and History*, Vol. II, No. 1 (October 1959), pp. 49–56; *Out of Our Past* (New York: Harper and Row, Publishers, 1984). Examples of writers holding the latter viewpoint include Eric Williams, *Capitalism and Slavery* (New York: Russell and Russell, 1961) and Theodore W. Allen, *The Invention of the White Race* (New York: Verso, 1995). Regardless of what factors caused the initial enslavement of Africans, it is generally agreed that the system, once it got underway, intertwined with racist ideologies that were meant to justify it.
85. Political systems in which notions of democracy coexisted with slavery and applied only to specific portions of the population; in the case of the United States and the West Indies, that portion of the white population—usually male—who met certain property qualifications. See, for example, Pierre van den Berghe, *Race and Racism* (New York: John Wiley and Sons, Inc., 1967), pp. 17–18.
86. See, for example, Curtin, *Two Jamaicas*; Lowenthal, *West Indian Societies*; Dunn, *Sugar and Slaves: The Rise of the Planter Class in the English West Indies, 1624–1713*; F. James Davis, *Who Is Black?: One Nation's Definition* (University Park: Pennsylvania State University Press, 1991).
87. This is not to argue that racial conditions in the United States are simple, but rather that structural conditions have abetted the attempt to simplify issues of race that are inherently complex.
88. He meant the whole process of social change beginning with the abolition of slavery in 1834 and ending in the attainment of independence in 1962.

89. For example, see National Research Council, *A Common Destiny: Blacks and American Society* (Washington, D.C., National Academy Press, 1989); Joe R. Feagin, "The Continuing Significance of Race: Antiblack Discrimination in Public Places," *American Sociological Review*, Vol. 56, No. 1 (February 1991): 101–116; Douglas S. Massey and Nancy A. Denton, *American Apartheid* (Cambridge: Harvard University Press, 1993). A good example of the numerous articles recounting episodes of antiblack discrimination to be found in the press is Lena Williams, "When Blacks Shop, Bias Often Accompanies Sale" (*New York Times*, April 30, 1991): 14 L.

90. See "The Face of Extremism Wears Many Guises—Most of Them Ordinary" (*Wall Street Journal*, April 28, 1995): A1.

91. See Kerr, *Personality and Conflict in Jamaica*, p. 95; Norris, *Jamaica, the Search for an Identity*, p. 10; Lowenthal, *West Indian Societies*, p. 2; Kuper, *Changing Jamaica*, p. 63.

92. See, for example, Stone, *Class, Race and Political Behaviour in Urban Jamaica*, pp. 111; 166; Bertram, "The Light and the Dark."

93. See Barnett and Ricketts, "Blacks in Multi-Racial Jamaica"; Rupert Lewis, "Blacks in the Corporate Economy" (*The Jamaica Record*, March 19, 1989): 2; Tracey, "Corporate Power Structure—The Stock Exchange"; Monroe, "The Left and Questions of Race in Jamaica"; Stone, "Race and Economic Power in Jamaica"; Segal, *The Black Diaspora*.

94. See Nettleford, *Identity, Race and Protest in Jamaica*, Ch.1.

95. It should be remembered that, with respect to questions of race, Jamaica closely resembles other countries in the West Indies.

96. For discussion of this tendency in American society see, for example, Patterson, "Toward a Future that Has No Past—Reflections on the Fate of Blacks in the Americas"; Davis, *Who Is Black?: One Nation's Definition*; Sharon Lee, "U.S. Census Racial Classifications: 1890–1990," *Ethnic and Racial Studies*, Vol. 16, No. 1 (January, 1993): 75–94.

97. Orlando Patterson, "Context and Choice in Ethnic Allegiance: A Theoretical Framework and Caribbean Case Study," in *Ethnicity: Theory and Experience*, ed. Nathan Glazer and Daniel Patrick Moynihan (Cambridge: Harvard University Press, 1975), pp. 305–349.

98. See, for example, Allen, *The Invention of the White Race*; Davis, *Who Is Black? One Nation's Definition*; Thomas Gossett, *Race, the History of an Idea in America* (Dallas: SMU Press, 1975); Jordan, *The White Man's Burden*; Lee, "U.S. Census Racial Classifications: 1890–1990"; Joel Williamson, *New People: Miscegenation and Mulattoes in the United States* (New York: New York University Press, 1980).

99. Reynolds Farley has shown that the rate of intermarriage between some members of these groups and whites is high. See "Questions About Race, Spanish-Origin and Ancestry: Controversial Issues for the Statistical System." Paper presented at the "Beyond Black and White" Conference, Washington, D.C., February 12, 1996.

100. See, for example, Douglas Hall, "The Ex-Colonial Society in Jamaica," in *Patterns of Foreign Influence in the Caribbean*, ed. Emannuel DeKadt (London: Oxford University Press, 1972), pp. 32–48; Lewis, "The Contemporary Caribbean: A General Overview"; Kaufman, *Jamaica Under Manley*, p. 44.

101. Richardson found that the college students ranked groups, from most acceptable to least, in the following order: black Jamaicans (i.e., those of primarily African ancestry), white Jamaicans, East Indians, Jews, Syrians, and Rastafarians. She attributed the poor showing of Rastafarians to the class prejudices of the middle class students who formed her sample. See Mary Richardson, "Out of Many, One People—Aspiration or Reality?," *Social and Economic Studies*, Vol. 32, No. 3 (September, 1983): 143–163.

102. In his study of second generation immigrants in San Diego and the Miami metropolitan area, Ruben Rumbaut found that Jamaicans expressed these contradictory sentiments very strongly. Jamaican students, along with the Asians he studied, reported the highest educational aspirations. Consistent with this finding, these groups displayed the highest GPA, and the highest ratio of homework-to-television watching hours. Moreover, Jamaicans and other West Indians evinced the highest self-esteem scores. However, the Jamaicans were also most likely to agree with the statement: "No matter how much education I get, people will still discriminate against me." On a 4-point scale, with 1 representing the least expectation of discrimination and 4 the most, Jamaicans scored, on average, 2.59. The next highest figures were 2.37 for Haitians and 2.31 for other West Indians. By way of comparison, Cubans averaged only 1.67. See Ruben G. Rumbaut, "The Crucible Within: Ethnic Identity, Self-Esteem, and Segmented Assimilation among Children of Immigrants," in *The New Second Generation*, ed. Alejandro Portes (New York: Russell Sage Foundation, 1996), pp. 119–170.

103. Carolyn Cooper, "Only a Nigger Gal!": Race, Gender and the Politics of Education in Claude McKay's Banana Bottom," *Caribbean Quarterly*, Vol. 38, No. 1 (March 1992): 40–54.

CHAPTER

2

Economics and Migration

Discussions of West Indians' attitudes toward race in America have to take into account the important role played by economic considerations. These considerations are the reverse side of the process of downplaying race in those societies. As has been shown for Jamaica, this process tends toward the maintenance of that island's economic status quo. However, downplaying race also encourages ordinary Jamaicans to conceive of the society's tensions as resulting, primarily, from class conflict, even as society prescribes a means—higher education—of improving quality of life within the existing class system. The reality, though, has been that for most of its history, Jamaica, like other countries in the West Indies, has been a colony; and, more to the point, a small, open economy in a worldwide capitalist system. The upshot of all this is that the island is poor and has never been able to fulfill the aspirations of most of its citizens. The consequence has been, along with other West Indian countries, a tradition of migration in search of a better life. The United States is only the latest target in a long list of countries that have seen West Indians as migrants. For many West Indians the United States represents the latest best hope of improving quality of life. This focus means that West Indian immigrants tend to subordinate other issues—including, as much as they can, race—to their overriding desire to better themselves. The concern which they express regarding race results largely from their eventual recognition of this issue's potential to disrupt their quest for self-betterment.[1] Because questions of economics are so central to West Indian immigrants, in this chapter I give an overview of how these concerns have shaped their immigration and their place in American society.

■ THE TRADITION OF IMMIGRATION

By the end of the nineteenth century, migration had become a solidly entrenched aspect of the culture of the various West Indian territories. This early migration, as well as that continuing today, has derived from the economic underdevelopment of the region. West Indians have consistently migrated to countries that have offered better employment opportunities and, in general, opportunities to increase their economic security. The initial movements occurred within the region in the wake of the abolition of slavery in 1834. In larger territories—such as Jamaica and Guyana—which had available (though, usually, lower quality) land, freed slaves withdrew from plantations and became peasant farmers. In those territories, this meant that the former slaves took, respectively, to the hillsides and to the coastal lowlands.[2] However, in most of the smaller islands of the eastern Caribbean, freed slaves who aspired to become independent cultivators had to look outside of their islands because of the nonavailability of land. Thus, from as early as 1837, freed slaves from Antigua were immigrating to Trinidad and Guyana, both of which suffered from chronic labor shortages. Well-established patterns of seasonal migration (i.e., migration taking place during the sugar season) developed between Nevis, Anguilla, St. Kitts, St. Lucia, Barbados, and Trinidad. From the 1860s onward, St. Croix, Puerto Rico, and the Dominican Republic were the recipients of such seasonal migrants. More permanent intraregional migration also occurred, as West Indians, seeking better paying jobs, spread throughout the Caribbean in a variety of service capacities (e.g., Barbadian school teachers in the Bahamas and Jamaican coachmen in Haiti).[3]

The 1850s saw the beginning of a trend which soon eclipsed intraregional migration in importance and was to continue until the 1920s: the movement to Central America. The construction of the Panama railway (linking the Atlantic and Pacific coasts) in the 1850s attracted upward of 5000 Jamaicans to that country.[4] This was followed in the 1870s by the building of the Costa Rican railway, in the 1880s by the construction of the Mexican railway, and, most important, in the same decade, by the first attempt at the construction of the Panama Canal. This initial French attempt sparked intense interest among West Indians, especially among Jamaicans. Thomas-Hope reports, for instance, that in 1882, 1000 Jamaicans per month were leaving the island and that 1883 saw a 100 percent increase such that 24,000 Jamaicans migrated to Panama. The failure of the first Panama Canal project in 1888 deflected West Indians toward their homelands and toward other Central American countries.[5] Costa Rica was a favorite destination, since demand for labor on railroad construction remained high. Moreover, that country had developed a settled West Indian (largely Jamaican) population through the Costa Rican government's efforts to retain foreign labor throughout the intermittent construction of the railway. These benefits took the form of small parcels of land that could be claimed simply by working them. The result was that by 1884, Jamaican immigrants controlled more than 120 banana farms located along the first twenty-five miles of railroad track.[6] West Indian migrants, therefore, moved not only from their homelands to various Central American territories but also within Central America itself.

The resumption of the Panama Canal project in 1904, under American leadership, underscored the fluidity of West Indian migratory patterns as, again, it proved to be an irresistible magnet for West Indians. Large numbers—especially Jamaicans and Barbadians—poured in. Thomas-Hope notes that over the thirty year period 1891–1921, at least 26,000 Barbadians migrated to Panama, resulting in a 17 percent drop in that island's population. Over the same time period, Roberts estimates that at least 28,000 Jamaicans sought employment in Panama.[7] But the movement of West Indians was by no means unidirectional, since countries other than Panama also saw significant inflows. The opening of the Venezuelan oil fields after 1910 pulled in thousands—especially from the eastern Caribbean. Similarly, between 1912 and 1927, 105,021 Jamaicans and Haitians poured into Cuba to work in the cane fields.[8] In time, these massive migratory movements elicited a negative response from governments of several Latin American countries. From as early as 1910, Venezuela had tried to bar the entry of blacks from the West Indies and formally did so in 1918. In 1923, Costa Rica followed suit, as did El Salvador in 1924. And in 1928, Panama passed an extremely restrictive immigration law which allowed a quota of only five persons per year.[9] With the coming of the Great Depression, more West Indians actually flowed back into the West Indies than migrated.[10] It was only after the Second World War that another massive outward flow took place, this time to the United Kingdom. However, after that country passed legislation in 1961 limiting immigration from the region,[11] West Indians started to migrate to the United States and Canada in large numbers.

Immigration to the United States

Although most West Indian immigrants in the latter portion of the nineteenth century went to Central America, some also found their way to the United States. These immigrants formed the first of three distinct waves of West Indians to have migrated to this country in the present century. The first lasted from around the turn of the century to the 1920s, the second from the 1940s to 1965, and the third from the late 1960s to the present. The initial wave of immigration from the West Indies to the United States developed in tandem with the region's banana and tourism industries. By 1889, steamships originating in New York City and Boston were regularly transporting tourists to, and bananas from, such islands as Jamaica, Haiti, and Cuba back to the United States, helping to early establish those two American cities—especially New York City—as centers of West Indian immigration.[12] Additionally, some West Indians who had gone to Central

America as contract laborers also later migrated to this country. In the first two decades of the present century, West Indians came to the United States in increasing numbers. This flow of West Indian immigrants fell off after the restrictive legislation of the National Origins system was implemented in 1924. It declined even more dramatically (and, as noted previously, actually reversed) with the coming of the Great Depression (see Table 2.1).

The timing of, and the numbers of people constituting, the second wave of West Indian immigration are uncertain. Some writers place the period as beginning in the late 1930s, whereas others place it somewhere in the 1940s.[13] Kasinitz notes that one reason for the questionable number of West Indian migrants who came during this period was the frequent use of British passports, and he places the total at no more than 3000 per year.[14] This small yearly total pales when compared to the large totals that have been registered in the wake of the 1965 Hart-Cellar Immigration Act, which ushered in the third wave of West Indian immigrants (see Table 2.2). The large numbers that are characteristic of the present period of West Indian immigration has resulted from several factors. The 1965 Act shifted the basis of immigration policy away from race and region of origin toward the reunification of families. It also imposed a 120,000 person per year ceiling[15] (with no per country quotas until 1976) on Western Hemisphere nations. As colonies, under the 1952 McCarran-Walter Act, West Indian countries had been limited to annual quotas of 100 immigrants per year. However, by the time the Hart-Cellar Immigration Act had been passed, many of these countries had already gained their independence.[16] They, therefore, became eligible to send much larger numbers of immigrants to the United States; and

TABLE 2.1 Black Immigrants to the United States: 1899–1937

Year	Total	Year	Total
1899–1900	1,126	1919–1920	13,997
1901–1902	1,426	1921–1922	15,121
1903–1904	4,560	1923–1924	19,797
1905–1906	7,384	1925–1926	1,685
1907–1908	9,861	1927–1928	1,911
1909–1910	9,273	1929–1930	3,060
1911–1912	13,480	1931–1932	1,067
1913–1914	15,081	1933–1934	262
1915–1916	10,236	1935–1936	518
1917–1918	13,677	1937	275

Source: Ira Reid, *The Negro Immigrant,* 1939 (Original source: Reports of the Commissioner of Immigration and the Secretary of Labor, U.S. Department of Labor. 1899–1937).

they had tremendous impetus to do so since the United Kingdom had severely restricted entry to West Indians in 1961. These facts, the presence of a sizable community of West Indians already resident in the country, and favorable preference categories[17] combined to sharply increase the number of West Indians migrating to the United States after 1965 (see Table 2.2). One measure of the importance of immigration to these countries is their immigration rate. In 1992, this figure stood at 113 per 10,000 for Guyana and 75.66 for Jamaica. These rates far outstripped all other countries which were major senders of immigrants in 1992. According to figures calculated by David Heer, the Dominican Republic, with a rate of 55.96, exhibited the third highest rate. At the other end of the spectrum, countries sending very large numbers of immigrants to the United States exhibited very low immigration rates. For instance, the Philippines registered a rate of only 9.58, Taiwan, 7.86, and China 0.33.[18]

■ WEST INDIANS IN THE ECONOMY

If West Indians migrate for economic reasons, traditionally this has meant settling and participating, primarily, in distinct regions of the country. The tristate region of New York, New Jersey, and Connecticut, along with Massachusetts, has historically drawn the largest numbers. The second largest concentration has developed in and around Miami, with smaller pockets occurring along the East Coast in Philadelphia, Washington, D.C. and its suburbs, and Richmond. Atlanta, Georgia, has also started to attract West Indian immigrants. The 1990 census reports that approximately 7 percent of foreign-born West Indians live in New England, 53 percent in the Mid-Atlantic states, and 27 percent in south Florida (which means, primarily, Miami and surrounding areas). However, the population is more concentrated than even these numbers would indicate, since the bulk of the West Indian population has always settled in New York City, and Jamaicans have long predominated.

While West Indians' spatial concentrations in certain regions of the country is clear, it is somewhat less obvious, at first sight, how to conceptualize the manner of their incorporation into the economy. West Indians have been characterized as possessing a particular propensity for starting small businesses. This view reflects a long tradition that, ultimately, is rooted in the experiences of the first cohort of West Indians to immigrate to America between 1900 and 1930. Ira De A. Reid noted as much in his classic study of the black immigrants of the period. He argued that immigrant blacks were a major force in the Harlem business community. Indeed, the belief in their acumen as businessmen became part of the standard package of stereotypes that was used to describe West Indians.[19] This particular stereotype has

TABLE 2.2 West Indian Immigrants to the United States: 1956–1995

Country of Birth	1956–1960	1961–1965	1966–1970	1971–1975	1976–1980	1981–1985	1986–1990	1991–1995	Total
Antigua	298	866	1,729	1,969	4,014	8,081	1,762	—	18,719
Bahamas	1,646	1,203	1,132	1,609	2,498	2,660	4,648	3,563	18,959
Barbados	1,514	1,992	7,312	7,878	12,603	9,406	8,076	5,366	54,147
Dominica	219	432	1,767	1,182	3,294	2,818	3,626	3,572	16,910
Grenada	216	602	1,907	2,388	5,182	5,254	5,325	3,832	24,706
Jamaica	6,518	8,335	62,676	61,445	78,476	100,560	136,222	90,731	544,963
Montserrat	253	531	877	932	959	700	651	—	4,903
St. Kitts	283	870	3,132	1,960	4,220	7,096	3,513	—	21,074
St. Lucia	116	481	884	1,305	3,560	2,964	3,146	2,906	15,362
St. Vincent	199	559	1,384	1,613	3,040	3,673	3,880	—	14,348
Trinidad	1,497	2,149	2,236	33,278	27,297	17,018	22,515	33,708	139,698
Guyana	896	1,239	5,760	14,320	32,040	37,271	52,649	34,134	178,309
Belize	677	1,213	2,945	2,591	4,646	13,204	10,320	5,848	41,444
Other W.I.[a]	2,731	650	3,031	2,919	4,243	2,416	3,156	11,962	31,108
Haiti	3,265	9,889	27,648	27,130	30,294	43,890	96,273	95,977	334,366
Total	20,328	31,011	124,420	162,519	216,366	257,011	355,762	291,599	1,459,016

Source: U.S. Department of Justice, *Statistical Yearbook of the Immigration and Naturalization Service,* 1991; 1995.
[a]Includes Anguilla, Aruba, British Virgin Islands, Caymans, Guadeloupe, "Leeward Islands," Martinique, "Netherland Antilles," Turks, "Windward Islands."

proved long-lived. For instance, Gilbert Osofsky's analysis of social life in early Harlem offered a similar assessment of West Indian immigrants.[20] At midcentury, Glazer and Moynihan, analyzing the place of blacks in the New York economy during the first half of the century, argued that, "if problems of incapacity for business prevailed among Negroes coming up from the South, it did not among . . . West Indians."[21] And a more recent *Economist* survey of the West Indies, refuting the notion that West Indians' racial origins explain the relative paucity of entrepreneurs in the region, posited that "Jamaican and Trinidadian businessmen are bywords for verve in America."[22]

In reality, though such enterprises certainly exist, West Indians are not particularly drawn to starting their own small businesses. Irma Watkins-Owens's recent analysis of West Indians in early Harlem paints a picture of a community that was dominated by white business interests which sought to forestall the development of African-American and West Indian–owned businesses. Against this backdrop of white economic hegemony, blacks—native and foreign-born—who operated businesses became race heroes for managing, in a small way, to carve out an independent economic niche for the black community. Overall, concludes Watkins-Owens, only a very small portion of the native black and West Indian immigrant communities engaged in entrepreneurial pursuits. She puts this figure at 2 percent for the former and 1 percent for the latter.[23]

These conclusions are not surprising considering that, traditionally, West Indians in their homelands have sought upward mobility, not through ownership of business, but through higher education designed to give access to prestigious professions. Historically, four professions have stood out: medicine, law, teaching, and the civil service. The first two, being particularly prestigious, have long been the focus of the cultural orientation toward higher education which was discussed in chapter 1. It is, in fact, the intensity of this orientation that has caused writers such as Adam Kuper and Diane Austin[24] to label the belief, among Jamaicans, in the uplifting powers of education an ideology; and which prompted the anthropologist M. G. Smith to criticize that same society for promoting, among the poor, aspirations toward high status occupations (such as medicine) which are unlikely to be fulfilled for the majority. Despite this criticism, he found that these aspirations have been actively facilitated by parents to whom, "occupational advancement alone offers upward mobility."[25] As has been shown by Violet Johnson in her study of entrepreneurship among West Indian immigrants in Boston, these immigrants have brought this mobility-through-occupation orientation with them to the United States. Pointing to their overall weakness in the business field,[26] she has argued that West Indian immigrants to Boston migrated in search of "middle-class" status, which they define as, "a stable, well-paying job, a respectable profession such as law or medicine, a good education for their children, and, finally, that paramount indicator of middle-class status—home ownership."[27] Census data for 1990 confirm the relative scarcity of self-employment among West Indians, as these data show the percentage of West Indians so employed to vary from 2 percent for the Guyanese to 4 percent for Trinidadians. These rates compare unfavorably to the overall rate for the whole country (7 percent) and to the rate for some other ethnic groups (e.g., 9.8 percent for Taiwanese immigrants).[28] However, West Indians' rates of self-employment closely resemble those of African Americans (see Table 2.3).

Ethnic Niches

Rather than focusing on self-employment, West Indians insert themselves in the economy through other ethnic niches. As described by Roger Waldinger, these niches consist of readily identifiable ethnic concentrations in particular sectors of the economy; or, more technically, industries "employing at least 1000 people, in which a group's representation is at least 150 percent of its share of total employment."[29] Waldinger advances this concept as part of a larger theory for explaining the place of ethnic groups in the New York City economy. He conceptualizes ethnic groups as occurring in something like a queue on an escalator. As groups at the top of the escalator move up, they make room for those below them. Thus, ethnic succession takes place. However, as he points out, the escalator analogy is misleading in one important respect, since it presents a picture of orderly ethnic succession. In reality, ethnic groups are to be found concentrated in niches, and those groups occupying more favorable niches are better able to exploit slots in the economy that become vacant as groups occupying them are pulled upward into better jobs. This bunching of ethnic groups into particular industries is advantageous since such niches can provide large numbers of jobs. These may not be particularly well paying, but they help those holding them to take "modest, gradual, but still significant steps up New York's economic ladder."[30] Moreover, ethnic niches also provide a degree of shelter from racial discrimination by presenting to job seekers, networks of coethnics who help to provide work where outsiders might not.

Though the picture presented by Waldinger is at odds with the view that ethnicity (defined broadly) is a declining force in the postindustrial United States, it accords with other research (e.g., on the role of ethnic enclaves in promoting upward mobility)[31] showing the continued salience of this factor. More important, for present purposes, it helps to explain the place of West Indians in the economy. As shown by Tables 2.4 and 2.5, ethnic concentration tends to be more pronounced among West Indian women.[32] Following the passage of the Hart-Celler Immigration Act in 1965, they carved out niches for themselves in two main areas: as domestics and in the health care field—especially nursing. One reflection of these

TABLE 2.3 Selected Social and Economic Characteristics of the American Population and British West Indian and Asian Immigrants: 1990

	Median Family Income	Percentage of Families Below the Poverty Level	Percentage of Group Pursuing Self-Employment	Labor Force Participation Rate	Education[a]	
					High School Graduates	College Graduates
Total U.S.	**35,225**	**10.0**	**7.0**	**65.3**	**77.6**	**21.3**
Whites	37,152	7.0	7.6	65.5	79.1	22.0
Blacks	22,429	26.3	2.0	62.7	66.2	11.3
West Indians						
Guyanese	36,278	10.6	2.0	74.2	69.5	15.8
Jamaicans	34,018	11.1	3.0	77.4	67.9	14.9
Trinidadians	33,206	12.7	4.0	77.2	74.1	15.6
Asians						
Indians	49,309	7.2	6.2	72.3	87.2	64.9
Taiwanese	47,126	11.2	9.8	59.4	82.5	43.0
Filipinos	46,698	5.2	3.1	75.4	91.6	62.2

Source: 1990 Census of Population: The Foreign Born.

[a]Persons 25 years and over.

TABLE 2.4 Occupational Distribution of Female Jamaican Immigrants in New York City, 1990 (Top 80 Percent of Occupations; N = 47,943)

Occupation	Percentage	Occupation	Percentage	Occupation	Percentage
Nursing aides, orderlies, and attendants	21.4	Managers and administrators	1.9	Child care workers, private household	1.0
Secretaries, typists, receptionists	8.4	Accountants and auditors	1.7	Hairdressers and cosmetologists	1.0
Registered nurses	7.5	Janitors and cleaners	1.7	Supervisors, general office	1.0
Maids, private household cleaners and servants	3.8	Licensed practical nurses	1.6	Sales workers, apparel	0.9
Computer operators (including data entry keyers) and programmers	3.6	Social workers	1.5	Family child care providers	0.8
Cashiers	3.5	Investigators and adjusters (insurance and noninsurance)	1.5	Health aides, except nursing	0.8

All administrative support, including clerical and file clerks	3.3	Sales workers, other commodities	1.4	Early childhood teachers' assistants	0.6
Teachers	3.0	Financial managers and officers	1.2	Managers, medicine and health	0.6
Bookkeepers, accounting and auditing clerks	1.9	Bank tellers	1.1	Personal service occupations	0.6
		Clinical laboratory and health technologists and technicians	1.1	Management related occupations	0.5
				Laborers (non-construction)	0.5
				Waitresses	0.5

Source: 1990 U.S. Census microdata sample.

TABLE 2.5 Occupational Distribution of Male Jamaican Immigrants in New York City , 1990 (Top 60 Percent of Occupations; N = 34,738)

Occupation	Percentage	Occupation	Percentage	Occupation	Percentage
Construction and other laborers, brickmasons and stonemasons	5.5	Cooks and miscellaneous food preparation	2.5	Housemen	1.2
Truck drivers	4.2	Automobile and other mechanics	2.4	Cashiers	1.2
Guards and police	4.2	Stock handlers, baggers, etc.	2.4	Administrative support occupations	1.1
Carpenters, painters, maintenance, and other construction	4.0	Plumbers, pipefitters and steamfitters, welders and cutters	1.9	Supervisors, production occupations	1.1
Janitors and cleaners	3.3	Accountants and auditors	1.8	Typists	1.0
Registered nurses	3.0	Computer programmers and operators	1.6	Construction supervisors	0.9
Managers/administrators	2.7	Sales and commodities	1.2	Real estate sales	0.8
Supervisors, proprietors, sales occupations	2.7	Electricians	1.2	Teachers, elementary schools	0.7
Taxicab drivers, chauffeurs, and bus drivers	2.7	Bookkeepers, accounting and auditing clerks	1.2		
Shipping, receiving, stock clerks, messengers	2.6	Administrative support/legal assistants	1.2		

Source: 1990 U.S. Census microdata sample

female concentrations has been that the post-1965 sex ratio among West Indian immigrants has been skewed in favor of women. This represents a reversal of the pre-1965 pattern when males typically took the lead in migrating to destinations such as Panama, Costa Rica, and to the United States as farm workers, business persons, and as students.[33]

Concentration in domestic work resulted from demand for such workers as white women moved, in larger numbers, into higher paying jobs outside the home. Judging from the experiences of West Indian domestics with whom this writer is acquainted,[34] networking appears to have been a key factor in the development of the concentration. Typically, while still living in the West Indies, these women would attempt to get Americans to sponsor them as domestics; or, lacking sponsorship but hearing of the possibility of better paying jobs than the ones which they held at home, they would come to the United States on vacation and, while here, try to obtain sponsorships. Since West Indians often had relatives and friends already working as domestics, obtaining such jobs became easier. The recommendation, by already employed domestics, of coethnics looking for similar work carried weight. Employers would naturally tend to defer to the judgment of employees with whom they had already developed a working relationship.

Once women had secured jobs as domestics, they would set about seeking other work in the same field, so that in some cases a single individual would juggle two or three jobs at the same time. This reflects the reality that West Indians—especially females—display very high levels of labor force participation (see Table 2.3), as well as multiple family members employed in the workforce (see Table 2.6).[35] However, in cases of multiple jobholding, one employer is usually regarded as the primary employer, and the others are seen as a means of supplementing income. The extent to which it is possible for West Indian women to juggle several jobs has depended on the exact nature and location of the primary domestic job. Where it involves residing in fairly distant suburban areas such as Westchester (New York) or

TABLE 2.6 Percentage Distribution of West Indian Workers per Family

	Number of Workers in Family		
	1	2	3 or More
Total U.S.	**28.0**	**45.5**	**13.3**
Guyanese	27.6	45.2	22.0
Jamaicans	28.0	45.9	20.5
Trinidadians	31.2	33.2	18.3
Haitians	31.6	42.5	19.9

Source: 1990 Census of Population: The Foreign Born

Tom's River (New Jersey) ("living-in" in the parlance of the domestics),[36] multiple jobs have usually been out of the question.

However, West Indian domestics have usually preferred living near other coethnics. This not only helps them to juggle different jobs but also keeps them close to their families. The latter has been an important consideration, since the West Indian pattern of sequential migration often leaves children emotionally vulnerable.[37] In the West Indies sequential migration has meant a situation where these "barrel children"[38] are reared by relatives—typically spouses, aunts, and grandmothers—until the children are reunited with the immigrant parent in the United States. Though the children's material needs are taken care of—especially through remittances sent back by the immigrant parent—children who have been left behind in the West Indies—even if only temporarily—sometimes develop emotional problems. At the extreme, these manifest themselves in premarital sex or even suicide; but as journalist Knolly Moses has noted, loneliness and a sense of abandonment seem to be the norm.[39] It is with an eye to this problem that immigrant women prefer to live near home after their children have migrated to join them: they are trying to reestablish bonds that have been strained by the immigration process. Another important reason is that immigration also tends to strain marital bonds, and female immigrants often fear that if they work for long stretches in distant suburbs their husbands will stray.[40]

As Palmer has noted, relatively speaking, domestic work has been declining in importance over the past few years.[41] However, the concentration of West Indian women in the health care field and in the lower level service sector is still evident. These concentrations—especially the former—reflect a combination of demand in the United States (enhanced by West Indians' fluency in English) and West Indian women's search for upward mobility through prestigious professions.[42] Overall, West Indian males exhibit less occupational concentration than do women. To the extent that this does occur, however, it is most evident in the construction industry (see Table 2.6). Waldinger has argued that concentration into this niche has resulted from West Indian males' exposure, prior to migrating, to the construction industry (for example, on sugar plantations). In this country, such exposure has combined with networking to expand the niche. Waldinger shows that some of the West Indian contractors he interviewed exhibit a preference for coethnics. The other side of this preference is a tendency—which other researchers have also found[43]—to view African Americans and Puerto Ricans as being less dependable workers.

Ethnic Niches and Racial Issues

The place occupied by West Indians in the American economy is, of course, central to their quest for an improved quality of life and to their sense of self.

They tend to be very goal oriented and perceive themselves as hard, competent workers. It would not be overstatement to say that, to a large extent, their lives in America revolve around their economic activities. But West Indians' role in the economy and their place in the society have long elicited more general interest. This attention has stemmed from the fact that as blacks who seem to be "successful," they provide an apparent test of the thesis that race has a particularly negative impact on blacks in America. If that is the case, this argument goes,[44] how does one explain West Indians' relative prosperity? The ancestors of both West Indians and African Americans originated in West Africa and both experienced slavery. Yet, according to this argument, the former have succeeded much better in their American quest for upward mobility. Overall, this seems to suggest that other factors are more important than race in determining the place of blacks in American society.

The obvious qualifications that arise with respect to this argument is what is meant by terms such as "successful" and "relative prosperity." Johnson's description of the goals of the West Indians whom she studied in Boston is worth repeating here, since it eloquently sums up West Indians' response to the question of what it means to be "successful." She notes that they are seeking stable and well-paying jobs; prestigious professions; a good quality education; and material rewards, especially homes.[45] While absolute levels of achievement with respect to these criteria are important (e.g., how much income an individual makes), what is perhaps even more important is the comparison of these levels with other situations and/or individuals. In this context, a crucial fact for West Indians is that they constantly compare their lives in America with their lives in the West Indies. Undoubtedly, from an economic perspective, many West Indian immigrants regard the United States as presenting more opportunities for improving quality of life than do their West Indian homelands. For them, America is always judged relative to where they came from.[46]

For proponents of the notion that West Indians test the role played by race in the achievement of blacks, the key comparison has not been with the West Indies but, rather, with African Americans. As noted previously, these comparisons started early in the history of West Indian immigration to the United States, with speculation as to whether West Indians are more business-oriented than African Americans. Such speculations and, more generally, the view that West Indians' socioeconomic standing shows that blacks do not face special problems, continue into the present. Among the more notable writers advancing this perspective have been Glazer and Moynihan,[47] Dennis Forsythe,[48] and Thomas Sowell[49]—all of whom see this overcoming of racism manifesting itself concretely in such things as greater business acumen, disproportionate representation in prestigious or leadership positions, and statistical indicators of socioeconomic well-being.

As mentioned earlier, Glazer and Moynihan view West Indians (especially those arriving earlier this century) as being particularly adept as businessmen. Echoing the sentiments of writers (e.g., James Weldon Johnson) who observed the first wave of West Indians, Glazer and Moynihan argue (in *Beyond the Melting Pot*) that, "West Indians' most striking difference from . . . southern Negroes was their greater application to business, buying homes, and in general advancing themselves."[50] These sentiments, along with those offered in a later work—*Ethnicity*—have influenced the views of other writers on the subject of West Indian achievement. In the latter work, Glazer and Moynihan posit that a group's social ranking depends on the extent to which its members successfully accord with a society's established social norms. Reflecting this perspective, Dennis Forsythe has argued forcefully that American culture is essentially materialistic, and various groups partake of this materialism (i.e., achieve success) to the extent that they reflect the core characteristics of the Protestant Ethic. He defines these as "rugged individualism and acquisitiveness, aggressiveness, ruthless competitiveness, pragmatism, rationalism and anti-traditionalism."[51] In his view, West Indians have been thoroughly imbued with this ethic by their majority status in their homelands, the educational system, driving ambition, and the selectivity of the immigration experience. Borrowing from sociologist Edna Bonacich,[52] he argues that they have viewed themselves as "sojourners" who are in the United States primarily to achieve material wealth and status. Thus, they tend to have a very instrumentalist focus. Like Glazer and Moynihan, Forsythe bases his argument on the idea of a small group having a disproportionate effect on their surroundings. For instance, he argues that "at no time . . . has the West Indian population in the United States amounted to anything more than 1% of the total Black population. . . . Yet in spite of this small numerical size they have made their presence felt and their voices heard in America." Specifically, this impact has been seen in their leadership roles, especially in the area of protest politics.[53] Because of this influence, Forsythe sees West Indians as spurring "Afro-Americans to continue their struggle to gain a greater share of the American capitalist culture, and to substantiate their claim to American citizenry."[54]

Thomas Sowell has also advanced the disproportionate effects and culture arguments to show West Indian success and that racial discrimination is not a large obstacle for blacks seeking upward mobility. To make his case, Sowell cites examples of West Indians who have had a significant effect on American life and, also, statistical data. For instance, in *The Economics and Politics of Race*, he shows that in the early 1970s, 31 percent of native black (compared to 24 percent of West Indian) families were headed by females. Similarly, in *Ethnic America*, using the "Family Income Index" (in which 100 represents the national average), he shows that in 1978, African Americans had a score of 64 but that of West Indians was

94—the point being that West Indians were close to the national norm despite their race.

Oscar Glantz's work is also noteworthy, inasmuch as it has compared African American and West Indian students at Brooklyn College on beliefs and values regarding achievement and race. He found that West Indian students exhibit significantly higher confidence in the possibility of obtaining a good job and in the social system's ability to treat blacks fairly. For instance, West Indians are less likely to view a teacher's race as significant in effective learning and the police as repressive, and they exhibit less cynicism with respect to the possibility of fundamental changes in American society. Moreover, these effects remain intact after controlling for class and gender.[55]

The theme of West Indians as high achievers has been picked up and reinforced in journalistic treatments of the subject. An example is James Traub's, "You Can Get It if You Really Want It"[56] in which it is argued that though racial discrimination is a factor for West Indians, they have been able to overcome it through application of their values and hard work. Similarly a series of articles in the *New York Times* by Sam Roberts has emphasized the finding that blacks in the New York City borough of Queens have attained income parity with whites. These articles posit that this achievement has resulted from the high labor force participation rate of black immigrants. Similar assessments are to be found in other articles[57] in the same paper and in an April 1995 series in *New York Newsday* on the black middle class in New York City.

Perhaps more than any other recent event, the extraordinary popularity and achievement of Colin Powell have greatly stimulated the viewpoint that West Indians are high achievers. His story—that of the poor child of immigrants who achieves wealth and power—reinforces a cherished view of immigrants. For instance, journalist Steven Roberts, writing in the August 31, 1995, issue of *U.S. News and World Report*, has argued that Powell is only one example from an immigrant clan that, seemingly, has been drawn inexorably to success. Noting that various members have become very wealthy businessmen,[58] physicians, judges, and ambassadors, he states that, "Colin Powell's vast extended family has lived a classic immigrant story, a classic American story. The experience of West Indian blacks in America is less familiar than that of Italians or Chinese or Jews, but it is no less remarkable."

Because of their focus on achieving upward mobility in this country, West Indians tend to agree with many of the foregoing arguments. It is unlikely that they would disagree with being told that they are "rugged individualists" and being compared with Colin Powell. However, West Indians, themselves—unlike much of the older literature on West Indian achievement—will quickly point out that there is another side to the issue of achieving upward mobility in the United States. This literature tends to imply that race is somehow irrelevant to West Indians, or that they effortlessly overcome such barriers. The reality is, though, that West Indians, like African-Americans, must constantly negotiate racial obstacles in the job market, and they do not overcome these easily.

Ivan,[59] one of the Jamaicans I interviewed, illustrates the two sides of the achievement coin. A surveyor by profession in Jamaica, he had managed, through networking with college friends, to continue working in this field upon migrating to America. In fact, he had been relatively successful, managing to obtain a series of high paying jobs and, finally, starting (with a relative) his own small construction firm. Like many of the Jamaicans I interviewed, he held strongly to the belief that West Indians[60] are high achievers, especially compared to African Americans.[61] Nevertheless, during our talk he complained, angrily, that racial discrimination has hindered his opportunities—and those of blacks in general—in this country. This is how he put it:

> No matter what you do the white man is always fighting the battle with the black man. . . . I try not to let it bother me too much, but it's there, I've come across [it] . . . . There are times . . . when you have to be conscious because it confronts you. There are things that you could get and you know definitely you did not get because of your race. . . . I have bid on jobs . . . in this city and have been told you didn't need certain forms and when the time came for me to start the job they say well you didn't submit certain forms, and they incorrectly said that form wasn't necessary; and I was the low bidder and didn't get the job.

A second example of the opportunities and discriminatory barriers that West Indians face in the job market comes from my interview with Jonathan. His class background was quite different from Ivan's. Where Ivan had grown up in a middle class Jamaican family, had been able to travel widely, and obtain a college education, Jonathan described himself as having received little education. In fact, he was a high school dropout. Afterwards, he gravitated into the printing trade but gradually concluded that that field did not offer much scope for upward mobility in Jamaica. Like thousands of other Jamaicans in the 1960s, he came to see migration to America as the way of achieving this mobility. In this country, Jonathan continued in the printing trade and did well financially. He estimated that after a number of years he was making between thirty-five thousand and forty thousand dollars in that profession. However, his job situation took a turn for the worse when the company for which he was working started losing money. He lost his job as a result and encountered great difficulty finding another in the same profession at a similar salary. He attributed this to two factors: foreign competition which made it more profitable for American printers to farm-out work to low cost countries and to racism. Addressing the process of searching for a job he commented:

Some of these places [at which he interviewed] . . . looked at me very strange as a black person, you know, when you tell them your skills and how much you worth. . . . I actually started on a job in Long Island . . . and there was a guy who liked me very well. He was a white guy and he said: "They pay you well and the union, they know that you can do the work." . . . These guys were talking about $5.00 to $6.00 an hour. . . . The guy assured me: . . . "Put it in for two days . . . and then we can evaluate [you]." It turned out that I worked there nearly a week because they were so fascinated with my work and wanted me to stay; but they were just ignorant to the fact that they should pay me [well] . . . because I was the only black at the time—so I just quit.

Because of the existence of such barriers to upward mobility, another branch of the literature on West Indian achievement—most of it more recent—has adopted a more cautious tone in assessing the progress of West Indians in this country. The neglect of structural considerations and a focus on culture (e.g., values) as being *the* force motivating upward mobility among West Indians has been the hallmark of the older literature on West Indian achievement. The newer literature on this subject has sought to bring structure back into the analysis, thereby creating a more balanced picture of West Indians. Two early examples of work pointing to the importance of structure are Lennox Raphael's, "West Indians and Afro-Americans" and Roy Bryce-Laporte's, "Black Immigrants, the Experience of Invisibility and Inequality." Both concur in arguing that while West Indians' single-minded focus on achievement results from their peculiar socialization in the West Indies and the self-selectivity of the immigrant experience, single-mindedness is a two-edged sword: It carries them far but promotes ethnocentrism and often blinds them to structural forces acting against both West Indians and African Americans.

Stephen Steinberg's *The Ethnic Myth* has also criticized the older achievement literature for focusing on culture at the expense of structure. Arguing that the social science literature tends to view West Indians as ethnic heroes, he notes that much that has been written about them falls in the realm of myth. A prime example of this is the belief in their tendency toward entrepreneurialism. At the same time, argues Steinberg, cultural explanations tend to ignore the issue of selectivity in immigration. Particular attitudes toward hard work, savings, investment, and education may, in fact, exist among some West Indians, but these exist in a migrant pool that has been creamed-off their respective societies. Thus, Steinberg does not deny that culture might be a useful variable in explaining achievement; rather, he doubts that it is an all-purpose explanation and implies that comparing West Indian immigrants and African Americans is erroneous because it juxtaposes two populations with different histories and socioeconomic profiles.

Farley and Allen, employing 1980 census data, have addressed the West

Indian/African American issue from a quantitative point of view. Among their findings is that although West Indians have outpaced African Americans in some areas (e.g., family income and levels of education), they have lagged behind in others (e.g., individual incomes). Overall, in the 1970s, West Indians and African Americans resembled each other much more closely than either group resembled whites or foreign-born Asians. Farley and Allen have interpreted this as showing weak evidence for the notion that West Indians are culturally superior to African Americans.[62] Suzanne Model's analysis of the same data set has led her to similar conclusions, although she has also shown the existence of complex dynamics with respect to gender. Her analysis has confounded the idea that West Indian immigrants outearn their African American counterparts. Indeed, among pre-1980 immigrants, some national groups (e.g., Jamaicans) earned less than their male African-American counterparts. West Indians and African-American men both earned substantially less than equally qualified whites. The situation was more complicated for women, since several nationalities equaled similarly qualified African-American women in earnings and, in fact, earned slightly more than similarly qualified white women.[63]

Model's more recent analysis of West Indian and African-American socioeconomic characteristics between 1970 and 1990 has confirmed the complexity of the situation vis-à-vis those two groups. Over that twenty-year period, West Indian labor force participation rates exceeded those of African Americans. However, earnings displayed a more complex pattern. While the mean income of African Americans consistently outpaced that of foreign-born West Indians, native-born West Indians consistently outearned African Americans—although that has started to change. For instance, in 1970, native-born West Indian men demonstrated mean earnings of $29,871 compared to $23,616 for African Americans. By 1980, the respective figures were $28,040 and $22,059; and by 1990 they were $26,093 and $26, 216. Data for women show a similar, though not as dramatic, trend, since, by 1990, native-born West Indians still held a $2500 advantage over their African-American counterparts. To make the situation more complex, Model's analysis has shown that the earnings of foreign-born West Indians overtake those of African Americans, but only after the former have lived in the country for several years.[64] Kalmijn's recent analysis of West Indians and African Americans arrived at broadly similar conclusions: namely, that Anglophone West Indians—but not those from other parts of the West Indies—outearn African Americans, but "the difference is not as spectacular in magnitude as is commonly believed. The advantage is not large enough, for example, to bring them on a par with white men."[65]

Overall, these and other similar studies[66] advise caution if West Indians and African Americans have to be compared with each other. They imply that a complex interweaving of cultural and structural factors affect black upward mobility. West Indians' belief in the efficacy of higher education is one cultural characteristic that has emerged from the peculiarities of their history; and, given the close correlation between level of education and earnings, this orientation is clearly functional. However, the educational systems of the various West Indian societies cannot actually accommodate all of the individuals who wish to seek higher credentials. One reflection of this is that the percentage of immigrants who are college graduates falls below that of the United States as a whole, and well below that of some Asian immigrants. The fact that, in most respects, West Indians are an intermediate population points to the importance of perspective where they are concerned. As Table 2.3 shows, their median family incomes are significantly higher than that of African Americans and they display significantly lower rates of poverty. These important accomplishments imply a certain level of "success," but could they be even more successful? (e.g., having even higher median family incomes). Are structural factors limiting their progress? Or as sociologist Roy Bryce-Laporte has put it: "When one considers the drive which black foreigners display . . . where would they have been in American social structure and what cultural esteem would their tradition have borne if they were not perceived or treated as blacks? Where would they have been permitted to live, work, study, and invest?"[67]

The analysis of West Indians' economic activities within the context of niches shows how structural forces shape and limit their options. Objectively speaking, their specialization in certain fields can both help or hurt their economic chances, depending on whether these niches are expanding or contracting. For instance, West Indian women initially gained a foothold in the health care field in New York City because of a fortuitous combination of factors. Increasing prosperity caused whites to move up and out of lower level health care jobs, even as demand for health care services was expanding. West Indians—especially women—filled this void because they were English-speaking, well-trained, and seeking expanded opportunities by migrating from their homelands. Waldinger has argued that though, in West Indian niches, the terms of compensation remain tilted in favor of whites, the health care field has enabled West Indian women to maintain very high levels of labor force participation.[68] Furthermore, Palmer has argued that these women are likely to continue to do well in the future, since the health care field is expected to expand over the coming decades. Thus, establishing a niche in health care has benefited West Indians.[69] In contrast, those West Indians who have migrated into public sector jobs are expected to do less well in the future, as this sector experiences budget cuts and increasing competition from other ethnic groups looking to secure a foothold in it. The indications are that blacks' concentration in the public sector, while it may have been helpful in the past, will increasingly make them vulnerable.[70]

Blacks are vulnerable, not only because they happen to occupy niches that may be declining, but also because of discrimination. Waldinger has shown that this is particularly true of the niche which West Indian men have carved out in the construction industry (recall the interview with Ivan). He argues that, overall, white ethnics have long resisted entry of blacks into that industry. Yet the fragmentation of the industry allows neophytes to enter and set themselves up as independent contractors. West Indians' premigration experiences in construction give them advantages over African Americans. However, as contractors, both groups suffer from the disadvantages of small size; lack of ongoing informal contacts with influential individuals in the industry (what one of his respondents referred to as the "golf course advantage"); and the outright refusal of some whites to do business with blacks. To cope with this discrimination, some black contractors resort to disguising ownership of their businesses. However, most seek to avoid the pitfalls of contracting in the private sector by bidding on public sector jobs; but rather than solve their problems, involvement in the public sector brings a whole new set of difficulties. For instance, it reduces their level of control over their workforce, since as Waldinger notes, "reliance on public work makes unionization a near inevitability for most black contractors."[71] This not only reduces the profit margins of these contractors but, also, it often gives them white workers who, because they resent having to work for blacks, may undermine productivity. These realities lead Waldinger to conclude that,

> ethnic differences among African-American and Caribbean blacks make for only partly diverging fates. Foreign origin may help the immigrants to get a start and secure a more skilled labor force, but it doesn't seem to provide much shelter from the force of discrimination; Caribbean immigrants were no less vocal than their U.S.-born counterparts when complaining of the opportunism of white developers and general contractors, and the racial animus that lay behind such behavior.[72]

Waldinger aptly uses the phrase "partially diverging fates" to describe the relative economic and social situation of African Americans and West Indians. It suggests that discussions comparing these two groups are best framed in terms of shades of difference, rather than clear-cut differences. This is not to deny the existence of distinct cultural differences between African Americans and West Indians. These cultural differences, along with other traits (e.g., being English-speaking) may give them something of a boost in some segments of the labor market. The fact that West Indians, overall, exhibit somewhat better social indicators than African Americans is significant and probably amounts to real differences in quality of life. However, to say that the fates of both groups diverge only partially implies that these fates join at some point. The connection is that both African

Americans and West Indians continue to experience invidious discrimination. The apparently better social indicators displayed by West Indians may disguise this commonality. For instance, it would be easy to conclude that their higher median family income implies that discrimination is less of a drag on West Indians than it is on African Americans. However, it could be argued that not less discrimination but other factors—in this case having multiple family members in the workforce and high labor force participation rates—explain these relatively high incomes. The point is that in determining the place of any group in the society, multiple factors must always be taken into consideration; but, in the case of blacks, race can never be ruled out, regardless of how successful they seem to be. Certainly, West Indians experience and perceive a great deal of discrimination directed toward them because of their skin color. While it is hard to quantify whether this is less or more than is the case for African Americans, racial discrimination in this country greatly concerns West Indians and has a definite impact on their lives.

■ CONCLUSION

Economics plays a crucial role in the lives of West Indians. It is the factor that originated and continues to motivate their long-standing pattern of worldwide migration. Like other immigrants who come to the United States, they have distinct goals and work hard to achieve these. However, multiple factors shape their actual place in the economy. Level of education, skills, and the size and quality of their networks are only a few of these factors. The fact that West Indians, like other groups, tend to cluster into distinct occupational niches is especially significant, since, depending on the particular historical period in question, these could help lift large segments of ethnic populations or drag them down. Niches show the continued significance of ethnicity in the labor market, especially with respect to networking. Theoretically, one of the things which such networks achieve is protection from out-group discrimination, as coethnics favor each other for jobs. How well groups realize this largely depends on the particular industries in which they happen to find themselves. In the case of blacks in the construction industry, for instance, this protection is only weakly realized because of a combination of a weak capital base, poor networks linking them to powerful players in the industry, and continuing discrimination. The latter factor, obviously long a particular concern for blacks in the United States, deserves to be looked at more closely for West Indians because of the tendency to view them as having demonstrated the demise of race for blacks in America. However, their actual experiences in this country show no such thing. Moreover, coming from societies that are more race-neutral than is the

United States tends to enhance the likelihood of them perceiving race as being a problem. Though social and economic differences remain vis-à-vis African Americans, both groups continue to be joined by common experiences of racial discrimination.

Notes

1. This is not to argue that West Indian immigrants are, necessarily, unconcerned with racial issues before they migrate; or that race is secondary to social class in importance. The race issue is latent in many West Indian societies, and, by the time they settle in the United States, immigrants have gained some idea of racial conditions in this country from relatives and friends who have already migrated, as well as from the news media. Moreover, some West Indians have already traveled to the United States on vacation before deciding to settle here. Still, new immigrants often possess only a vague understanding of racial issues in the United States. Based on the interviews I conducted and my interaction with West Indians, it seems that those immigrants who are newly arrived express mixed feelings about this country. These consist of a combination of some knowledge regarding the treatment of blacks, vague fears that they could also experience discrimination, and a desire to achieve upward mobility. The latter sentiment tends to predominate, since self-betterment is usually the key reason for migrating in the first place. Also, it should be remembered that their whole socialization tends toward the suppression of viewing issues from a blatantly racial perspective. Among the immigrants I interviewed, this orientation was as evident among the newly arrived, as among those who had lived here for several years. The difference, in the case of the latter, is that they had come, over time, to view issues from a more consciously racial perspective. In other words, their racial experiences in this country had transformed their vague feelings with respect to racial issues into strongly held opinions.
2. Richardson has noted that this was also true of the Windwards. See Bonham Richardson, *Caribbean Migrants* (Knoxville: The University of Tennessee Press, 1983).
3. See, for example, Richardson, *Caribbean Migrants*; "Slavery to Freedom in the British Caribbean: Ecological Considerations," *Caribbean Geography*, Vol. 1, No. 3 (May, 1984): 164–175; Elizabeth Thomas-Hope, "Caribbean Diaspora—The Inheritance of Slavery: Migration from the Commonwealth Caribbean," in *The Caribbean in Europe*, ed. Colin Brock (London: Frank Cass and Company Limited, 1986), pp. 15–35; Peter D. Fraser, "Nineteenth Century West Indian Migration to Britain," *In Search of a Better Life: Perspectives on Migration from the Caribbean*, ed. Ransford W. Palmer (New York: Praeger, 1990), pp. 20–37.
4. Gisela Eisner, *Jamaica: 1830–1930* (Manchester: Manchester University Press, 1961), p. 147; Fraser, "Nineteenth Century West Indian Migration to Britain."
5. Thomas-Hope, "Caribbean Diaspora," p. 16. This writer also points out that some West Indians elected to remain in Panama, thereby laying the groundwork for a West Indian community in that nation.

6. Charles W. Koch, "Jamaican Blacks and Their Descendants in Costa Rica," *Social and Economic Studies*, Vol. 36, No. 3 (1977): 339–361.

7. Thomas-Hope, "Caribbean Diaspora," p.17; G. W. Roberts, *The Population of Jamaica* (London: Cambridge University Press, 1957), p. 139. While the number of West Indians moving to Panama and other places during this period of early migration was undoubtedly large, one needs to exercise caution in interpreting them. The nonexistence of accurate records has forced researchers in this area to rely, at least partly, on estimates. Consequently, stated migration figures sometimes diverge significantly. For example, Dawn Marshall ["A History of West Indian Migrations: Overseas Opportunities and 'Safety-Valve' Policies," in *The Caribbean Exodus*, ed. Barry B. Levine (New York: Praeger, 1987), p. 22] states that between 1904 and 1914, 60,000 Barbadians migrated to Panama. However, Thomas-Hope, (ibid., p. 17) implies that only 26,000 migrated over the thirty-year period, 1891–1921.

8. This total was calculated from figures presented by Ira De A. Reid in *The Negro Immigrant* (New York: Columbia University Press, 1939), p. 65.

9. Ibid., pp. 61–63; Margaret Byron, *Post-War Caribbean Migration to Britain: The Unfinished Cycle* (Aldershot: Avebury, 1994), p. 35.

10. For instance, social scientist W. F. Maunder ["The New Jamaican Emigration," *Social and Economic Studies*, Vol. 4, No. 1 (1955): 38–61] has presented data which show that Jamaica registered a net loss of 145,304 people from 1881–1921. However, from 1921 to 1943, it recorded a net inflow of 25,766. Afterwards, the flow returned to its normal pattern of having more Jamaicans leave the island than return. Thus, for the period 1943 to 1954, the island recorded a net loss of 32,716 Jamaicans. See, also, Gisela Eisner, *Jamaica: 1830–1930*, Table X, p. 147, and Gilbert Osofsky, *Harlem: The Making of a Ghetto* (New York: Harper and Row, 1966), p. 135.

11. See, for instance, Dennis Dean, "The Conservative Government and the 1961 Commonwealth Immigration Act: The Inside Story," *Class and Race*, Vol. 35, No. 2 (October–December 1993): 57–74.

12. Roberts, *The Population of Jamaica*; Richardson, *Caribbean Migrants*.

13. For example, Philip Kasinitz [*Caribbean New York* (Ithaca: Cornell University Press, 1992), p. 25] dates the second period from the late 1930s to 1965. However, W. F. Maunder ("The New Jamaican Emigration") and George C. Abbott place the beginnings somewhere in the 1940s. See, George C. Abbott, "Estimates of the Growth of the Population of the West Indies to 1975," *Social and Economic Studies*, Vol. 12, No. 3 (1963): 236–244.

14. Data presented by Maunder ("The New Jamaican Emigration") for Jamaican immigrants for a portion of this period tend to support Kasinitz's estimate. Maunder has argued that for the period 1943–1954, 20,000 Jamaicans migrated to the United States. Over that eleven-year period, this would mean that the average per year was approximately 1800; and since Jamaicans have always composed the bulk of West Indian immigrants, it is unlikely that the total per year was much higher than this or exceeded Kasinitz's estimate.

15. This overall ceiling, although a boon for newly independent countries in the Western Hemisphere, actually represented a step backward for long-independent

countries of the region, since they had traditionally been subject to no ceiling at all. In 1978, the separate ceilings for Eastern and Western Hemispheres were combined into a single world ceiling of 290,000.

16. Jamaica gained its independence on August 6, 1962; Trinidad on August 31 of the same year; Guyana on May 26, 1966; and Barbados in November 1966.

17. The McCarran-Walter Act established a preference system consisting of five categories: First preference went to the highly skilled (and their spouses and children) whose services were needed by the United States. Second preference went to the parents, and unmarried sons and daughters of American citizens; third preference to spouses and unmarried sons and daughters of permanent residents; fourth preference to married sons and daughters and siblings of American citizens; and a fifth nonpreference category went to immigrants not entitled to any of the preceding categories. Under the 1965 Act, first preference went to the unmarried sons and daughters of American citizens; second to spouses and unmarried children of permanent residents; third to professionals with "exceptional ability"; fourth to married children of American citizens; fifth to brothers and sisters of American citizens; sixth to skilled and unskilled workers in occupations felt to be in short supply in the United States; seventh to refugees; and an eighth nonpreference category encompassed all those who did not fit any of the preceding seven categories. See, John A. Ross, ed., "Immigration Policy," in *International Encyclopedia of Population*, Vol. 1 (New York: The Free Press, 1982), pp. 309–314.

18. The immigration rate is figured by dividing the number of legal immigrants arriving from a country by its population. See David Heer, *Immigration in America's Future* (Boulder: Westview Press, 1996), p. 152. It should also be remembered that sizable numbers of illegal immigrants from the West Indies are to be found in the United States.

19. Reid offers a lengthy list of these stereotypes. These included the ideas that West Indians were crafty and not to be trusted in business matters; oversensitive to racial slights; arrogant; clannish; troublemakers; and incessant talkers. See Ira De A. Reid, *The Negro Immigrant* (New York: Columbia University Press, 1939), pp. 107–108.

20. *Harlem: The Making of a Ghetto* (New York: Harper and Row, Publishers, 1966).

21. Nathan Glazer and Daniel Patrick Moynihan, "The Negroes," in *Beyond the Melting Pot*, ed. Nathan Glazer and Daniel Patrick Moynihan (Cambridge: The M.I.T. Press, 1970), p. 34. In forming these opoinions, Glazer and Moynihan relied on James Weldon Johnson's description of early West Indian immigrants to Harlem. In *Black Manhattan* (New York: Plenum Publishing Corporation, 1930, p. 153) Johnson argued that immigrants from the British West Indies, "average high in intelligence and efficiency. There is practically no illiteracy among them, and many have a sound English common school education. They are characteristically sober-minded and have something of a genius for business, differing almost totally, in these respects, from the average rural Negro of the South."

22. "Columbus's Isles: A Survey of the Caribbean" *The Economist* (August 6, 1988), p. 18.

23. Irma Watkins-Owens, *Blood Relations* (Bloomington: Indiana University Press, 1996).

24. Adam Kuper, *Changing Jamaica* (London: Routledge and Kegan Paul, 1976); Diane J. Austin, *Urban Life in Kingston, Jamaica: The Culture and Class Ideology of Two Neighborhoods* (New York: Gordon and Breach, 1987).

25. M. G. Smith, *The Plural Society in the British West Indies* (Berkeley: The University of California Press, 1965), p. 219.

26. For other discussion of this see, for instance, Philip Kasinitz, *Caribbean New York* (Ithaca: Cornell University Press, 1992) and Roger Waldinger, "Ethnic Business in the United States," in *Immigration, Multiculturalism and Economic Development,*" ed. R. J. Holton (Flinders: Flinders University of South Australia, 1987), pp. 99–112.

27. Violet Johnson, "Culture, Economic Stability, and Entrepreneurship: The Case of British West Indians in Boston," in *New Migrants in the Marketplace,* ed. Marilyn Halter (Amherst: University of Massachusetts Press, 1995), p. 60.

28. At 18 percent self-employed, Korean immigrants display a higher rate than all other groups.

29. Roger Waldinger, *Still the Promised City?* (Cambridge: Harvard University Press, 1996), p. 95. Also, see Waldinger, "The 'Other Side' of Embeddedness: A Case-Study of the Interplay of Economy and Ethnicity," *Ethnic and Racial Studies,* Vol. 18, No. 3 (July 1995): 555–580; Suzanne Model, "The Ethnic Niche and the Structure of Opportunity: Immigrants and Minorities in New York City," in *The "Underclass" Debate: Views from History,* ed. Michael B. Katz (Princeton: Princeton University Press, 1993).

30. Waldinger *Still the Promised City?* p. 318.

31. See, for instance, Ivan Light, *Ethnic Enterprise in America* (Berkeley: University of California Press, 1972); Alejandro Portes and Robert D. Manning, "The Immigrant Enclave: Theory and Empirical Examples," in *Competitive Ethnic Relations,* ed. Susan Olzak and Joane Nagel (Orlando: Academic Press, Inc., 1986), pp. 47–66; Alejandro Portes and Alex Stepick, "Unwelcome Immigrants: The Labor Market Experiences of 1980 (Mariel) Cuban and Haitian Refugees in South Florida," *American Sociological Review,* Vol. 50: (1985): 493–514; Alejandro Portes, Alex Stepick, and Cynthia Truelove, "Three Years Later: The Adaptation Process of 1980 (Mariel) Cuban and Haitian Refugees in South Florida," *Population Research and Policy Review* 5 (1986): 83–94; Alejandro Portes and Alex Stepick, *City on the Edge: The Transformation of Miami* (Berkeley: University of California Press, 1993); Sanford J. Ungar, *Fresh Blood: The New Americans* (New York: Simon and Schuster, 1995); Silvia Pedraza, "Cuba's Refugees: Manifold Migrations," in *Origins and Destinies,* ed. Silvia Pedraza and Ruben G. Rumbaut (Belmont: Wadsworth Publishing Company, 1996), pp. 263–279; Guillermo J. Grenier and Lisandro Perez, "Miami Spice: The Ethnic Cauldron Simmers," in *Origins and Destinies,* ed. Silvia Pedraza and Ruben G. Rumbaut (Belmont: Wadsworth Publishing Company, 1996), pp. 360–372.

32. See, also, Waldinger, *Still the Promised City?*; Philip Kasinitz, "From Ghetto Elite to Service Sector: A Comparison of the Role of Two Waves of West Indian

Immigrants to New York City," *Ethnic Groups*, Vol. 7: (1988): 173–203; Ransford Palmer, *Pilgrims from the Sun* (New York: Twayne Publishers, 1995).

33. For instance, G. W. Roberts and D. O. Mills used official documents filled out by Jamaicans traveling abroad between 1953 and 1955 to gauge their reasons for travel. The largest category belonged to those traveling for purposes of vacation. Seventy-three percent of those indicating travel for this reason were women. However, men dominated all other categories. After "vacationing," the second largest category consisted of those migrating permanently in search of employment (i.e., "immigrants" in the conventional sense of the word). Sixty percent of those falling in this category were males. Traveling for "business" represented the third largest category found by Roberts and Mills. Eighty-eight percent of those indicating this as the main reason for travel were males. Travel for purposes of study was the fourth category in Roberts and Mills's study. Sixty-one percent of those citing study as the primary reason for travel were males. The post-1965 period of immigration has seen a reversal of this male-dominated pattern. The 1980 census reported the overall male/female ratio for Jamaican immigrants was 78.9. See G. W. Roberts and D. O. Mills, "Study of External Migration Affecting Jamaica, 1953–1955," *Social and Economic Studies*, Vol. 7, No. 2 (June 1958):1–350; Reid, *The Negro Immigrant*, p. 236; Monica Gordon, "Dependents or Independent Workers?: The Status of Caribbean Immigrant Women in the United States," in *In Search of a Better Life: Perspectives on Migration from the Caribbean,* ed. Ransford Palmer (New York: Praeger 1990), pp. 115–138; Ransford Palmer, *Pilgrims from the Sun* (New York: Twayne Publishers, 1995).

34. The following description draws upon the writer's interaction with some of these women and on other works discussing West Indian domestics. These include Margaret Prescod-Roberts and Norma Steele, *Black Women: Bringing It All Back Home* (London: Falling Wall Press, 1980); Thomas Kessner and Betty Caroli, *Today's Immigrants: Their Stories* (New York: Oxford University, 1982); Nancy Foner, "Sex Roles and Sensibilities: Jamaican Women in New York and London," in *International Migration: The Female Experience,* ed. Rita James Simon and Caroline B. Brettel (Totawa: Rowman and Allanheld, 1986), pp. 133–151; Aubrey W. Bonnett, "The New Female West Indian Immigrant: Dilemmas of Coping in the Host Society," in *In Search of a Better Life: Perspectives on Migration from the Caribbean,* ed. Ransford Palmer (New York: Praeger 1990), pp. 139–149; Monica Gordon, "Dependents or Independent Workers?"

35. An example of these high labor force participation rates would be the former student of the writer—a Jamaican immigrant—who had three jobs. A full-time nursing student, she worked in a hospital part-time, in a library part-time, and delivered newspapers in the mornings.

36. A typical "live-in" job will take a woman away from home for a whole week. This means that, at most, they see their families only on weekends. In the writer's experience with such women, such jobs have lasted for months or even years at a time. See, also, Nancy Foner, "Sex Roles and Sensibilities: Jamaican Women in New York and London," in *International Migration: The Female Experience,* ed. Rita James Simon and Caroline B. Brettel (Totawa: Rowman and Allanheld,

1986), pp. 133–151; Bonnett, "The New Female West Indian Immigrant: Dilemmas of Coping in the Host Society."

37. Palmer has conceptualized West Indian migration as a circular process in which West Indians immigrate sequentially (i.e., one or two family members at a time). The process is completed when the entire family is reunited in the United States. Along similar lines Basch, Schiller, and Blanc and Sutton have argued that the migration of West Indians must be viewed within the context of "transnationalism." By this, they mean that West Indian immigrants find themselves embedded, simultaneously, in social networks and the economies of their home societies and the United States (or other countries to which they have migrated). See Linda Basch, Nina Glick Schiller, and Cristian S. Blanc, *Nations Unbound: Transnational Projects, Postcolonial Predicaments, and Deterritorialized Nation States* (Amsterdam: Gordon and Breach Publishers, 1994); Constance Sutton, "The Caribbeanization of New York City and the Emergence of a Transnational Socio-cultural System" in *Caribbean Life in New York City: Sociocultural Dimensions*, ed. Constance Sutton and Elsa M.Chaney (New York: Center for Migration Studies of New York, Inc., 1987), pp. 15–30.

38. So-called because of the West Indian practice of sending barrels filled with food, clothes, and other consumer items to relatives in the West Indies.

39. Knolly Moses, "The 'Barrel Children,' " *Newsweek* (February 19, 1996), p. 45.

40. For instance, see Foner, "Sex Roles and Sensibilities: Jamaican Women in New York and London"; Bonnett, "The New Female West Indian Immigrant: Dilemmas of Coping in the Host Society."

41. Palmer, *Pilgrims from the Sun*, pp. 80–81.

42. The latter means that nurses tend to constitute a significant portion of West Indian immigrant women entering the country as professional and technical workers. It also means that some women who start off as domestics later seek upward mobility, in stages, in the health care field. One sequence which this writer has observed among some West Indian women is that which takes them from being domestics, to lower level health care workers (e.g., working in nursing homes), to being nurse's assistants and, in some cases, registered nurses.

43. For example, see Nancy Foner, "The Jamaicans: Race and Ethnicity among Migrants in New York City," in *New Immigrants in New York*, ed. Nancy Foner (New York: Columbia University Press, 1987), pp. 195–218. Also, see chapter 4.

44. See, for example, Sowell below.

45. Johnson, "Culture, Economic Stability, and Entrepreneurship: The Case of British West Indians in Boston," p. 60. The 1990 census reports that 44 percent of Jamaicans own their own homes. This compares to 49 percent for all foreign-born immigrants and 65 percent for native-born Americans.

46. See, for example, Foner, "Sex Roles and Sensibilities: Jamaican Women in New York and London"; Gordon, "Dependents or Independent Workers?: The Status of Caribbean Immigrant Women in the United States."

47. *Beyond the Melting Pot.*

48. "Black Immigrants and the American Ethos: Theories and Observations," in *Caribbean Immigration to the United States*, ed. R. S. Bryce-Laporte and Delores Mortimer (Washington, D.C.: The Smithsonian Institution, 1976), p. 55.

49. See, for example, *Ethnic America: A History* (New York: Basic Books, 1981); *Markets and Minorities* (New York: Basic Books, 1981); *The Politics of Economics and Race: An International Perspective* (New York: William Morrow, 1983); *Civil Rights: Rhetoric or Reality?* (New York: William Morrow, 1984).

50. Glazer and Moynihan, p. 35.

51. Forsythe, "Black Immigrants and the American Ethos: Theories and Observations," p. 55.

52. Edna Bonacich, "A Theory of Middleman Minorities," *American Sociological Review*, Vol. 38 (1973): 583–594.

53. Forsythe, p. 68.

54. Ibid., p. 75.

55. Oscar Glantz, "Native Sons and Immigrants: Some Beliefs and Values of American Born and West Indian Blacks at Brooklyn College," *Ethnicity* 5 (1978): 189–202.

56. Harpers (1982): 27–31.

57. For instance, see Adam Nossiter, "A Jamaican Way Station in the Bronx" (*New York Times*, October 25, 1995): B1.

58. For instance, Bruce Llewellyn, a cousin of Powell, owns *Essence Magazine*, a successful Coca-Cola bottling plant, and a television station.

59. The names used throughout the book to identify the West Indians whom I interviewed are pseudonyms.

60. Jamaicans living in the United States tend to view all immigrants from the West Indies as being, essentially, alike. Therefore, they often use the nation-specific term *Jamaican* interchangeably with the larger panethnic term *West Indian*.

61. For similar views, see, for example, Nancy Foner, "The Jamaicans: Race and Ethnicity among Migrants in New York City," in *New Immigrants in New York*, ed. Nancy Foner (New York: Columbia University Press, 1987), pp. 195–218; and Thomas Kessner and Betty Caroli, *Today's Immigrants: Their Stories* (New York: Oxford University Press, 1982).

62. *The Color Line and the Quality of Life in America* (New York: Oxford University Press, 1989).

63. Suzanne Model, "Caribbean Immigrants: A Black Success Story?" *International Migration Review*, Vol. 25 (Summer 1991): 248–275.

64. Suzanne Model, "West Indian Prosperity: Fact or Fiction?" *Social Problems*, Vol. 42, No. 4 (November 1995): 535–552.

65. Mattijs Kalmijn, "The Socioeconomic Assimilation of Caribbean American Blacks," *Social Forces*, Vol. 74, No. 3 (March 1996): 928.

66. For example, see Kasinitz, "From Ghetto Elite to Service Sector: A Comparison of the Role of Two Waves of West Indian Immigrants to New York City"; Nasser Daneshvary and R. Keith Schwer, "Black Immigrants in the U.S. Labor Market: An Earnings Analysis," *Review of Black Political Economy*, Vol. 22, No. 3 (Winter 1994): 77–98.

67. Roy S. Bryce-Laporte, "Black Immigrants, the Experience of Invisibility and Inequality," *Journal of Black Studies* 3, No. 1 (1972): 50.

68. Roger Waldinger, *Still the Promised City?*; also, see Philip Kasinitz, "From Ghetto Elite to Service Sector: A Comparison of the Role of Two Waves of West Indian Immigrants to New York City"; Ransford Palmer, *Pilgrims from the Sun*.

69. For instance, relying on Department of Commerce data, he shows that between 1988 and 2040, overall employment in the health care field is expected to increase by about 15 percent and average earnings by approximately 65 percent. See Palmer, *Pilgrims from the Sun*, p. 80.
70. See, for example, Waldinger, *Still the Promised City?*; Kirk Johnson, "Black Workers Bear Big Burden as Jobs in Government Dwindle," *New York Times* (February 2, 1997): A1.
71. Waldinger, p. 291.
72. Waldinger, p. 296.

CHAPTER

3

Encountering Race In America

One striking, long evident feature of the literature on West Indian[1] immigrants in America has been its dualistic focus on achievement and the barriers—especially of a racial nature—to achievement affecting these immigrants. This dualism reflects real contradictions in the life experiences of very goal-oriented immigrants who are living in a society which simultaneously espouses such goal seeking while, in many instances, actively hindering the actual attainment of these goals.[2] Noting, however, the presence of this dualism is not to argue that the various facets of the West Indian experience in America have been given equal treatment. Instead, as shown in the previous chapter, some of the most well known writings on West Indians have emphasized achievement over barriers to achievement. However, to a considerable extent, this focus on achievement presents a one-sided view of West Indians. A fuller understanding of this group requires a focus not only on the positives but also on the unpleasant aspects of their experiences in this country. Of these, the encounter with race is, undoubtedly, the most significant.

As shown by such writers as Reid, Lennox, Bryce-Laporte, Foner, Kasinitz, and Waters,[3] West Indians' encounter with racial discrimination is an integral part of their lives in America. This is the case because negative stereotypes regarding individuals who have been socially defined as blacks are deeply ingrained in the society, and West Indians (most of whom fit this definition), no less than African Americans, feel their impact. This impact derives from the lived experience of racial discrimination and takes on even greater force in the case of West Indians because they are socialized to ignore race. In their pursuit of upward mobility in this country, they find themselves blindsided by problematic racial issues. Understanding these issues from the point of view of West Indians means seeing the issues from the perspective of the societies from which these immigrants come. The basic truth is that West Indians' debate with American notions of race is conducted in terms of norms that have been established by the peculiar historical, demographic, and ideological circumstances of their home societies. They view race in America through distinctly West Indian eyes. Because West Indians' prior notions of, and experience with, racial discrimination differ substantially from those prevailing in this country, they experience persistent difficulty dealing with explicit racialism. These difficulties center on the following specific areas of concern: (1) surprise at the salience of race in American life, (2) a wide range of negative racial encounters, and (3) continuing difficulties coping with racial discrimination. Ultimately, many West Indians, in response to these difficulties and as a means of understanding them, develop a heightened consciousness of race. Race ceases to be the background variable that it is in many West Indian societies and becomes self-evidently more important.

However, West Indians' struggles with race have wider significance beyond what they say about West Indians themselves. These struggles also illustrate the larger truth that blacks—especially upwardly mobile ones—routinely encounter contradictions in their everyday lives. West Indians, for instance, find America to be a "land of opportunity" and, in fact, often espouse social values that, in this country, would be labeled "conservative." This conservatism is evident, for example, in their feelings about welfare. It would not be overstating to say that with respect to this issue, their sentiments often recall the biblical injunction that "if a man does not work, he should not eat."[4] However, embracing these values does not prevent them from encountering, daily, racial discrimination. Similarly, upwardly mobile African Americans find that achieving educationally, occupationally, and materially often does not protect them from invidious treatment because of race. Consequently, I end this chapter by arguing that the contradictions experienced by West Indians can be generalized to the larger black population and are an important reason for the discontent to be found among many blacks. These facts are noteworthy because they are counterintuitive. Some writers[5] argue that upward mobility among blacks (African-American and West Indian) necessarily implies the diminishment of racial discrimination. However, upward mobility and discrimination not only can but do coexist, and much black middle class discontent stems from the tension between the theoretical class location of these upwardly mobile blacks and the discordant experiences of racial discrimination which they frequently encounter.

■ APPREHENDING THE SALIENCE OF RACE

In his seminal description of the lives of the first wave of West Indian immigrants, sociologist Ira Reid showed how their different culture, socialization as part of a majority population, and their varying perception of race led to problems when they migrated to the United States. Marcus Garvey was the most famous example of this difficulty. Coming from a society deeply mired in racism, he developed a philosophy which sought, as historian Gordon Lewis has stated, to "wipe out the inherited inferiority complex and facelessness of the Negro in a white world."[6] Unfortunately, Garvey assumed that light skinned blacks in America played a similar role in this country to those in Jamaica. In reality, where the latter had developed the entrenched habit of viewing themselves as different and superior to those of darker skin, light skinned blacks in America had been forced by crushing racial discrimination to view themselves as part of the larger black masses.[7] Garvey's misperception led him to tailor his appeal for racial solidarity around dark skinned blacks and to castigate those of lighter skin—such as Du Bois— whom he viewed with suspicion. This only tended to further intensify the intraethnic conflict taking place between West Indians and African Americans in the early decades of this century.[8]

This conflict was only one manifestation of a basic difference in outlook originating in the differing historical experiences of the two groups. On a deeper level, despite racial discrimination in their own societies, West Indians just could not get used to its relatively harsher tone in the United States. As Reid, speaking of early West Indian immigrants noted, they quickly realized that they had come into a completely different social milieu. The result was deep disillusionment, as their previous enthusiasm for America was replaced by surprise and anger. For instance, he gave the example of the immigrant who having been taken to "nigger town" upon his arrival reported: "It was the first time I had heard that opprobrious epithet employed. . . . Already I was becoming rapidly disillusioned. . . . How unlike the land where I was born. . . . There, colored gentlemen were addressed as gentlemen; here as 'niggers.' "[9]

A half-century after the publication of Reid's book, we find West Indians offering very similar sentiments. For instance, in her analysis of the experiences of Jamaican immigrants in America, Nancy Foner has shown how migration to America creates a new consciousness of color among these immigrants.[10] As she notes, this does not mean that Jamaicans lack color consciousness before they migrate. Indeed, that aspect of Jamaican culture is well known; but, as shown previously, the demographic predominance of blacks and the ideology of nonracialism have tended to mute traditional color consciousness—especially among postindependence Jamaicans. This leaves Jamaican immigrants—and West Indians, in general, whose societies have seen similar transformations—badly prepared for dealing with America's blatant racialism.[11] These immigrants' assertion that they only discover what it means to be black after coming to America is a recognition that African ancestry carries far more serious consequences in this country than it does in their home societies.

My own research among Jamaican immigrants confirms the continuing difficulties West Indians have apprehending the salience of race in this country. In interview after interview, these immigrants expressed a consistent sense of puzzlement, frustration, and anger at their racial experiences. An instructive case which not only illustrates these attitudes but also the tensions existing between upward mobility and racial discrimination concerns the highly educated technician whom I interviewed in Brooklyn. In the United States only about two years at the time of the interview, he embodied the stereotype of the immigrant "go-getter." Having graduating from college with honors, he migrated to this country and obtained advanced degrees in different disciplines. These enabled him to obtain a job, in the technical department, of one of America's foremost corporations.

However, his professional career stood in stark contrast to problems pertaining to his race. When I spoke with Harry,[12] he expressed continuing difficulties making the transition from Jamaica, where his race was never an issue, to the United States, where it frequently was. He could not understand why people did not always judge him on the basis of his qualification and performance instead of on his skin color. In truth, and reflective of the experiences of African Americans, the reality was more complex than this, since the esteem accorded him fluctuated, depending on his exact location.[13] In his office, his colleagues respected him for his technical expertise and he was on friendly terms with them. However, at times, the security guards at his workplace acted suspiciously toward him, questioning his right to be in the building. This outraged him because he viewed himself as being far more educated than they were, yet, in his interpretation, they refused to respect him because of his skin color. As far as the security guards were concerned, his technical skills and ambition were far less important than how he looked.

The irony of the situation only deepened Harry's anger—and he *was* angry, advocating, for instance, that since whites consistently stereotype blacks as criminals, the latter should live up to the reputation by deliberately behaving aggressively toward whites. His rationale was that the typical white person has little respect for blacks and this can be increased only by instilling fear through aggressive behavior. In talking with this immigrant, it became obvious that this extreme response was merely one of many possible responses in what was, in fact, a struggle to come to terms with racism in America. For instance, he advocated another strategy which resulted from an encounter with the police. Walking one night near his home, a police patrol stopped him, inquiring what he was doing out on the street at night. He answered by presenting his work identification badge. Because his association with the particular corporation seemed to impress the officers, the badge took on increased significance in his view and he insisted on taking it wherever he went, in case he was ever, again, asked to validate his presence.[14]

Inasmuch as it was impossible to permanently display this badge, the shortcomings of this strategy are obvious. Nevertheless, the important points to note here are: (1) Harry's variable status depending on location and (2) his difficulties coping with the increased salience of race in America. Other West Indians have reported similar difficulties. The following excerpts illustrate this point. A thirty-seven-year-old computer programmer, Ralph, had this to say about getting around in New York City:

> Race was important [in Jamaica] but not on a day to day basis. The difference I find is that when you get to America, you have to start thinking about race when you walk into the store. . . . In Manhattan you walk into a store; you'll find that people will be following you around: Things like that you have never been accustomed to. To me, what has been a shocker here is to walk on the train and for women to clutch their handbags. That has never happened to me before. So you realize that you have to develop a . . . thick skin . . . because if you have never been taken as a thief before and all of a sudden you have to deal with this! That has been, to me, my worst problem to overcome since I have been here.

One thirty-nine-year-old truck driver, James, put the problem this way:

> I am just here four years now [and] . . . I am going to honestly tell you— America is not what I expected. . . . I am having a problem getting adjusted to the American system, per se. Because up here . . . the lifestyle that is America is not me, honestly. . . . It might be too fast for me or maybe it's the city I am in. Maybe it's because I am in New York.

Often one finds, as in the following examples, struggles with race mixed with appreciation for the opportunities brought about by migration. Joel, a fifty-one-year-old accountant, noted that,

> it's a good country. I have lots of opportunities. I have . . . two sons born here. . . . I knock America from a racial standpoint, because, personally, I don't feel it will ever be truly integrated. But I would never say that I would never come back here, or whatever, because as I said it has a lot of opportunities to offer and you can make it here. I think the biggest problem in America is the racial problem.

Similarly, Elton, a thirty-year-old chemist, stated:

> I think we [West Indians] refuse . . . to really get caught up in the whole racial issue . . . although we are being treated the same way racially. Our thing is . . . to forge ahead just the same. . . . Since . . . we . . . grow up . . . [with] a more socio-economic issue in the West Indies—we are not that

sensitive to racism; although some, you know, is pretty blatant that you just can't refuse from knowing that it is racism.

■ RACIAL ENCOUNTERS AND COPING STRATEGIES

If West Indians' difficulties apprehending the salience of race in America consisted merely of abstract comparisons between this country and their homelands, there would be little problem. In reality, these comparisons take on a pressing nature because of the experiences of these immigrants. These experiences, which range from the subjective (e.g., feelings of anxiety about being in particular neighborhoods) to the blatant (e.g., discrimination in the workplace, verbal and physical abuse), mirror those reported by Feagin and Sikes in their study of African Americans.[15] This implies that West Indians' racial encounters are only one manifestation of a set of problems that afflict blacks generally. To make sense of West Indians' self-reported racial experiences, I present in Table 3.1 a typology which combines West Indians' racial encounters with their strategies for coping with these encounters. It is based on the idea that racial encounters consist of at least two aspects: actions or attitudes projected by particular agents (referred to henceforth as racial agents) and the responses to these by individuals who perceive themselves to be the intended targets. In each encounter, agents are characterized as behaving in an active or passive manner, and their targets are conceived as responding in a similar manner. This yields four categories: Confrontation (aggressive racism, aggressive response), Assertion (passive racism, aggressive

TABLE 3.1 A Typology of Racial Encounters

Actions/Attitudes of Racial Agents	West Indians' Reactions	
	Active	Passive
Active	CONFRONTATION 1. Insults/threats 2. Physical altercations	PRAGMATISM Encounters with the police
Passive	ASSERTION 1. Refusal to interact, give service, form friendships 2. Denial of promotions	RESIGNATION 1. Encounters in public places (e.g., avoidance by women) 2. Being watched

response), Resignation (passive racism, passive response), and Pragmatism (aggressive racism, passive response).

Confrontation describes situations in which racial agents approach West Indians in an overt, aggressive manner. The latter perceive this to be the case and respond in kind. Examples include situations in which West Indians perceive themselves as being physically attacked, threatened, or insulted. *Assertion* describes situations in which racial agents, while not approaching West Indians in an overt way, nevertheless affect them adversely because of their race or ethnicity. West Indians perceive these situations in a negative light and react assertively. Examples include situations in which racial agents (usually whites) refuse to serve West Indians or to promote them on the job. *Resignation* is similar to Assertion in that racial agents do not overtly approach West Indians but nevertheless affect them negatively. The latter, while understanding this, nevertheless choose to avoid confrontation. The preeminent example of this is that situation where whites deliberately avoid blacks in public. The final category, *Pragmatism*, describes situations in which racial agents approach West Indians aggressively but the latter, fearing the consequences of a similar response, opt for a subdued reply. Encounters with the police are the main example of this type of situation.

These categories, being built on the actual empirical examples derived from my research, do not exhaust the full range of possible coping mechanisms. Other responses to each of the categories are possible. For instance, although they are usually respectful of the police, West Indians could respond to aggressive police tactics in kind. Such a response would, according to the typology, have to be properly labeled as Confrontation. In the case of Resignation, West Indians usually shrug off situations in which whites avoid them, reasoning that any other response would be difficult to sustain. But they could, in fact, confront such individuals. In that case, the response would have to be moved to the Assertion category. A more important limitation of the typology, though, is the fact that it does not illustrate a key West Indian response to racial discrimination: the development of a racial consciousness over time. In the long run, this crucial coping strategy enables West Indians to make sense of situations for which their socialization in the West Indies has not prepared them. I will delay my discussion of this strategy for coping with racial discrimination until after I have elaborated the typology.

It is also important to note that the typology overlaps with some very useful discussion of these same issues that have been put forward by other writers. Of particular importance in this context is Richard Jenkins' discussion of the social construction of ethnic identity.[16] Following others in the field,[17] Jenkins posits that the construction of ethnic identity is a dualistic process which involves questions of self-definition that emanate from within ethnic groups; and external definitions that are imposed by powerful outsiders. However, arguing that the first dimension of identity construction has been overplayed, Jenkins wishes to shift emphasis to the second. Consequently, he has presented a typology which shows the contexts in which the process of the external imposition of identity (or "social categorization") can occur. These range along an "informal"/"formal" continuum; with the former referring to relatively unstructured situations in which social categorization takes place and the latter to highly regulated structures (e.g., the census) within which powerful outsiders seek to define the ethnic identity of others.

The informal end of this continuum bears particular relevance to the present discussion; for Jenkins presents, as the epitome of this, what he refers to as "routine public interaction." He defines this as, "the face-to-face interaction that occurs outside ongoing social relationships and within the gaze of others."[18] In these situations, some individuals can seek to categorize others by appropriating, with or without their knowledge, explicit signals of ethnic identity (e.g., skin color) or nonverbal cues to such identity (e.g., stereotyped behaviors). The actual attempt to impose an ethnic identity can manifest itself in several ways, ranging from violence, through verbal abuse, to ethnic jokes. The racial experiences that have been reported by West Indians may be interpreted as attempts by outsiders (primarily whites) to impose, on them, a stereotypical identity as "blacks." By this, I mean unwarranted expectations about character and behavior that these outsiders expect to flow from the simple fact of possessing African ancestry. Such attempts become particularly powerful in public places, because, as Feagin and Sikes have shown in *Living with Racism*, the *site* in which racial discrimination occurs significantly impacts blacks' ability to cope. As shown earlier in the case of Harry, the workplace (e.g., office) can offer a certain amount of protection from racial discrimination. However, this protection declines as blacks move into public places. In those situations strangers enjoy much greater freedom to make unflattering assumptions about, and treat blacks, unfavorably.[19] At the same time, blacks are at their weakest defending against discrimination that takes place in public. For West Indians, particularly, discrimination in public places represents situations where they have the least ability to redefine the content of "blackness." That is, they would like to make the point that African ancestry and, for instance, achievement, and "good behavior" (e.g., being law-abiding) are in no way contradictory. However, public places offer little scope for making such connections, since, in such situations, blacks often find themselves being judged categorically and negatively.

Confrontation

West Indians are not shrinking violets. In fact, the opposite is true: in seeking their ambitions they are often quite assertive. Speaking of Jamaicans, historian Gordon Lewis noted as much in *The Growth of the Modern West Indies* when, in critiquing Alexander Bustamante,[20] he spoke of the "Busta personality ... with its tremendous braggadocio, its personification of the Jamaican folk hero, the spider-man Anansi who survives in a hostile world by cunningly exploiting the weaknesses of his enemies."[21] Jamaican political scientist Carl Stone echoed similar sentiments in seeking to account for Jamaicans' drive to succeed. According to Stone, "Black Jamaicans have acquired an international reputation for being aggressive, pushy, self-confident and self-assertive and for fighting against any efforts to treat them as inferior."[22] In the 1980s, the media exaggerated these characteristics by overemphasizing the "posse" menace. Frequent stories appeared to the effect that dangerous Jamaican drug gangs had entered America and were spreading throughout the country.[23] Although such drug activity does exist, the allegation has been made that these media reports led to the Manhattan District Attorney creating a list with the names of thirty thousand Jamaicans who had been involved in even minor offenses.[24] Simultaneously, the popular media advanced very unflattering stereotypes of West Indians in films such as *Marked for Death* and *Predator II*.[25]

Despite these media exaggerations, it is true that West Indians, in general, have gained a reputation for being outspoken in the face of discrimination. In an often-cited example, Reid showed that in the early days of West Indian immigration (up to the late 1930s), the Pullman Coach Company refused to hire these immigrants because they would not accept insults from white passengers. He also noted that, at times, West Indians faced with racial discrimination would retort by appealing to the British Embassy for protection. This is ironic, because, at the time, the British were practicing their own brand of racial injustice in the West Indies. Nevertheless, the point is important, because it illustrates the extent to which West Indians, even in the midst of racial discrimination in their home countries, had accepted the idea that race was relatively unimportant in those islands.

My interview with Pete, a retired carpenter, confirmed accounts of the assertive attitudes of early West Indian immigrants. Migrating to America in 1945, he found himself pressed into the war effort helping to build troop ships. However, in New York City after the war he experienced discrimination despite his skills as a carpenter. He recounted that he breached these barriers only by being persistent and forthright. On one occasion, having been turned down for a job, he barged into the foreman's office and demanded that as a skilled carpenter who belonged to the carpenters' union, he should be hired by the company. Told by the foreman to leave, he refused and was eventually rewarded with the job he sought when the former relented.

On another occasion, while traveling in the South during the Jim Crow era, he was refused service in a restaurant. Outraged, he found the nearest police officer (who ignored him) and complained about his treatment, holding up as proof of the injustice of the whole affair, his credentials as a good law-abiding citizen who was demanding only ordinary rights held by whites. A black person who had been socialized in this country would have expected such discrimination in the Jim Crow South, and is most unlikely to have sought justice from the police. However, Pete, like many early West Indian immigrants, spoke of being born "under the British flag"; and an integral aspect of his place of birth, in his estimation, was the expectation of fair play and a respect for law and order. In other words, he had thoroughly embraced the West Indian belief that, in judging people, race is much less important than such factors as character, education, wealth, and skills. The clash between this optimistic perspective and the actual treatment of blacks in Jim Crow America proved to be very jarring.

Although some of the Jim Crow era's more blatant manifestations of antiblack sentiment (e.g., segregated water fountains) are no longer in evidence, racial discrimination has by no means disappeared and modern-day West Indians have their own stories to tell. The most graphic example of Confrontation would be situations in which West Indians engaged in actual fights because of racial friction. One example of this fighting was the construction worker who found himself in a brawl with Eastern European coworkers who, he reported, constantly insulted him with racial slurs and actually attacked him. Another example of fighting stemming from racial insults comes from my interview with Mark, a bus driver. He stated that in the five years since he had migrated to America, he had already been involved in one serious physical altercation related to race. This confrontation was rather dramatic and, eventually, involved some of New York City's top political figures. It began as a traffic incident, while doing his usual rounds as a bus driver. In Bensonhurst, Brooklyn, he had stopped so that a motorist at an intersection could make a left turn in front of his bus. The motorist behind him, irate over being held up, initially expressed his displeasure by blowing his horn repeatedly. However, when the bus proceeded down the road, the disgruntled motorist sped up and cut in front of it. After emerging from the car, the motorist proceeded to assail Mark with a variety of racial slurs. Events proceeded downhill from there.

Mark stated that, having cut off the bus, the white motorist shouted, "You . . . nigger, what the hell you doing here?" (i.e., in Bensonhurst). In response Mark left the bus and confronted the motorist with equally strong words. He continued:

> He run . . . into his car for a baseball bat [stating]: "I'll break your . . . skull
> . . . ; no nigger is supposed to be in this area." . . . I said: "Look man, I go
> anywhere. And this is not the days of . . . Mississippi or down in the Midwest
> when you used to catch black people and hang them by the neck. . . . This

is 1980;[26] this is New York." And then I went back into the bus. I said look: "I think I am stupid just like you to come out and argue with a trash like you because you don't have no sense." When I went back into the bus he feel a bit pissed-off and he took out his baseball bat and he start to smash about three of the glass [windows] on the side of the bus. . . . I came out and I stood in front of the car to take his plate number. . . . Then he backed the car up and drive the car toward me so I got to jump out the way.

Mark explained that the racial insults caused him to become increasingly angry, and he reacted dramatically when the motorist tried to take his life.

I jumped on the hood of the car because I feel like I want to break the guy's neck. I eventually lost control of myself. . . . When you think about somebody say something to you that hurt you a lot. . . . And it's the first time, I said, I ever been confronted [with racism] and I don't like it. . . . Thinking about what I read from my boyhood days coming about what black people . . . suffer . . . and when he . . . said: "nigger" . . .—this man look on me as dirt. . . . I jumped on the front of the car and tried to grab his head through the window; so he wind the glass up and drive a couple blocks.

By his own assessment, he overreacted to the situation and, once over the shock and anger, wanted to forget the incident. However, in December of the previous year (1986), a fatal attack by a mob of white adolescents on three blacks in Howard Beach, Queens, had greatly increased racial tension in the city.[27] Consequently, so-called "bias crimes" had attained a high profile, and the city administration, anxious to stem further escalation in racial tensions, pressured him to bring charges against the white motorist. He refused because he wished to avoid becoming entangled in the legal system. Furthermore, since he had not been seriously injured—despite the attempt on his life—he saw no need to press charges. Indeed, it was the bus company which ultimately pressed charges on the motorist for the damage he had inflicted on their property. Still, Mark found it impossible to extricate himself from the politics of the situation, since the city administration, anxious to show that it was doing something about racial violence, continued to pressure him to file bias charges. This pressure ranged from the subtle (a personal interview with the District Attorney) to the blatant (the threat that he would be jailed for contempt of court if he refused to testify before a grand jury). Ultimately, he gave in to the pressure and testified before the grand jury. The motorist received a one-year suspended sentence and was required to compensate Mark for "embarrassment" and the bus company for damaging its property.

More typically, insults of this type do not lead to actual fights, but West Indians, nevertheless, respond to them directly. Reflecting the attitudes of earlier West Indian immigrants, one respondent insisted that West Indians "don't get better treatment . . . they demand it! The West Indians are very assertive and . . . the way that [the] average American will take an insult; the average West Indian is more cool with it. In other words, he doesn't get flustered."[28] Something of this attitude emerges in the following incident, recounted by Joel, the accountant to whom I referred previously:

> I go to the track one day a year—the Belmont stakes. . . . There are . . . benches around the place that you can sit on; not reserved, not paid for. Everybody pays $5 and you go into the clubhouse. . . . We were feeling a little tired and we went . . . to sit down. . . . And we sat and these people started to tell us that these seats were reserved. So we said, "Look, these seats are not reserved. If you want to reserve a seat you have to pay extra because I have one of the tags." . . . And this redneck guy looked around and told us that . . . he used to . . . kill people like us; meaning he used to kill black people! . . . I told the guys [the whites] that if they thought that the seats were reserved, then go get the police to come, to see if we would get up. The argument abated because they can't bully you. It's a situation where if you don't know, they can bully you. But we stayed because the seats were not reserved.

In this instance, Joel and his friends, faced with the threat of racial violence, responded by refusing to yield the disputed seats. In the face of potential violence, they held up their tickets—proof of the legitimacy of their claim to the seats.

Another, somewhat amusing, example comes from the experiences of a subway motorman. While shopping in a small grocery store, he found himself being followed by the proprietor. Exasperated, he finally confronted the woman and pulled out his wallet, showing her all his credit cards. He reported telling her that he had more than enough funds to buy whatever he wanted and, therefore, did not have to steal from her. His ploy worked, since the proprietor stopped following him. A fifth example will suffice to illustrate this feisty attitude. James, the truck driver who was cited above in reference to the difficulties of life in America, insisted during our interview that he dealt with racial discrimination very forthrightly. As he stated, "On my job I show them that I don't take no nonsense from nobody . . . my boss, nobody. . . . They respect me as a person; they come and speak to me as a man." To prove his point he recalled that after working at his company for a number of months, the business was taken over by the owner's son. However, unlike his father, the son disliked black customers and discriminated against them. Disturbed by these actions, James confronted the son, reminding him that these same customers constituted the backbone of the business. Fortunately for him, the father came to the same conclusion after noticing that the company had started losing business. This perception, combined with the fact that James was regarded as a valuable worker, helped to save his job.

Assertion

Assertion resembles Confrontation, since it also describes situations in which West Indians respond directly to situations that they perceive as affecting them negatively for racial reasons. The difference in the former is that the racial agents involved are not directly approaching the West Indians. Thus, Assertion describes subtle, institutionalized racism. Often, this racism assumes the form of avoidance. While, prima facie, this might seem harmless, West Indians often perceive such avoidance as injuring them. "Injury," here, is being used in a broad sense, since the data show that it ranges from wounded sensibilities to actual economic penalization. Below, I will present several examples which illustrate this range.

The first example shows how avoidance can offend the sensibilities of some West Indians. One respondent recalled that during the period in which he worked as a security guard, white security guards routinely refused to associate with the black ones. He decided to breach this barrier because he felt that it was foolish for the two groups not to associate with each other simply because of color. Thus, he started inviting himself to lunch with the white guards and eventually became friendly with all of them. At another job, after work one day, he invited one of his white colleagues to a tavern for a drink. Taken aback by this request, the colleague expressed even greater reluctance when he realized that this meant going to Flatbush. The white colleague's response was that since the Flatbush section of Brooklyn is overwhelmingly black, his life would be in danger. The Jamaican was offended by this perception and determined even more strongly that he would show his white colleague that black skin does not equal criminality. He ended the story by noting that, indeed, his white colleague at the end of the day reported feeling somewhat differently about blacks.

While this account sounds somewhat idealized, there is no reason to doubt the Jamaican's veracity. More importantly, his response to avoidance reflects the difficulty many of these immigrants have dealing with people in an overtly racial way. Since this rarely ever happens in Jamaica, confronting it routinely in America takes getting used to. In addition, the example underscores the tendency of some West Indians to view themselves as role models. Although directed chiefly at African Americans, role modeling also—as in this instance—finds whites as a target. In the foregoing case, role modeling asserted itself in the Jamaican seizing the initiative to prove to a somewhat hostile white that his fears about black people were unfounded. This demonstration accounts for the satisfaction expressed by the respondent when he reported that after leaving the tavern, his white colleague had gained new insight into the character of blacks.

The second example of avoidance goes somewhat beyond wounded sensibilities, since it involves a situation where a Jamaican was deprived of a service to which he was entitled. Neil, a social worker, recounted the follow-ing incident:

> I was on [a] plane from Miami to Washington and the hostess . . . walked around just before the aircraft took off, distributing magazines. And I was sitting in my seat by myself; very cool, very professional. And she walked past me: she don't give me no magazines. . . . I was the only black person on the flight. When she was coming back, I simply leaned forward and I said: "I can read!;" . . . just like that, and she gave me a magazine.

In this instance, Neil perceived himself as having been unjustly overlooked because of his race. The hostess, by avoiding him, had diminished the plea-sure to be derived from the flight. Moreover, she added to his discomfort by conveying the distinct impression that he had been singled out for bad treatment because of his race. She implied by overlooking only him that he was less worthy than the other passengers. Neil responded by asserting his rights as a fee-paying passenger.

In the third instance of avoidance, the stakes were much higher. As hurt-ful as wounded sensibilities and the denial of service are, they do not com-pare in impact to situations in which such avoidance threatens to undermine the individual's economic security. Many of the Jamaicans I interviewed ex-pressed great anger about workplace discrimination. In such instances, an-guish is particularly severe, because, as noted previously, West Indians place economic self-improvement at the top of their agenda. Moreover, such dis-crimination attacks a central aspect of their identity: the notion that they are serious, hard-working individuals who advance on the basis of merit. This belief reflects the tendency of West Indian societies to downplay race and to emphasize education as *the* means for social advancement.[29] West Indians have deeply internalized the idea that merit is the only proper basis for up-ward social mobility. As Al, an engineer, complained:

> I think a man should be qualified for a job. . . . I don't want a job because I'm black. I want a job because I'm qualified. . . . If you make an applica-tion here [for a job], they want to know your race. What the hell with my race?! I feel right away that you're going to judge me off of that and I am at a disadvantage there. I'm a man! Do I have the qualifications? That [is what] you must find out.

Moreover, this emphasis on merit and hard work is the basis on which some West Indians claim to be able to act as role models for some African Americans; their explicit message being that West Indians are achievers, and that by adopting similar attitudes, those African Americans whom these West Indians perceive as being less than "successful" can also prosper.

Because of this general outlook, West Indians experience deep dismay when they encounter the irony of whites judging them using particularistic criteria while they, themselves, are emphasizing merit. This tends to lead to hard feelings. For instance, there is the case of another engineer, Gordon, who had to struggle to obtain promotion. He noted:

> For promotion, I had a hard time. I remember once . . . I was assistant to this guy for a while and he was promoted and I thought, well, I'm going to succeed this guy; just fit into his slot. But I was there, still acting. Then this . . . Irish guy said: "You know . . . the chief is looking around for someone from outside." I said: "What!" Because, you know, in Jamaica we were taught that you go up by merit. . . . So I thought that since I was there they wouldn't look for somebody [from] outside. It was a shock to me. . . . I was doing the work but I would be in charge of all whites. . . . They didn't want me to do that. . . . I said [to his superior]: "Give it to me now and if I don't prove myself within one month you can fire me". . . . I waited about another three weeks. . . . But I had to fight!

The problem, here, is that Gordon's superior, having indicated approval of his job performance, allowed him to labor under the assumption that he would obtain a promotion. Anger and feelings of betrayal resulted when it emerged that the superior was actively trying to subvert Gordon. Once he realized that his job was at risk, he set about building a case as to why he should be promoted. In so doing, Gordon brought the whole process out into the open so that his superior would be accountable for his actions. Gordon forced him to focus on objective standards; to keep or fire him on that basis. Once the situation had been exposed, the superior reluctantly decided to abide by these principles and allow the promotion. Ultimately, however, the experience left Gordon so embittered that he resigned his position and opted for self-employment.

Seeking out other jobs is one way in which West Indians attempt to cope with frustrating workplace situations. Others stay put for various reasons and develop deeply pessimistic attitudes. Those who leave often see higher education and migration as desirable options. Faced with barriers in America, West Indian immigrants often reason that they can overcome if only they gain enough credentials. Thus, for instance, we have the case of Cliff, a twenty-eight-year-old insurance salesman, who expressed great dissatisfaction with his white colleagues. In his view, they "walked around like demigods," belittling blacks and obstructing their upward mobility in the company. His solution to the problem was to enroll in the company's advanced insurance classes, with the eventual aim of establishing his own agency. In other instances, the desire for higher education is combined with a desire to change not only jobs but also physical location. Here the impetus is often twofold: escape the undesirable job (or other) situation and move to a part of the country that seemingly offers greater opportunities for blacks and a better quality of life. Among West Indians this usually means moving to such areas as Silver Spring, Maryland, Richmond, Atlanta, Miami, and Houston. Older West Indians view Florida, especially, as an ideal place to which to retire, since it combines a semitropical climate and proximity to the West Indies.[30]

Resignation

As in the case of Assertion, avoidance lies at the heart of Resignation. The difference is that whereas in Assertion West Indians respond directly to perceived threats, in Resignation they do not; either because they cannot, or because adopting a passive response effectively insulates the West Indian individual against racial discrimination. The stereotypical situation in which West Indians (especially men) find themselves unable to respond to racial discrimination is that where other individuals avoid them in public places. This might take the form—as noted previously in the case of Ralph—of women tightening their grip on their purses; or crossing the street on the approach of West Indians. The suspicion and hostility underlying such responses become magnified if, for work-related reasons, West Indians have to work in the homes of whites. Under such conditions they are subject to intensified scrutiny. Thus, Adam, a technician for a large computer company, noted his experiences upon visiting the home of a customer with a malfunctioning machine:

> On the job . . . two of us went out to the field, in Brooklyn . . . to this lady's house. Anybody's house you go to, you know your eyes wander. From what I have heard, she is upset about that; not just [me] alone; me and the other fellow [also black]. We went two different times. It's like, she's looking right in your eyes and if you switch from the machine to the side, she gets nervous.

As the technician explained it, the customer became upset because she felt that the two black men had allowed their eyes to wander too much. As a result, she lodged a formal complaint with the men's supervisor.

Only little reflection is needed to see why, in such circumstances, West Indians are unable to offer a pointed response. The technicians were constrained by institutional boundaries. They had visited the customer's home in a professional capacity as representatives of their company and, therefore, were fairly powerless to challenge preconceived notions about the character of black men. As seen from the example, even the passive response which they displayed was not enough to allay the woman's fears. She reported them merely because she concluded that they had seen more than they should have. Potentially, if the men had taken issue with her version of events they could have faced the loss of their jobs.

Instances where individuals avoid West Indians in public places present a more difficult problem. Its essence is that West Indians (or the blacks in general who are the usual target of such behavior) cannot prove conclusively that other individuals avoided them merely because of their approach. It could, in fact, be that an individual, seeing another approaching, crosses a particular street for completely nonracial reasons. And even if West Indians could conclusively ascertain such knowledge, on what basis would they accost the person who had crossed the street? If we compare this situation to the case of an individual who is denied promotion because of racial discrimination, we can see that in the latter case a set of rights and mutual obligations exists. Employees are supposed to put in an honest day's work, and employers, when they promote, are supposed to do so on the basis of merit. If, as in the case given above, employers refuse to promote because of particularistic criteria such as race, a case can be made that the employer has breached the norms (and possibly the laws) governing workplace behavior. Obviously, individuals walking on the street are not bound by any such arrangements. Consequently, the most West Indians can do is live with the uncomfortable suspicion that they have been stigmatized because of their race.

Because of such discomfort and—more pointedly—the fear which it engenders, some West Indians seek to preempt racial discrimination by avoiding settings dominated by whites. An example of this avoidance is the salesman who stated that before he enters restaurants, he always examines the clientele first to make sure that at least a few blacks are evident. If such is not the case, he will avoid the restaurant out of fear that he will be subject to racial discrimination. This behavior finds general and more important expression in the tendency to approach white neighborhoods cautiously. Events in New York City in the 1980s—from the killing of a black transit worker in Gravesend to the slaying of a black youth in Bensonhurst[31] (to name only a few of the more well known examples)—certainly gave West Indians (and minority individuals in general) cause to worry. The Howard Beach case is particularly noteworthy in this instance, since it had not been lost on the Jamaicans whom I interviewed that though skin color seems to have been the factor triggering the incident, the young man who was killed was Trinidadian. In their eyes, this was clear proof that bigots do not esteem ethnicity more highly than black skin.[32]

The responses of the Jamaicans I interviewed, with respect to travel into white areas of the city, reflect the general air of caution surrounding such trips. To the extent that they can, the Jamaicans avoid such areas entirely.[33] However, since many West Indians must work in these areas, avoidance is often not an option. In such cases, they try to be prepared for anything that might happen. An example was the mechanic who noted that, in the wake of the Howard Beach incident, he traveled with a baseball bat in his service truck. He intended, should he be attacked, to retaliate in kind. The following excerpts illustrate West Indians' caution in approaching white neighborhoods. Leon, a forty-year-old accountant, stated:

We were doing an audit once where we had to go into a white neighbor-hood—Marine Park. . . . I was there with my white supervisor and we were driving the state car and he said: "You know, the only blacks around here are maids and gardeners, so when they see a black person driving through they get very fearful." . . . And it was a little scary because, in fact, we were out there for a few hours and I didn't see no black people coming out of those homes. . . . I wouldn't go there in the nights by myself.

Dewey, a fifty-eight-year-old civil servant, stated:

I don't socialize at night. I made a mistake and socialized once and I said to myself I would never do it again. A white chap . . . was working for me and he said: "There's this pub . . . " It was in this white neighborhood. About 11:30 I said: "Look, I have got to go." He said: "No, no problem; nobody is going to worry you. Sit down." So 12:30 I said: "I have got to go." And when I stepped out and I looked around. I said: "My god, I don't see any black people at all. . . . This is no good!" So I went back in-side and I said, look: "Walk me to my car." So he said: "Why?" I said: "I don't see anybody looking like me out there. And people been coming in and getting a few drinks and I know that these Irish, when they have a few drinks, they want to have a little fight. Plus they see a lone black guy around there—bait, right?" And I jumped in the car and drove home and I would never do that again. That's asking for trouble.

And there was this from Bob, the thirty-three-year-old manager of an elec-tronics store:

I know for a fact that in the Bay Ridge section of Brooklyn, after a certain time of night, if you are a minority do not go in there! . . . You can be . . . accosted racially and you'll have a police officer look in the other direction. So there are certain areas, certain stores that are closed out to me. . . . One of my best friends . . . actually shakes . . . [whenever he has] . . . to go into Bay Ridge.

These sentiments, though somewhat effective in avoiding racial dis-crimination, carry a high cost: the deliberate truncating of some of the free-doms associated with living in a democratic society. Some of the Jamaicans following this strategy had even—at least on the surface—convinced them-selves that they did not experience racial discrimination. However, as the in-terviews wore on, it usually became evident that the notion of limiting oneself for fear of reprisal grated on them and the underlying anger would begin to emerge. The clearest expression of this anger emerged in an interview with a chemist who lived in one of the city's outlying suburbs. Although suc-cessful and rather conservative,[34] he felt deep anger at racial injustice. Thus, after meeting the writer at the train station, he insisted on detouring through a number of rather exclusive-looking neighborhoods and justified this ex-cursion with the assertion: "Let me show you where black people can't live!"

Similar observations about the anger produced by racial discrimination can be made of those Jamaicans who felt limited in their ability to respond to perceived racial discrimination because of institutional or situational constraints. They felt a deep sense of frustration that judgments were being made about them over which they had no control. As in the case of discrimination in employment, irony deepened the wound, since respect for law and order (drug posses notwithstanding) has been one of the bedrock values of both colonial and postcolonial West Indian culture.[35] It has been part and parcel of the set of values that is pushed by the educational system. Therefore, the West Indians found it doubly galling that regardless of their social class or age, others impugned their integrity.

Pragmatism

The Jamaicans' responses to the police illustrate the collision between their conservative social values and a realization that their skin color singled them out for, at minimum, greater police scrutiny and, at worst, brutalization. My interview with Nelson, a high level manager for a New York State agency, typified these contradictions. Although, as I will show later, he expressed strong criticism of racial discrimination against blacks, he directed even stronger criticism against the black community for allowing the family unit to become weakened by fostering indiscipline. In his estimation, overcoming the problems afflicting some African Americans had to begin by inculcating such measures as increasing discipline, reducing the incidence of female-headed households, and, most important, emphasizing education:

> Koreans have come in; the Vietnamese have come in; I look at every group that has come in . . . and have made it. And we are still at the back of the bus. Now, you have to ask yourself: . . . "Why are we still there with all this twenty six, twenty seven million people that we have . . . Is the white totally responsible why we are still at the back?" We are more than fifty percent responsible for being at the back of the bus because of the fact that some of us who have escaped the situation . . . close the door behind us and forget that the masses are still there. . . . What do we really expect . . . in our families? In the first place, we don't have the family unit: We are a matriarchal society. . . . The family unit is so weak that we aren't going any place. . . . We got to go back from that family unit and build . . . ourselves by education and economics. . . . [But] we . . . ignore what's going on and say . . . we want to go to Washington and we want to march. . . : Where is it bringing us?

Contrary to what might be expected from such sentiments, though, Nelson held a rather low opinion of the police, illustrating the contradictions afflicting upwardly mobile blacks who must still face invidious judgment based on race. I inquired about the police's relationship with the black community:

> It's not good and I am not blaming them one hundred percent for it but
> . . . the system is corrupt. . . . It's a corrupt system and in . . . the black
> community we are stereotyped. Your skin is black and therefore you are
> supposed to be so and so and so and so. You talk to them, they really want
> to talk down to you. You could have ten Ph.Ds. . . . You have some of them
> who'll tell you who you are and what you are based solely on the color of
> your skin.

Although police brutality was not common among the Jamaicans whom
I interviewed, it was not unknown. A fifty-seven-year-old insurance salesman stated:

> I have never placed myself in a position where I get any mistreatment from
> the police. I am very docile. A friend of mine . . . got his foot broken. . . .
> These cops were patrolling the area and he stopped to make a phone call
> to his wife, to tell her that he was on his way. The cops came, saw him in
> the phone booth and they asked him: "What you doing in the phone
> booth?" This guy was very dominant. . . . And he said . . . : "When you go
> into a phone booth, what do you do?" And they beat him, broke his foot
> and arrested him. . . . He sued them, but he still walks with a limp.

In the continuum of possible police responses from greater scrutiny to brutalization, some combination of the former and discrimination—and intermediate state—usually applied. The insurance salesman provided an example
of greater scrutiny. He told how on occasion, while driving home through
the suburban neighborhood in which he lived, he was followed by a police
car which pulled up behind him in his driveway. The policemen left only
after he convinced them that the house belonged to him.

In the context of this discussion, discrimination by the police refers to
situations in which they go beyond mere suspicions and physically appre-
hend individuals for racial reasons. While this is difficult to prove objectively,
several of the Jamaicans interpreted their encounters with the police in this
light. In their opinion, the police disproportionately target black men. The
West Indians understood that young blacks disproportionately commit certain types of crime, but they, themselves, severely criticized such criminality,
arguing that it was damaging to the image of blacks, as a whole. Indeed,
the stereotype of black criminality is one of the reasons why some West
Indians seek to distance themselves from some African Americans (and, for
the same reason, from some younger recent West Indian immigrants).
However, some of the Jamaicans found that such distancing does not shield
them from police suspicions. To take one example: a courier reported that
a police officer, after stopping him on the highway, pointed a gun at him,
issued a variety of racial slurs, and conducted a body search. He found nothing and, eventually, allowed the respondent to go on his way.

Since only one of the Jamaicans reported that he felt especially targeted for being Jamaican, it is reasonable to believe that such police behavior might be more related to the widespread imputation of criminality to young black men. One says "might," since not every encounter between a white police officer and a black individual is necessarily racial. Nevertheless, race so suffuses the history of these encounters that most of the Jamaicans perceived them as such. Interestingly, criticism of police behavior went beyond race, since some of the Jamaicans felt that, in general, the police are "power struck." That is: although white officers are more likely to target blacks, such behavior also characterizes some nonwhite officers as well. Overall, the viewpoint offered by Stan, a thirty-five-year-old tax accountant, sums up the attitude of many whom I interviewed. In his opinion the police, rather than protecting all citizens equally, really serve to protect whites from blacks. Consequently, they display a relatively benign face in white neighborhoods but a harsh one in black areas of the city.

The meeting of law and order impulses and suspicions that the police treat blacks unfairly produced responses combining acknowledged need of the police, distrust, and passivity in dealing with them. The latter stemmed from the knowledge that the police, unlike ordinary citizens with a racial animus, have the power to fashion racial encounters in their favor. In such situations, it is unlikely that the black person would win. Rupert, a contractor, illustrated this viewpoint neatly:

> My encounters with the police [have been] very interesting. When I am approached by the cops, I am approached just as [in the] everyday [situation] where the cop pulls over a black person and their hands are on [their] guns. . . . This is the way I see it: They are expecting some type of hostile response or something. Now, I am calm and I am relaxed. I communicate with them in a manner which will take them by surprise. . . . [I speak] very slow[ly] and easily. I will say: "What can I do to facilitate your request?" . . . Right away, hostility and that kind of aggression that was up front is slowly lowered. It disintegrates into nothing and it becomes rather more amicable. I understand that they are doing their job . . . so there's no need for that, but because I am black, I have to be . . . approached with the routine of aggression.

Other responses revealed more cynicism. Dewey, the civil servant, opined:

> There are a lot of black kids who commit misdemeanors and they are being handcuffed and hauled off to jail and become statistics. Meanwhile, the white kids are being slapped on the wrist and sent home. I know that for a fact because I have police friends. . . . As a matter of fact there is one who was telling me that this white boy was in trouble and they call[ed] his parents and said: "Look we can't . . . lock-up this guy because . . . he's a handsome fellow and he's going to be raped in there. So we can't put him in jail." So we see that over and over: . . . whites commit a lot of crime and get away with it because the cops turn [away], but when . . . [it's a] black,

> he's [the policeman's] there . . . We have a lot of blacks who are in jail who
> . . . are being incarcerated . . . because they are black.[36]

Similarly, Adam, the computer technician, offered the following opinion of the police:

> I fear them. Some stories I have heard about what the cops do, what they can do, what they are capable of doing: You fear them. Don't get me wrong. If a crime is committed, I'm calling them. I would even go to the precinct and talk to them. [But] down there on the street, it's like I have a different respect for them. Those guys have your lives in their hands: They can give you a trumped-up charge anytime.

Still other responses showed anger. One respondent, a police officer before he migrated to the United States, stated that the police are

> far away from the people; number one, they don't set any example. . . . Number two, they are not out there as . . . peace officer[s]. To me, they are there more to throw a person in jail; more than trying to encourage a person, or want a person not to do wrong. . . . I think they are . . . more partial to the white people and they are quicker to give the black guy trouble. And they just feel to themselves that they are just God himself. They don't have any respect for people.

At times, the law and order component of the Jamaicans' socialization came through very clearly, overriding concerns about police mistreatment of blacks. The predominant sentiment among these Jamaicans was that young black males commit a disproportionate amount of crime; therefore, the police justifiably target them. The following excerpt presents a sampling of this viewpoint:

> The law and order that is in this country is not right. . . . A man look at you and kill you, and him go to prison [for] a few years and he is back out. . . . You take, for instance, this girl in Central Park[37] . . . those guys should face the electric chair. . . . You see, you've got to kill out [this] type of element that is coming-up. . . . These children have sense [are responsible]. . . . If they want to sex [rape] that woman, they have sense. . . . It could be your sister; it could be your mother; it could be your wife; it could be your daughter. . . . These are the types of things that [have] got to stop.

■ RACIAL CONSCIOUSNESS

Although West Indians employ several strategies to cope with racial discrimination, it could be argued that these are only short-term remedies for an entrenched problem. With respect to race, perhaps the greatest difficulty faced by West Indians is that they are socialized to deemphasize its importance. Because of this, they are constantly surprised by the blatancy with which race is played out in the United States.[38] Much debate currently exists as to whether America is becoming a more "color-blind" society; but an often overlooked fact is that West Indians,[39] coming from societies with lower levels of racial tension, almost inevitably perceive the United States as being very race conscious. It there was one theme that came through consistently and clearly in my interviews with the Jamaicans, it is that they experience great difficulty adjusting to the notion that in routine, everyday situations, they must take race into account. Over time, continued exposure to racial discrimination causes many West Indians to shift their paradigm from a nonracial one to one that is more explicitly racial. By this, one means that West Indians: (1) come to understand that race permeates all facets of American life; (2) expect to have unpleasant encounters because of race; and (3) often become pessimistic that the United States will become "color-blind" any time soon. In other words, the understanding that they may have had about race prior to migrating goes from being fairly abstract to being experiential and more consciously life-shaping.

To make this point, though, is only to scratch the tip of a complex situation. Saying that, over time, West Indian immigrants become more conscious of race is not to say that this process is either easy or, necessarily, desired. As journalist Malcolm Gladwell has noted, many West Indians would prefer to ignore the whole issue of race.[40] That sentiment came through very clearly in my interviews. The problem is that the society will not allow them to forget. Moreover, the development of greater consciousness of race among West Indians does not negate their overriding goal of achieving upward mobility. One of the central paradoxes of the West Indian experience in the United States is that they believe that racial discrimination is widespread but that this discrimination coexists with the possibility for upward mobility. In practical terms—as the Jamaicans explained it—this coexistence means that West Indians try to maximize their opportunities—educational, financial, material, and occupational—within whatever barriers exist. This does not mean that they agree with racial discrimination; but, rather, that they view racial barriers as long-term and try, as much as is possible, to take control of their own lives by preparing themselves in ways that will enable them to prosper in a capitalist economy.

The Jamaicans whom I interviewed ran the gamut from the minority who absolutely resisted viewing issues in racial terms to the majority who argued that though it *should* not be the case, race certainly *is* a factor in their everyday lives. A good example of strong resistance to thinking about issues in racial terms comes from my interview with Bogle, a fifty-eight-year-old small business man. He had migrated from Jamaica in 1962 and through hard work had managed to thrive. Residing, at first, in Flatbush, he eventually moved to a predominantly white suburban neighborhood after concluding that rising crime rates had made Flatbush unlivable. Initially—as he explained it—the whites in the neighborhood into which he moved expressed hostility at the idea of a black family moving in. However, all this changed when they discovered that the family was West Indian. Previous hostility melted away and was replaced by a very welcoming attitude.

Although this account sounds idealistic, Bogle expressed a strong conviction that whites are more accepting of West Indians because they have a reputation for being law abiding, hard working, and so on. He related the story of his move to the white neighborhood as a way of explaining why, in his opinion, race thinking is bad. Had he adopted that perspective, he argued, he would have limited his vistas and not moved into a pleasant neighborhood out of fear of discrimination. But, as it turned out, the whites accepted his family because of the positive stereotypes associated with West Indians. Merit, diligence, politeness, and respect rather than race thinking were, in his view, the keys to attaining upward mobility in America. Because of this view, Bogle expressed great anger at those blacks who, in his opinion, insisted on seeing everything through the lens of race. He related that the defining moment in the crystallization of this antirace perspective occurred at a social gathering at his house. At this party, an African-American friend upon hearing that the Jamaican family enjoyed ballet questioned why such a "white" art form would be of any interest to blacks. Bogle stated that he reacted with disgust to thinking which he considered crass and limiting and broke the friendship with that particular individual.

Religion and/or ideology can also douse racial feelings. For instance, there was the case of the deeply religious, activist conservative family[41] which severely criticized any sort of race thinking. Holding up as models for blacks to follow, Jerry Falwell, George Bush, and capitalism, they argued that liberalism, allied with a focus on race, was hindering rather than helping American blacks. While not denying the existence of racial discrimination in America, they held that a focus on hard work within the context of a free market and biblical principles would ultimately be most beneficial to blacks. The former, in their view, would assure the prosperity and independence (from hostile racial forces) of blacks, while the latter would assure God's blessing.

Although these Jamaicans expressed their antiracialist sentiments very forcefully, they were unusual in their insistence on the absolute meaningless of race. More typically, the Jamaicans pragmatically distinguished between the *ought* and the *is*. This differentiation produced in them an internal conflict as they realized that, to make sense of their American experiences, they would have to embrace a more consciously racial point of view. They seemed to admit this necessity reluctantly, sadly, and with more than a little pessimism. Mitchell, a thirty-two-year-old financial consultant, illustrates this:

I still can't fathom why, because of the color of your skin, certain privileges are not available to you. I still can't understand it; I just can't understand it. . . . When you come here it's almost like after a while you learn to accept your fate. . . . So for instance, if you know you are not going to be welcome in certain places, you just don't go there . . . because you alone cannot fight this war. . . . And this situation has been here long before we came here and it will be here . . . for as long as I can see into the future. So it's just a matter of working within the system to extract the benefits that you will need for yourself. That's how I see it.

The development of heightened consciousness of race is also associated with a great deal of anger. Neil, the social worker to whom I referred previously, explained how he coped with persistent anger at racism by sublimating that anger:

The first experience you have of someone reacting to you vis-à-vis skin color . . . makes you angry. But that was when you were 24. I am now 45. I can't get angry every time a racist incident comes up in front of me. I [would] go crazy. . . . It all depends on the extent to which you decide that you are going to understand a situation and develop a set of controls. In other words, racism doesn't anger me less now, and I am not a whit less concerned now at 45 than I was at 24. What I have deliberately gone through is a series of experiences and also [a] looking into myself to basically temper my reaction and deal with it.

Some of the strategies for tempering reactions to racial discrimination—notably avoidance and adoption of religious/ideological viewpoints—have already been noted. Another possibility is to view racism as part of a historical trend. In this way, the individual depersonalizes racial discrimination and views himself or herself as only one of millions who have suffered such a fate. Thus, as some of the Jamaicans explained it, all blacks in white dominated societies share similar experiences; and the only difference between West Indians and African Americans is that the former disembarked from the slave ships a little sooner.

Still, the continuous experience of discrimination can be offset only so much and it tends to leave lasting scars on West Indians. Several of my interviews illustrated how these scars developed over a period of time. A good example of this was Jerry, a young minister. He had arrived in the United States at age twenty, after having attended college in the West Indies. The immediate cause for his coming was his receipt of a scholarship with which he planned to further his education. Intending, at first, to specialize in one of the "hard" sciences, he eventually shifted to the study of religion and psychology. This took him, first, to a small prestigious liberal arts college, and later to an ivy league university where he received an advanced degree.

Jerry indicated that while in Jamaica, his outlook had been "socialistic,"[42] having been drawn to the People's National Party's attempts to empower the poor. At this stage of his life, social inequality as manifested in class differentials was the issue which engaged him. Coming to America put an entirely new spin on that issue as he started to recognize the relationship between inequality and race. He became much more race conscious than he had been in Jamaica. At first, the factors that led to this mentality were not necessarily dramatic. He indicated, for instance, that the simple act of fill-ing out forms made him realize the premium Americans place on race. In Jamaica, this routine act had held no racial significance, but in America he was regularly required on forms to state his race. This forced him to start thinking in racial terms, a tendency that was accelerated by the fact that the society seemed to be saturated with a consciousness of race. He cited the media as being particularly significant in this regard. Attending a succession of prestigious private schools really drove home the point that race matters, because he found himself part of a distinct minority. Many of the whites with whom he interacted focused first on his skin color and, only secon-darily, on his other characteristics. This behavior ranged from outright dis-criminatory treatment to well-meaning professors informing him that, as a foreigner, he could not really appreciate the difficulties that faced African Americans. Reacting with suspicion to what he saw as attempts to co-opt foreign blacks by ostensibly evaluating them more positively than African Americans, he threw himself into campus politics, espousing various pro-black causes.

The end result of his experiences since migrating was a mentality which saw far more similarities than differences between West Indians and African Americans. This was not a negation of his "West Indianness," since, sur-prisingly, he argued in favor of dating but not marrying African American women. His rationale was that marriage is a chancy proposition and the like-lihood of it succeeding is greatly enhanced when the individuals involved share commonalties. West Indians and African American matches would en-counter severe culture clashes that would doom the marriages. Moreover, he argued that since American society, in general, is permissive, he would raise his child to embrace West Indian values, because he viewed these as placing greater emphasis on discipline.[43] Nevertheless, he argued that it would not trouble him if people identified him with African Americans. As he stated:

> If the term black was in there it wouldn't bother me at all. . . . I was black before I was Jamaican. Black is just who I am, and prior to any other knowl-edge I had of myself, I was black.

Hence, he concluded:

> There are areas in which our different histories meet. Whether it was a "class-ist" exploitation or it was racial exploitation—it was exploitation. . . . People

were dehumanized and are still being dehumanized. I think there is more common ground between us than there are differences. . . . We tend to overemphasize the differences rather than looking for the common ground which we can build on.

Consistent with his emphasis on his racial identity, upon leaving graduate school, he deliberately chose to pastor a church in an inner-city area, viewing this choice as a means of asserting control over his life in a society that constantly sought to belittle blacks, regardless of their achievements or ethnicity. Pastoring in the inner city was a way of establishing a "comfort zone" in which he did not have to constantly justify his presence to suspicious whites. He stated that over the years he had changed from a position of relative racial innocence to a point where he felt little desire to interact with whites on an ongoing basis. Far more important to him was the fact that many blacks had acute spiritual, social, and economic needs that were going unmet. Among his inner-city congregants were people who accepted him implicitly and he, in turn, felt a greater fulfillment in his life knowing that he was helping to meet their needs.

While this minister had arrived at a position of relative contentment with the issue of race, other Jamaicans continued to feel lingering bitterness. As was true in several cases, this stemmed from unfortunate racial experiences on the job. A case in point was Stanley, the forty-year-old technician, who, at the time of the interview, worked for a very large multinational corporation and, before that, for its even larger corporate parent. Like many other Jamaicans, prior to migrating to America he had grown very comfortable with being a member of a majority group in a society which lay great stress on upward mobility through merit. These facts are important because they left him quite unprepared for dealing with the racial conflict which he encountered in the United States.

In 1970, a year after he migrated, he obtained the job as technician in one of the first cohorts of blacks to be brought into the company under affirmative action. As he explained it, the company had long been dominated by the stereotypical "old boy's network" of white males and run in a militaristic fashion (for instance, employees who missed their assigned duties were referred to as being "AWOL"). Blacks were not welcomed. The first inkling Stanley had of this was when a piece of equipment which he had approved as usable was sabotaged and he was blamed for putting defective equipment into operation. He claimed that this was one example of incidents of harassment to which black workers were subjected and which were designed to get them fired. To the obvious question of how he knew that his white coworkers had deliberately sabotaged the equipment after he had approved it, he replied that thirteen years after the fact, a white colleague apologized to him for doing it but insisted that he had only been following

orders from management. However, since he never found out which manager had ordered the sabotage, the apology only increased his feelings of
discomfort.

Instead of firing him over the incident, Stanley's superiors transferred
him to another building. His new coworkers, being primarily younger
whites—and ones influenced by 1960s popular culture at that—exhibited a
decidedly more laid-back culture than his previous coworkers.

> The technicians that I worked with in the new area were better educated
> and they had higher social class, so they were less afraid of me, per se. But
> . . . the office where I was leaving from, they were definitely threatened by
> me because I guess for their own self-worth they needed to believe that
> blacks were lower, less intelligent. . . . But for these [new coworkers] to
> have an intelligent black working for them: It wasn't a problem. They would
> boast about me. . . . I felt confident to go in and work on anything with-
> out having to know that anybody was going to go behind my back. They
> were . . . all young . . . into the peace movement . . . crazy about black music
> and into getting high: They were . . . hippies.

Despite his more pleasant environment, over the years Stanley had several other unpleasant encounters with his superiors. These stemmed from
their refusal to promote him. Indeed, as he described it, his was only one
example of a corporate culture that was openly hostile to blacks.[44] One expression of this hostility was that minority workers' attempts to redress their
grievances usually resulted in them being transferred or fired. He stated:

> I have considered going to the Human Rights Commission and taking the
> case against them about being passed over; over and over and over again.
> Then usually what happens to people who do that is that you get trans-
> ferred to some [other] area. It's like you win the battle but lose the war.
> It has happened before where the black guys got together and said: "We've
> got to do something about this; they're doing this too far." And they ac-
> tually presented their case . . . and the next week they were gone!

As a result of events such as these, many of the blacks at his company
had become very disillusioned. Stanley, himself, had become extremely conscious of race and, in fact, had become known to his supervisors as one who
tended to see everything through the visor of race. For instance, he stated
that early in his career at the company, when he first started to realize how
important race was compared to Jamaica, he tried to cope by doing as much
reading as he could to educate himself about the history of blacks and race
in America. During this period, he would often bring in articles to show his
coworkers to educate them as to the difficulties blacks have faced in America.
If anything, however, this tended to work against him, as his supervisors
wanted to avoid, as much as possible, open discussion of racial issues. This
lack of response has only served to embitter him further, and, when I interviewed him, he reported that he had become quite cynical, regarding him-

self as an "old soldier" whose singular efforts could not make much difference against the culture of a multibillion dollar corporation. He described what was required to achieve promotion in his company, indicating that he was not interested in conforming and that, in any case, such conformity would hardly benefit blacks:

> Basically, you have to become white; you have to play by the white rules. You can't be this, "Free South Africa!" You can't be a radical; you can't be, "This country is unfair to blacks." You have to close your eyes to all that and just try to become a gear in the machine. . . . All the black people who have been with the company twenty, thirty years: none of them are really happy or self-fulfilled. . . . There are whites who have been with the company the same length of time and they come in in the morning. They are smiling; they are happy; they are fulfilled. They've gotten their expectations. . . . Most of the blacks . . . have become so bitter [that] they only do what they have to do to keep their jobs. . . . They feel that they have been used or abused in some way and the only option of getting back is not to do anything.[45]

Because of all this, Stanley perceived America, in general, and whites, specifically, very negatively. Contrasting West Indians and African Americans, he blamed systemic racial discrimination against the latter, in the context of minority status, for the differences in attitudes between the two groups; and argued that even second and later generation West Indians were more likely than the foreign-born to succumb to what he perceived as societal pressures promoting notions of black inferiority:[46]

> If you were educated in Jamaica; you became an adult in Jamaica, you . . . have gotten to a certain point where nobody can negate you [because you] . . . already . . . know your capabilities. . . . It's . . . your second generation, your third generation [West Indians who] . . . are being given the same indoctrination [as] the American blacks who we can't understand. We as Jamaicans come here—as Africans, as Trinidadians, as Barbadians, or whatever. We can't understand: How come they don't have any pride? How come they can allow this to happen? You know, they have all this opportunity around them and they haven't done anything. . . . We are all the same, so the only thing that's different is that they came to a country where there was a white majority and we went to a country where we [were] a black majority and the things that they did to them here, they could not get away with doing with us there because . . . we would only take so much. You can only push the majority so far before they rise up and tear you limb from limb. But when you are a minority, no matter what they do to you, you have to sit quietly and take it. . . . The system is meant to keep them there.

In fact, he was even more pessimistic than this, arguing that whites, perceiving blacks to be the source of much of their everyday troubles—preeminently crime—would, if they could, happily get rid of all of them.

I think America is a white country and I see Jamaica as a . . . black country, and if I am a black man then I don't really have a choice . . . : This is
never going to be my country. I would like it to be but . . . I perceive it
on my job among the . . . middle class whites who come in from Long
Island or New Jersey or Pennsylvania, or whatever, that the only reason
New York City is not what it used to be is because blacks are taking over.
That's the reason why there is so much crime; that's the reason why you
can't park your car; that's the reason why you can't have a radio in your
car: It's because the blacks are here: . . . There is that danger [as] . . . more
of them come to believe that . . . the only reason there are problems is because of these foreigners, these blacks who are not supposed to be here;
and if somehow you could find a way to get rid of them, then everything
is going to be great—America is going to be perfect; America is going to
be the Garden of Eden.

■ GENERALIZING THE WEST INDIAN EXPERIENCE

The racial experiences of West Indians in the United States are significant
because they affect the ongoing quality of life of these individuals.
Discrimination, for them, is not an abstract notion but, rather, an ongoing
struggle to maintain their dignity and to attain their hopes and desires against
hostile, entrenched societal attitudes and actions. Put in this way, it is clear
that West Indians often resemble African Americans and, therefore, West
Indians attitudes and experiences take on larger meaning. With respect to
this, the key question has always been: What does the presence of West
Indians say about the socioeconomic status of African Americans in the
United States? For obvious historical reasons, race has been posited as the
factor that disproportionately shapes blacks' position in American society.
West Indians' relatively good showing on certain economic indicators (e.g.,
median family income and percentage falling below the poverty line) implies
that the role played by race is exaggerated. However, West Indians, themselves, believe that racism is a major obstacle in their quest for upward mobility. Moreover, writers who have taken a comprehensive view of West
Indians have shown that: (1) in accessing their performance, several inter-
related factors must be accounted for and (2) race still remains significant.[47]
If West Indians say anything about the place of African Americans in
American society it is not that race is now unimportant. Rather, it is that
race remains crucial and intertwines with other key factors impinging on socioeconomic status—e.g., presence in ethnic niches that are expanding or
contracting; years of schooling and schooling in particular disciplines; and
intangibles such as self-confidence, deferral of gratification, and persistence.
As Thomas Pettigrew has noted, the socioeconomic status of blacks in
present-day American society is best accounted for, not by race or class sep-

arately; rather, both factors "jointly determine ("interact") the shape of present-day American race relations."[48]

The intertwining of race and class to which Pettigrew alludes points to the contradictory forces that shape the place of blacks—West Indians and African Americans—in present-day American society. A well-publicized incident clearly illustrates these contradictions. In April 1993, several black employees of the Secret Service were snubbed by service people at a Denny's restaurant in Annapolis, Maryland. It later emerged that this incident, far from being isolated, was only one manifestation of a corporate policy that was meant to discourage blacks from patronizing these restaurants. Because they were viewed as being likely to leave without paying, all blacks were placed in a "high risk" category. Translated in individual stores, this designation meant the institution of such discriminatory policies as demanding payment up front, reneging on special offers when blacks tried to take advantage of them, deliberately offering them slow service, placing them in undesirable locations within the restaurants, and literally locking doors— known euphemistically as "blackouts"—when blacks were on their way into the restaurants. All of these tactics were directed only at blacks, and all Denny's employees—including blacks—were pressured to comply. Failure to do so meant job termination.[49]

Although Denny's eventually settled charges brought against it by the Justice Department for $54.4 million, the case is important because it shows how blacks are often singled out for discriminatory treatment; and this discrimination tends to be categorical: at Denny's, for instance, blacks, regardless of gender, age, special circumstances, or occupation, found themselves discriminated against. Thus, adolescents found themselves targeted, but so did handicapped individuals, and federal judges. Most importantly, though, the Denny's case is a metaphor for race relations in modern-day America: increased opportunities for some segments of the black community mixed with continuing high levels of discrimination. The black Secret Service agents, for instance, found themselves in jobs which a few decades ago they were unlikely to have held. Yet, having obtained such jobs, they could not take it for granted that their elevated status would result in greater respect.

This interpretation of the current state of race relations in America finds support in several places. For instance, in the comprehensive assessment of the condition of blacks in the United States—*A Common Destiny: Blacks and American Society*—Gerald Jaynes and Robin Williams argue that, "The status of black Americans today can be characterized as a glass that is half full—if measured by progress since 1939—or as a glass that is half-empty— if measured by the persisting disparities between black and white Americans since the early 1970s."[50] They show that according to a host of statistical indicators—e.g., education, incomes and living standards, social and political participation—the well-being of blacks has improved noticeably since the 1940s. But because this has also been true of whites; because the economic progress of blacks has stagnated since the 1970s; and because of continuing prejudice and discrimination, inequality still exists between the two groups (see Table 3.2). They conclude that because of its central role—especially with respect to blacks—in American history, "race is likely to retain much of its saliency as a feature of American society for some time to come." This will be even more the case, they posit, as demographic changes in the society cause Americans to become ever more conscious of race.[51]

This consciousness is likely to be more complex than in the past. Sociologists Lee Sigelman and Susan Welch's analysis of black Americans' views of racial inequality in the 1990s illustrates this. They found that blacks: (1) perceive widespread discrimination against themselves by whites, (2) are far more likely than whites to perceive such discrimination, (3) believe that discrimination is the major reason why they continue to experience a variety of social ills, ranging from finding adequate housing to securing good jobs, (4) make an exception in the case of education, where they perceive little or no discrimination, and (5) agree that a degree of self-help is necessary in order for blacks to enhance their quality of life.[52] More recent surveys—e.g., the 1996 survey of 1200 blacks by Yankelovich Partners and the 1997 Gallup Poll on Black/White Relations—tend to support these findings. The Yankelovich survey found that 72 percent of blacks believe that

TABLE 3.2 Selected Socioeconomic Characteristics of the White and African-American Populations: 1960–1995

Year	Median Family Income[a]		Percentage of Families Below the Poverty Line		Percentage Completing Four or More of Years High School[b]	
	Whites	Blacks	Whites	Blacks	Whites	Blacks
1960	27,617	15,287	14.9	—	43.2	20.1
1970	37,772	23,170	8.0	29.5	54.5	31.4
1980	40,561	23,469	8.0	28.9	68.8	51.2
1990	43,044	24,980	8.1	29.3	79.1	66.2
1995	42,646	25,970	8.5	26.4	83.0	73.8

Source: U.S. Bureau of the Census, *Statistical Abstracts of the United States,* 1996.
[a]In current dollars.
[b]Persons 25 years and over.

government programs do not go far enough to help blacks; 58 percent believe that conditions are getting worse for them; and 48 percent believe that
failure of blacks to appropriate available opportunities is a more serious problem for the group than is discrimination by whites.[53] Similarly, the Gallup
poll found blacks to be more pessimistic—and increasingly so in some cases—
than whites on a variety of issues, ranging from the possibility for getting
any kind of job to acts of discrimination in public and private spheres. For
instance, 79 percent of whites but only 46 percent of blacks believed that
blacks enjoy equal access to whites as far as obtaining any kind of job is concerned. Forty-five percent of blacks, but only 14 percent of whites, believe
that blacks are treated less well than whites on the job; and 60 percent of
blacks, but only 30 percent of whites, believe that the police treat blacks less
fairly than whites.[54]

From the white perspective, the perception of race is also more complex. For instance, in *The Scar of Race*, Piazza and Sniderman argue against
the view that America suffers from a single race problem; maintaining instead that several issues of race, allied with political ideology, constantly influence the reactions of white Americans. The latter, they claim, still willingly
endorse a wide range of negative stereotypes of blacks and, contrary to widespread perceptions, long-standing racial questions—such as the debate over
the use of government to ensure equal treatment for blacks—have not been
resolved. Thus, to some extent, the perception of racial progress is an illusion: Americans have not resolved old racial problems only to be confronted
by new ones. Instead, they are still grappling with the old problems, even
as newer ones emerge. Still, Piazza and Sniderman express optimism, because they argue that prejudice no longer dominates, across-the-board, the
reactions of white Americans. First, racism is not an integral aspect of core
American values. Second, whites are pliable on racial issues, the measure of
this being the ease with which they can be talked out of positions that they
have taken on such issues. Third, some opinions which seem, ostensibly, to
be based on race, really reflect political ideology. Consequently, racial problems are not only multiple, they are also inherently political rather than pri
marily moral.

Blacks—including West Indians—would probably take issue with the optimistic view that racism is not as deeply embedded in American society as
it seems to be. Sigelman and Welch and the Yankelovich survey, for instance,
point toward notable black pessimism on matters of race. As shown by Feagin
and Sikes, this pessimism is rooted in the actual everyday experiences of
blacks, which constantly remind them just how significant race is. Without
necessarily denying the complexity of race as an issue, these and the similar
experiences of West Indians cast doubt on optimistic assessments of race in
present-day America. For instance Piazza and Sniderman argue that, "the
test of whether people are committed to racial equality . . . is whether they

can be talked out of it easily."[55] However, it could be argued that the real test of commitment to racial equality lies in the extent to which actual behavior, rather than the espousal of a belief in equality, reflects equal treatment. Similarly, not taking into account blacks' experiences can result in puzzlement over the apparent discrepancy between statistical indicators showing some blacks doing well and pessimism with respect to race. For instance, Abigail Thernstrom has written: "Two nations, black and white, separate and unequal, was the Kerner Commission's description of America in 1968. The good news is that the inequality has been dramatically reduced. The median income of black married couples with children is now only slightly lower than that for all American families. Since 1970, residential segregation has dropped sharply in 11 of the 15 metropolitan areas with the largest black populations. . . . The media let the problems of the underclass define black America when by some measures many blacks are doing well."[56]

However, even upwardly mobile blacks are quite likely to encounter mistreatment because of race. Ironically, as shown for some of the West Indians I interviewed and by writers such as Cose, Feagin and Sikes, and Nelson,[57] upward mobility might actually sharpen blacks' perception of racism, as they encounter treatment that is inconsistent with their status. They feel a sense of betrayal as they realize that adhering to the society's norms for achieving upward mobility does not necessarily insulate them from invidious treatment because of race. Race comes to stand out more clearly as the factor causing mistreatment. This explains why, for example, Nelson, the high level manager at the New York State agency, could simultaneously criticize blacks for not trying hard enough to attain, as he had, upward mobility, and castigate the police for being racist; or why Jerry, the inner-city minister, having attained degrees from several elite universities, could have reached the pinnacle of the educational system and yet express deep pessimism on racial matters. These contradictions make sense only if objective statistical indicators of success are combined with a recognition that, on a day-to-day basis, blacks experience discrimination and this leads to a certain amount of disillusionment.

This disillusionment has costs. Pessimism with respect to the possibility of blacks fully incorporating into American society as true equals is one manifestation. The reaction of some blacks to the verdict in the first O. J. Simpson trial can be read as one example of a lack of faith in the society's institutions. Another cost worth mentioning is support for extremist views in segments of the black community. While support for groups such as the Nation of Islam probably derives from several sources, one of them is very likely the day-to-day problems of blacks. These problems are multiple and do not all reduce to race. For instance, problematic patterns of behavior—e.g., out of wedlock births—are an important issue with respect to some of the black poor. Another key issue revolves around the question of whether some poor blacks exhibit attitudes—e.g., not being punctual for work—that work against their advancement.[58] Yet another cause for concern is the feeling among some young blacks that performing well in school amounts to "acting white."[59] As shown, for example, by Sigelman and Welch and the Yankelovich survey, blacks believe that their own attitudes and behaviors are important to achieving material success in American society. Still, it is important to note that though these issues are not, necessarily, inherently racial, they do intertwine with race; so much so that they often become wrapped up with the sense of disillusionment felt by many blacks. For instance, if it is true that some blacks do not exhibit behaviors that would help them succeed in a modern economy, it is also true that employers often generalize such attitudes to all blacks and refuse to hire them.[60] Given this, it is not difficult to see how some blacks could adopt pessimistic attitudes toward the larger society.

The Nation of Islam is one vehicle for the expression of blacks' sense of disillusionment. But not all, or even most, blacks will take such a route. The reality is that the separatist[61] tendencies of the Nation of Islam have to climb, uphill, against traditional assimilationist sentiment within the black community. West Indians, for instance, because of their focus on "making it" in America, will likely view Colin Powell, rather than Louis Farrakhan, as their prototype.[62] Moreover, as a black "leader," Farrakhan has traditionally fallen fairly low on the totem pole. For instance, in the *Black Anti-Semitism Controversy*, sociologist Hubert Locke has shown that in a 1986 sampling of black evangelicals, Farrakhan registered a low third behind Andrew Young and Jesse Jackson, and just ahead of Benjamin Hooks and Walter Fauntleroy.[63] And the Yankelovich survey, though showing a 4 point increase in "favorable" rating for Farrakhan over a similar 1994 survey (52 to 48 percent), still found him lagging substantially behind Coretta Scott King (83 percent), Jesse Jackson (82 percent), Johnnie Cochran (75 percent), and Colin Powell (70 percent). Moreover, Farrakhan's "unfavorable" rating of 30 percent was exceeded only by that of Clarence Thomas, who had an "unfavorable" rating of 37 percent.[64]

Despite all this, Farrakhan cannot simply be dismissed. A moral critique can be leveled against him for making extreme statements against groups ranging from assimilated blacks to Koreans.[65] However, this critique often seems to miss the important point that structural problems systematically affecting large segments of the black community and a failure of will to sincerely tackle these problems perpetuate Farrakhan's existence. Without these structural conditions, Farrakhan would have little appeal to many blacks.[66] Surveys show that while most blacks believe that racism created their problems in the first place, they also believe that, to some extent, they are masters of their own fate. Farrakhan provides an outlet for both the anger some blacks feel at being discriminated against and a desire to control their own destinies. And this appeal—despite antagonistic statements against other groups—cuts across class and ethnic lines within the black community, because blacks, regardless of class or ethnic origin, find that they must daily contend with attitudes and behavior which imply that they are inferior. It is probable that if Farrakhan did not exist, sooner or later someone like him would arise within the black community. It seems that the surest way to eradicate the sentiments expressed by someone like a Farrakhan is to actually and effectively tackle the structural barriers besetting blacks in American society.

■ CONCLUSION

Discussions of West Indian immigrants have, over the years, shown that the West Indian experience in America is multifaceted. At least two distinct and contradictory trends are discernible: West Indians focus on achievement and their difficulties incorporating into a racial order that tends to relegate those of African ancestry to the bottom of the social hierarchy. Although both facts appear throughout the literature, the former has often been highlighted. This gives the mistaken impression that West Indians are oblivious to racial problems in the United States; or that these problems are minimal. However, some discussions have shown that this is not the case. Without taking away from West Indians' focus on achievement, these discussions have also pointed out that racial problems are significant and inevitably entangle West Indians. In fact, far from being oblivious, West Indians spend a significant portion of their everyday lives dealing with antiblack attitudes and discrimination. They find this difficult, because, being socialized to minimize race, they would, in fact, like to be oblivious to it. However, the realities of everyday life cause West Indians to distinguish between the "ought" and the "is": while they try to ignore race as much as possible, it is a constant factor that must be dealt with.

West Indians' actual racial experiences show them to be quite similar to African Americans. Indeed, while real cultural differences exist between the two groups, both find that often—especially in public places—outsiders construct for them a common identity: "black." West Indians—like African Americans—practice a range of strategies for dealing with racist attitudes and racial discrimination. Perhaps the single most important of these—and perhaps the most difficult—is the development of a greater consciousness of race. Through this they are better able to comprehend experiences that, otherwise, make little sense. However, greater consciousness of race among West Indians does not negate their focus on achievement. Indeed, their presence tends to show that opportunities for upward mobility for blacks exist but that these commingle with, rather than displace, racism. Thus, West Indians help to illustrate the complexity, especially for blacks, of race in present-day America.

Notes

1. I use "West Indian" and "Jamaican" interchangeably, since, objectively speaking, the latter are very typical of immigrants from the English-speaking Caribbean. This is also true from a subjective point of view, since the Jamaicans whom I interviewed perceived little difference between themselves and other Anglophone West Indians.
2. For instance, a distinct trend in the post–Civil Rights period is for whites to embrace principles of equality but not the actual policies needed to implement these principles. See Howard Schuman, Charlotte Steeh, and Lawrence Bobo, *Racial Attitudes in America* (Cambridge: Harvard University Press, 1985); James P. Kluegel, "Trends in Whites' Explanations of the Black-White Gap in SES," *American Sociological Review*, Vol. 55, No. 4 (August 1990): 512–525; Lee Sigelman and Susan Welch, *Black Americans' Views of Racial Inequality* (New York: Cambridge University Press, 1991); Paul M. Sniderman and Thomas Piazza, *The Scar of Race* (Cambridge: Harvard University Press, 1993); Howard Schuman and Charlotte Steeh, "The Complexity of Racial Attitudes in America," in *Origins and Destinies*, ed. Silvia Pedraza and Ruben G. Rumbaut (Belmont: Wadsworth Publishing Company, 1996), pp. 255–269.
3. See, for example, Ira De A. Reid, *The Negro Immigrant* (New York: Columbia University Press, 1939); Lennox Raphael, "West Indians and Afro-Americans," *Freedomways* (Summer 1964): 438–445; Roy S. Bryce-Laporte, "Black Immigrants, the Experience of Invisibility and Inequality," *Journal of Black Studies* 3, No. 1 (1972): 29–56; "The New Immigration: A Challenge to Our Sociological Imagination," in *Sourcebook on the New Immigration*, ed. Roy S. Bryce-Laporte (New Brunswick: Transaction Books, 1980), pp. 459–474; Nancy Foner, "Sex Roles and Sensibilities: Jamaican Women in New York and London," in *International Migration: The Female Experience*, ed. Rita James Simon and Caroline B. Brettel (Totawa: Rowman and Allanheld, 1986), pp. 133–151; "The Jamaicans," in *New Immigrants in New York*, ed. Nancy Foner (New York: Columbia University Press, 1987), pp. 195–271; Nancy Foner, "Race and Color: Jamaican Migrants in London and New York," *International Migration Review* 19 (1985): 708–722; Philip Kasinitz, "The Minority Within: The New Black Immigrants," *New York Affairs*, Vol. 10, No. 1 (Winter 1987): 44–58; *Caribbean New York* (Ithaca: Cornell University Press, 1992); Mary Waters, "The Role of Lineage in Identity Formation Among Black Americans," *Qualitative Sociology*, Vol. 14, No. 1 (1991): 57–76; "Ethnic and Racial Identities of Second-Generation Black Immigrants in New York City," *International Migration Review*, Vol. xxviii, No. 4 (1994): 795–820.
4. 2 Thessalonians 3:10. This exact phrase was quoted by one respondent as he tried to explain why he opposed welfare. However, other respondents advanced similar objections to welfare. These sentiments can be generalized across the West Indian immigrant population. See, for instance, James Traub, "You Can

128 CROSSCURRENTS: WEST INDIAN IMMIGRANTS AND RACE

Get It if You Really Want It," *Harpers* (1982), pp. 27–31; Thomas Kessner and Betty Boyd Caroli, *Today's Immigrants: Their Stories* (New York: Oxford University Press, 1982); Jonathan Mandell, "The Changing Face of New York Caribbean Leaves Its Mark on City Dreams" (*New York Newsday*, April 5, 1995): A6; Mary Waters, "Lost Children of the Caribbean," (*New York Newsday*, April 12, 1995): A28.

5. The key representative of this view is W. J. Wilson's influential *The Declining Significance of Race* (Chicago: University of Chicago Press, 1980).

6. Gordon Lewis, *The Growth of the Modern West Indies* (New York: Monthly Review Press, 1968), p. 176.

7. Ira Reid, *The Negro Immigrant*; Lewis, *The Growth of the Modern West Indies*, pp. 167–196; Davis, *Who Is Black? One Nation's Definition* (University Park: The University of Pennsylvania Press, 1991).

8. Reid, *The Negro Immigrant*, pp. 147–155.

9. Reid, ibid., p. 189.

10. Foner, "Race and Color: Jamaican Migrants in London and New York"; "The Jamaicans: Race and Ethnicity among Migrants in New York City." For a journalistic view see Vivienne Walt, "Caught between Two Worlds: Immigrants Discover Success, Racism in the U.S" (*New York Newsday*, April 15, 1988): 9–27.

11. See David Lowenthal, *West Indian Societies* (London: Oxford University Press, 1972). Lowenthal and other writers (e.g., Mel Thompson) have pointed out that the United States is not unique in this regard. West Indians face similar problems accommodating themselves to blatant racial discrimination in Europe and Canada. For evidence of this see Thompson, "Forty-and-One Years On: An Overview of Afro-Caribbean Migration to the United Kingdom," in *In Search of a Better Life: Perspectives on Migration from the Caribbean*, ed. Ransford Palmer (New York: Praeger, 1990), pp. 39–70; Anthony H. Richmond and Aloma Mendoza, "Education and Qualifications of Caribbean Immigrants and Their Children in Britain and Canada," in *In Search of a Better Life: Perspectives on Migration from the Caribbean*, ed. Ransford Palmer (New York: Praeger, 1990), pp. 73–90; Francois Raveau, "An Outline of the Role of Color in Adaptation Phenomena," in *Color and Race*, ed. John Hope Franklin (Boston: Beacon Press, 1968), pp. 98–111.

12. A pseudonym.

13. Edward Ransford and Joe Feagin and Melvin Sikes have demonstrated the significance of location with respect to the racial episodes blacks experience. One aspect of this is that discrimination varies in intensity depending on how "protected" a site is. It increases in intensity as blacks move from more to less "protected" sites. For instance, blacks with professional jobs, while working in their offices experience some protection from discrimination because of their credentials. However, in public where such credentials are difficult to establish they may find themselves harassed by individuals who relegate them to a low status because of their skin color. See Edward H. Ransford, *Race and Class in American Society: Black, Chicano, Anglo* (Cambridge: Schenkman Publishing Company, Inc, 1977); Joe R. Feagin, "The Continuing Significance of Race: Antiblack Discrimination in Public Places," *American Sociological Review*, Vol. 56, No. 1

(1991): 101–116; Joe Feagin and Melvin P. Sikes, *Living with Racism: The Black Middle Class Experience* (Boston: Beacon Press, 1994).

14. The African Americans whom Feagin and Sikes interviewed for their study of coping with racial discrimination reported experiences and coping strategies that closely resemble those displayed by Harry.

15. Feagin and Sikes, *Living with Racism*.

16. "Rethinking Ethnicity: Identity, Categorization and Power," *Ethnic and Racial Studies*, Vol. 17, No. 2 (April 1994): 197–223.

17. Notably, Fredrik Barth, "Introduction," *Ethnic Groups and Boundaries*, ed. Fredrik Barth (Boston: Little, Brown and Company, 1970), pp. 9–38.

18. Jenkins, p. 211. The complete typology of social categorization, running from informal to formal reads as follows: routine public interaction, sexual relationships, communal relationships, membership of informal groups, marriage and kinship, market relationships, employment, administrative allocation, organized politics, and official classification (p. 210).

19. Accounts of antiblack discrimination in public places are a media staple. These accounts show that the problem is widespread and cuts across class and ethnic lines. For instance, journalist Lena Williams ["When Blacks Shop, Bias Often Accompanies Sale," (*New York Times*, April 30, 1991): A1] has shown how such well-known blacks as actress Debbie Allen and syndicated columnist Julianne Malveaux have encountered discrimination in public. Allen, shopping in a Beverly Hills store, encountered a clerk who refused to show the actress certain items because of the clerk's assumption that Allen would not be able to afford them. Similarly, Malveaux was falsely accused of switching price tags on an expensive silk dress. Williams also reports the case of a twenty-year-old chef's helper who, seeking to invest $1000 in a bank in Tamarac, Florida, was reported by bank employees as a potential robber. As a result, he was accosted and questioned by the police for almost one hour. Williams's article drew a number of equally revealing letters from blacks who had had experiences paralleling those which she mentioned in her article. See "Prejudice Is Still a Fact of Life for Blacks," (*New York Times*, May 17, 1991). Similar accounts are to be found, for instance, in Jerelyn Eddings's "The Covert Color War," *U.S. News and World Report* (October 23, 1995): 40–44.

20. One of the architects of the modern two-party system in Jamaica, through his founding of the Jamaica Labour Party and Bustamante Industrial Trade union in the late 1930s-early 1940s.

21. Lewis, *The Growth of the Modern West Indies*, p. 180.

22. Carl Stone, "The Black Self-Concept," in *Carl Stone on Jamaican Politics and Society*, ed. Carl Stone (Kingston: The Gleaner Company, 1989): 96.

23. Laurie Gunst has maintained that the focus on Jamaican drug posses arose from the Bureau of Alcohol, Tobacco and Firearms efforts in the 1980s to fend off moves to disband it. To do this, that agency exaggerated the idea of an international Jamaican organized crime conspiracy, thereby providing a rationale for the ATF's continued existence ["The Jamaican Posses Had Nothing to Lose" (*New York Newsday*, March 6, 1995): A23]. Other examples of the focus on posses include the following: George Volsky, "Jamaican Drug Gangs Thriving in U.S. Cities" (*New York Times*, July 1987): A17; Michael Roberts, "Jamaicans

on DA's Drug List," (*Carib News*, March 21, 1989): 3; Tony Best, "DA Denies Existence of List" (*Carib News*, March 21, 1989):3; Michael Massing, "Crack's Destructive Sprint Across America" (*New York Times Magazine*, October 1, 1989): 38–62; and Michael Roberts, "Jamaican Drug Gangs Targeted" (*Carib News*, March 6, 1990): 4.

24. The list caused a stir within the Jamaican community for several reasons. Its timing (around the same time as a rash of stories about Jamaican drug posses), targeting of a specific group, and flimsy rationale (it included the names of even those Jamaicans who had infringed such minor rules as selling hot dogs without a permit) seemed an obvious attempt to stigmatize the whole community (*Carib News*, March 6, 1990): 4. Apparently, such efforts have continued into the present. A recent article in one ethnic newspaper detailed recent efforts by the New York City Police Department to compile lists of West Indians who have been booked or arrested. See Virginia Turner, "Jamaicans Outraged! New York Police Targeting West Indians" (*The Weekly Gleaner*, January 24–30, 1997): 1.

25. The plot of the former film was especially egregious inasmuch as it traded in blunt stereotypes and carelessly confused cultures for dramatic effect—for instance, having Rastafarians practice Santeria. The tensions existent between Rastafarianism and folk religions relying on magic (let alone ones from fairly alien cultures deriving from the Hispanic Caribbean) have been documented by Barry Chevannes in *Rastafari: Roots and Ideology* (Syracuse: Syracuse University Press, 1994).

26. He really meant 1987, since the incident happened the year before I interviewed him.

27. On December 19, 1986, a white gang chased and beat three black men (at least two of whom were of Caribbean descent) who found themselves, at night, in the white enclave of Howard Beach, Queens. One of the blacks—Michael Griffith—ran onto a highway and was killed. The motives appeared to be distinctly racial, since the gang shouted racial epithets as they chased the black men. Several members of the white gang were later convicted—in sentences ranging up to eighteen years—for their part in the incident. See, for example, "Two Howard Beach Sentences Begin," (*New York Newsday*, April 24, 1990): 3.

28. This response is, obviously, ethnocentric, given African Americans' long struggle against racism.

29. See, for instance, Richard Stengel, "'Off to a Running Start' " (*Time*, July 8, 1995): 41.

30. The fear of being stigmatized by the criminality associated with drug posses and dislike of poorer, more- recent West Indian immigrants might serve as an impetus for some West Indian immigrants to seek a better quality of life in cities outside such traditional West Indian strongholds as New York City. See, Karen DeWitt, "Immigrants Look Outside New York for a Better Life" (*New York Times*, September 4, 1990); Garry Pierre-Pierre, "Heading to Florida, Nearer the Homeland" (*New York Times*, July 13, 1993): B 3.

31. White enclaves in Brooklyn with histories of racial conflict.

32. See Walt, "Caught between Two Worlds: Immigrants Discover Success, Racism in the U.S."

33. It should be noted that though West Indians often live alongside African Americans in segregated areas of the city, they also live in integrated neighborhoods. Because of the violence that arose between blacks and Jews in August of 1991, Crown Heights is, perhaps, the most well known of these neighborhoods in New York City (though its high proportion of Hasidic Jews and West Indians probably renders its ethnic mix atypical). The violence, which lasted four days, resulted after a car in a Jewish procession mounted a sidewalk and killed a seven-year-old black child. This precipitated the slaying of a rabbinical student by a group of young blacks. Crown Heights came to symbolize the racial and ethnic strife that has afflicted New York City in recent years. However, this violence was exceptional in its breadth, since most of the time blacks (including West Indians) and Jews in this area coexist in a tense peace (the writer is a long-time resident of the area). In the writer's experience, the area is integrated in the sense that blacks and Jews live, literally, next door to each other. However, little social interaction occurs between them.

34. These sentiments came through strongly in his strident criticism of Michael Manley's turn to socialism and the fact that Rastafarians have gained mainstream acceptance in Jamaica and abroad. He regarded with distaste, the idea that, in the minds of many Americans, Jamaica is associated with Rastafarianism and marijuana.

35. However, some of these societies do register high levels of crime.

36. This response, of course, represents Dewey's perception of the issues under discussion.

37. The sensational Central Park jogger case of 1989 in which a gang of black adolescents were accused of brutally raping a white woman.

38. For instance, an acquaintance of the writer related to him her dismay upon going through a job interview at a New York City firm in the early 1980s. She reported being so stunned at the blatancy of the racism involved in the process that, upon emerging from the building, she found herself screaming, on the street, in anguish. Another female acquaintance who has lived in a southern metropolis for several years has constantly complained, to the writer, about the racism that she finds in churches. In Jamaica, she had been deeply committed to the church and, with respect to this, viewed issues from a strictly spiritual/doctrinal point of view. However, in the city in which she lives she has found that race often overrides doctrine, with white Christians rebuffing her efforts to join their congregations.

39. This is probably also true, in general, for immigrants who hail from societies with lower levels of racial tension than are to be found in the United States.

40. Malcolm Gladwell, "Black Like Them," *The New Yorker* (April 29 and May 6, 1996): 74–81.

41. I interviewed two members of the family.

42. An orientation toward the leftward end of the ideological spectrum probably predisposes some West Indians toward identifying, more readily, with African Americans. While this did not always come through clearly in the interviews, in a few instances it did. One respondent stated quite forthrightly that he had been a PNP supporter in Jamaica; in America he favored Democrats because he viewed them, like the PNP, as being more likely to advance the cause of blacks; and, he

added, if he lived in the United Kingdom he would support the Labour Party for the same reason.

43. See, for instance, Ceilia Dugger ["A Cultural Reluctance to Spare the Rod" (*New York Times,* February 29, 1996): B1] on the clash between the West Indian belief in corporal punishment and many Americans' reluctance to punish children in this manner.

44. This respondent's explanation of a corporate culture that has been hostile to blacks is credible, because the writer, independently, interviewed two other individuals who worked for the same corporation, but at different tasks and in different locations. Both corroborated Stanley's account of corporate hostility to blacks. One of these respondents actually resigned, in anger, from the corporation after it failed to promote him, and the other, at the time of our discussions, was considering doing so.

45. Stanley's obvious overstatement is a manifestation of his anger.

46. For research partially supporting this viewpoint see Mary Waters, "Ethnic and Racial Identities of Second-Generation Black Immigrants in New York City," *International Migration Review,* Vol. xxviii, No. 4 (1994): 795–820.

47. For, example, Foner, "Race and Color: Jamaican Migrants in London and New York City"; Monica Gordon, "Dependents or Independent Workers? The Status of Caribbean Immigrant Women in the United States," in *In Search of a Better Life: Perspectives on Migration from the Caribbean,* ed. Ransford Palmer (New York: Praeger 1990), pp. 115–138; Nasser Daneshvary and R. Keith Schwer, "Black Immigrants in the U.S. Labor Market: An Earnings Analysis," *The Review of Black Political Economy* (June 29, 1994): 77–98; Roger Waldinger, *Still the Promised City?* (Cambridge: Harvard University Press, 1996).

48. Thomas Pettigrew, "Race and Class in the 1980s: An Interactive View," *Daedalus* 110 (1981): 233–255. Perhaps the area in which race remains most obviously important is residential segregation. Many studies have shown that such segregation is extensive and specifically targeted at blacks—including West Indians. For instance, Denton and Massey's study of segregation in the decade 1970–1980 ["Trends in Residential Segregation of Blacks, Hispanics, and Asians, 1970–1980," *American Sociological Review* (Vol. 52, 1987): 802–825] shows that in 1980, San Francisco saw the black–white index of dissimilarity (0 representing complete integration and 100 complete segregation) standing at 71.7. The respective figures for Asians and Hispanics were 44.4 and 40.2. The black–white index was even higher in other cities. In Milwaukee, it stood at 83.9, 87.8 in Chicago, and 90.6 in Gary-Hammond, Indiana. Other groups in these cities exhibited a lower index. For instance, the Asian–white index of dissimilarity stood at 10.8 in Milwaukee, 12.0 in Chicago, and 7.0 in Gary-Hammond. Denton and Massey concluded that the pervasiveness and durability of antiblack segregation over long periods of time suggests that, "blacks are apparently viewed by white Americans as qualitatively different and, by implication, less desirable as neighbors, than members of other racial or ethnic groups" (p. 832). To investigate this hypothesis, they examined segregation among Hispanics, since this category exhibits a wide range of phenotypes. They found that: (1) overall, Hispanics experience less segregation than blacks and (2) among Hispanics, segregation tends to increase as the proportion of dark-skinned Hispanics increases.

As a result, dark skinned Hispanics, like blacks, experience high levels of segregation from other groups, including light skinned Hispanics (p. 832). See, also, "Racial Identity among Caribbean Hispanics: The Effect of Double Minority Segregation on Residential Status," *American Sociological Review*, Vol. 54, No. 5, (1989): 790–808.

Other writers have obtained similar results. Farley and Allen ["Changes in the Segregation of Whites from Blacks during the 1980s: Small Steps Toward a More Integrated Society," *American Sociological Review*, Vol. 59 (1994): 23–45], for instance, have shown that, on average, the index of dissimilarity is 20 percentage points higher for blacks, compared to Asians and Hispanics. Moreover, the old industrial cities of the Northeast tend to exhibit the highest levels of segregation. In contrast, smaller cities in the South and West—especially university towns and those with military bases—tend to exhibit lower levels. For instance, between 1980 and 1990, the fifteen most segregated cities (mostly Northeastern and Midwestern) exhibited an average dissimilarity score of 84, while the fifteen least segregated cities (mostly Southern and Western) exhibited an average score of 45.

Alba, Denton, Leung, and Logan's (1995) study of neighborhood change in the New York City region between 1970 and 1990 tends to support these findings. Focusing on the impact of immigration on New York City neighborhoods, they found the following: (1) very few neighborhoods remain homogeneous, since, increasingly, whites find themselves living side by side with Hispanics, Asians, and blacks; (2) at the same time, all-minority neighborhoods occupied only by blacks and Hispanics are increasing in number. Although neighborhoods are increasingly likely to be heterogeneous, some groups—especially blacks—stand a much greater chance of being excluded because whites and Asians resist their presence. Indices of dissimilarity show that blacks are much more segregated from whites than are Asians and this fact has hardly changed (indeed, increased for blacks) in twenty years. Thus, in 1970, for the entire New York City region, the black–white index of dissimilarity stood at 80.7 compared to 53.9 for Asians. By 1990, the figures were 81.5 and 46.9. See Richard Alba, Nancy A. Denton; Shu-yin J. Leung; and John R. Logan, "Neighborhood Change under Conditions of Mass Immigration: The New York City Region, 1970–1990," *International Migration Review*, Vol. 29 (Fall 1995): 625–656.

Both scholarly studies and popular accounts demonstrate that West Indians resemble African Americans as far as residential segregation is concerned. Roger Waldinger has shown that in 1980, the index of dissimilarity between African Americans and non-Hispanic whites stood at 67.8; between Jamaicans and non-Hispanic whites at 71.1; and between other West Indians and these whites at 68.7. In contrast, the score for Chinese immigrants and non-Hispanic whites was 50 and for East Indians and these whites, 38.8. Waldinger's data show—in a finding confirmed in the later study by Conway and Bigby—that West Indians in New York City exhibit a high degree of spatial concentration and often live in close proximity to traditional black neighborhoods. For instance, in Waldinger's study, the index of dissimilarity between West Indians and African Americans stood at 38.6. See, Waldinger, "The Old Neighborhood Revisited," *New York Affairs*, Vol. 10, No. 1 (Winter 1987): 1–13; Dennis Conway and

Ulathan Bigby, "Where Caribbean Peoples Live in New York City," in *Caribbean Life in New York: Sociocultural Dimensions*, ed. Constance R. Sutton and Elsa M. Chaney (New York: Center for Migration Studies, 1987), pp. 74–83; Foner, "Race and Color: Jamaican Migrants in London and New York City." Accounts in the press support these findings, with a number of reports showing West Indians to have been the victims of deliberate bias—including violence—in their search for homes. See, for instance, William Douglas and Merle English, "Bitter Memories for Hate Victims" (*New York Newsday*, February 14, 1990): 8; Sara Rimer, "Block's First Blacks: Ashes to an Open House" (*New York Times*, February 17, 1991): A1; Balford Henry, "Jamaican Priest Victim of New York Racism" (*The Jamaican Weekly Gleaner*, August 4–10, 1995): 20.

49. Stephen Labaton, "Denny's Restaurants to Pay 54 Million in Race Bias Suits" (*New York Times*, May 25, 1994): A1; Howard Kohn, "Humiliation, Sunny Side Up" (*New York Times Magazine*, November 6, 1994): 42–80.

50. Gerald D. Jaynes and Robin Williams, ed., *A Common Destiny: Blacks and American Society* (Washington, D.C.: National Academy Press, 1989), p. 4.

51. Ibid, pp. 5–6.

52. Sigelman and Welch, *Black Americans' Views of Racial Inequality.*

53. A cautionary note should be added here, since the survey asked blacks to self-identify their social class. Jervis Anderson, "Black and Blue," *The New Yorker* (April 29 and May 6, 1996): 62–65.

54. The sample consisted of 3036 adults. See, "Black/White Relations in the United States," *The Gallup Poll Social Audit, Executive Summary* (June 10, 1997).

55. Piazza and Sniderman, *The Scar of Race*, p. 141.

56. Abigail Thernstrom, "Two Nations, Separate and Hostile?" (New York Times, October 12, 1995): A23.

57. Feagin and Sikes, *Living with Racism*; Ellis Cose, *The Rage of a Privileged Class* (New York: HarperCollins, 1993); Jill Nelson, *Volunteer Slavery* (Chicago: The Noble Press, Inc., 1993).

58. See, for instance, William J. Wilson, "The American Underclass: Inner-city Ghettos and the Norms of Citizenship," The Godkin Lecture, delivered at John F. Kennedy School of Government, Harvard University (April 26, 1990).

59. See, for instance, Signithia Fordham, "Racelessness as a Factor in Black Students' School Success: Pragmatic Strategy or Pyrrhic Victory?," *Harvard Educational Review*, Vol. 58, No. 1 (February 1988): 54–84; Signithia Fordham and John Ogbu, "Black Students' School Success: Coping with the Burden of 'Acting White,'" *The Urban Review*, Vol. 18, No. 3 (1986): 176–205; Seth Mydans, "Black Identity versus Success and Seeming 'White,'" (*New York Times*, April 25, 1990): B9.

60. Wilson, "The American Underclass: Inner-city Ghettos and the Norms of Citizenship"; "Work," (*New York Times Magazine* (August 18, 1996), pp. 26–52; Philip Kasinitz and Jan Rosenberg, "Why Enterprise Zones Will Not Work," *City Journal* (Autumn 1993): 63–69; Jonathan Kaufman, "Immigrants' Business Often Refuse to Hire Blacks in Inner City" (*Wall Street Journal*, June 6, 1995): A1.

61. Ironically, widespread antiblack segregation undercuts the valid critique against separatism. While calls for separatism are mostly rhetoric and localized, segre-

gation represents a form of separatism that is actual, systematically enforced, and widespread. It is also a vital part of the antiblack sentiments that cause disillusionment among some blacks.

62. The other reason, of course, is that Powell is a coethnic who has achieved the success which many West Indians desire.

63. This survey, commissioned by the William O. Douglas Institute, consisted of convenience samples of 189 volunteers from black churches in Seattle, St. Louis, and Buffalo. Two-thirds of these were female, 70 percent between the ages of twenty-six and sixty, 40 percent had received more than fifteen years of education, and 53 percent earned less than $20,000 per year. Polled—among others things—on the esteem they had for various black public figures, 36 percent gave Andrew Young the highest rating, 27 percent Jackson, 5 percent Farrakhan, 4 percent Benjamin Hooks, and 2 percent Walter Fauntleroy. On the other hand, Farrakhan received the bulk of the highest unfavorable rating, with some 29 percent of respondents giving such a rating. The next highest rating went to Jackson, with 9 percent (Locke 1994, pp. 49–58).

64. Anderson, "Black and Blue," p. 64.

65. See Michael A. Fletcher and Hamil R. Harris, "Rift between Farrakhan, Jewish Leaders Resurfaces" (*Washington Post*, October 14, 1995):1.

66. A number of commentators have put forward this point of view. Following the "Million-Man March" of October 16, 1995, many voices emerged expressing concern that Louis Farrakhan has seemingly become legitimated. Some of these (for example, reporter Clarence Page on the October 17, 1995, edition of the McNeil/Lehrer News Hour) have explicitly linked his popularity with antiblack racism. Others, while not making the explicit connection with race, have argued that the society's ignoring of the dire conditions existing in many black communities has created a vacuum that has been filled by Farrakhan. See, for example, Russell Baker, "He Filled a Vacuum" (*New York Times*, October 17, 1995): A25.

CHAPTER
4
Attitudes Toward African Americans

The tight integration of the West Indies into the communication networks emanating from North America ensures that little which transpires in this country will go unnoticed in the former region. This means, among other things, that many West Indians certainly possess a knowledge of racial conditions in the United States prior to migrating here. Perhaps more important, their relatives have quite likely communicated to them a more intimate knowledge of these conditions. Still, a large gap separates knowledge from experience. Being forced to deal with discrimination regularly raises, for West Indians, issues for which abstract knowledge does not prepare them. Among the most important of these issues is the problem of identity in a heterogeneous society. Where, before, they had been Trinidadians, Barbadians, or Jamaicans, in the United States it is not immediately obvious what they will be. The strong nationalism present in many West Indian societies reduces the salience of the identity issue in those societies. As shown previously, West Indians take very seriously the idea that, regardless of their ultimate origins, they form a united whole under the national banner of whatever society they happen to be living in. In the United States, however, West Indians' national identity prior to migrating becomes much less important than their racial identity.

From a theoretical point of view, identity becomes a problem because, rather than being a given, it is negotiated in specific social contexts. Some individuals find themselves with several valid identity options, while others may have only a few. Some may enjoy great freedom to tailor their identity according to specific preferences; while other individuals find that outsiders impose particular identities and minimize personal choice. Research in this area has shown that Americans who trace their ancestry to Europe tend to enjoy the greatest freedom to determine their identity and to shift between a number of different identities. For instance, Herbert Gans and Richard Alba[1] have shown that where claiming allegiance to particular European ancestries—e.g., Italian—once brought a certain degree of discrimination, this is no longer the case. Americans of European origin—especially those tracing their ancestry back to eastern and southern Europe—are now quite assimilated. Under such conditions, ethnicity becomes "symbolic" in the sense that identifying with a particular ancestry entails little cost and is less an integral aspect of the self than it once was. Instead, ethnicity begins to revolve around social phenomena—e.g., festivals and cuisine—that, while important, are transient. Mary Waters's research among Americans of European descent has shown how the lessened salience of having particular European ancestries enables these Americans to opt for ethnic identities to which they may have some legitimate claim; or to eschew that and regard themselves as unhyphenated Americans. For instance, a child with ancestors from, say, Germany and Ireland could claim German ancestry, Irish ancestry, or downplay both and emphasize his or her "Americanness." Stanley Lieberson has argued that the haziness surrounding issues of ethnic identity for Americans of European ancestry derives in no small part from the inevitable gaps in knowledge, regarding ancestry, that develop over time. The further back in time an individual goes, the less certain is that individual of his or her ancestry. Over time, these gaps in knowledge make it easier for the individual to lose—without effort to maintain it—a sense of special attachment to particular identities. Thus, Lieberson found, for instance, that white southerners, because of the earlier migration of their ancestors to the United States, demonstrate the greatest tendency to view themselves as unhyphenated "Americans."[2]

Individuals of African ancestry differ markedly from all this. Rather than enjoying freedom to define themselves to reflect the full range of their ancestries, they have imposed on them by society the label "black." The operative principle has been the rule of *hypodescent*—the so-called one-drop rule—whereby all individuals, with even remote African ancestry, become defined by society as "black."[3] This rule has sought to subsume West Indians as well, but they have traditionally viewed it as problematic. Their societies never developed racial lines quite as rigid as those in this country. Moreover, a larger number of variables—notably social class—have been included in definitions of race. Consequently, they have enjoyed greater freedom to self-define their identities. More important, the negative stereotypes imputed, by Western culture, to African ancestry have not become as entrenched in the West Indies as they have in America. Therefore, as Kasinitz has pointed out, for West Indians, assimilating into American society implies giving up greater freedom for less and embracing negative stereotypes.[4] Because of this concession, West Indians' attitudes toward African Americans is a particularly important aspect of their encounter with race in America. These attitudes demonstrate that notions of race vary cross-culturally and that ethnic identity is flexible: in the case of West Indians, shrinking or growing depending on the particular issues that are being considered at any one time.

Basically, West Indians' relationship with African Americans revolves around the process of distancing and identification, sometimes leading to a synthesis of the two. Because of the restrictions and stereotypes associated with American notions of "blackness," West Indians wish to establish themselves as being different from the society's perception of African Americans. They want to be viewed by the society as "West Indians," an identity which encompasses pride in African ancestry, a focus on achievement, and somewhat conservative values. On a negative note, this attempt at identity construction sometimes involves the holding of negative stereotypes of African Americans. The irony of West Indians holding such stereotypes is that, since the society promulgates them against blacks, in general, West Indians also find themselves being stereotyped. Over time, their experiences with racial discrimination convince many that attempts to distance from African Americans are both futile and morally wrong. West Indians and African Americans, it turns out, must daily face common problems resulting from race. Thus, though some West Indians would distance themselves from African Americans, they find that racial issues which affect both groups singularly, pull them together. Or, put another way, where race becomes *the* issue, West Indians often conclude that the relevant identity to hold is "black," rather than "West Indian"—a position, it must be noted, which results from a combination of imposition of identity (e.g., the "one-drop rule") by powerful outsiders and choice. Taken together, these facts mean that West Indians find themselves caught between powerful cross-pressures of ethnic separatism and racial identification.

■ SOCIAL DISTANCING

West Indians' reluctance to assimilate into the larger African-American community can easily be misinterpreted as a wholesale rejection of the latter group. In reality, it stems from an attempt to avoid the imposition of a more restrictive identity than that to which they are accustomed. Or to put it another way: they are attempting to preserve the broader identity options inherent within West Indian culture. This attempt causes them to have complex attitudes toward African Americans. At their crudest, these attitudes embrace ethnocentrism, and the resulting tensions have become folklore. As noted previously, Ira Reid's seminal study, *The Negro Immigrant*, outlined these tensions in great detail. He argued that in the 1920s and 1930s, West Indian immigrants in Harlem, unused to blatant discrimination, often sought to put social distance between themselves and African Americans. The mechanisms for achieving this varied but always involved the ideas that West Indians were foreigners and that racial conditions in the West Indies were better than those in America. Thus, when they mourned the death of British kings

(George V in 1936) or celebrated the coronation of successors (George VI in the following year), West Indians were symbolizing their allegiance to a foreign—and in their minds, better—tradition. The same was true of their complaints to the British embassy and their militancy in the face of discrimination. Gilbert Osofsky painted a similar picture when, speaking about 1920s Harlem, he noted that: "Most Negro immigrants felt a strong attachment to their homeland. They demonstrated an 'exaggerated' nationalism in America—a buffer against the strangeness of the new culture and the hostility they experienced." The result was to increase intraethnic strife, as African Americans resented West Indian standoffishness.[5]

These mechanisms served at the time to put psychological—if not physical—distance between West Indians and an unpalatable situation. The irony is that the British in the West Indies were skillfully practicing their own brand of racial injustice. For instance, in his discussion of the political and social climate of early-twentieth-century Jamaica, Keith Henry argued that though white racism had a brutal edge in that country, the British manipulated anti-American feeling to mollify a sullen, poverty-stricken black population. Through the press, they highlighted and routinely condemned the lynchings of African Americans.[6] Similarly, historian Ken Post stated that, "it was quite sincerely denied by capitalist spokesmen that either class or racial strife were Jamaican problems, or else suggested that the latter, at least, was something about which decent people did not talk." Such sentiments were blamed on foreign elements—specifically, at the time, returning migrants who were accused of having acquired color consciousness in the United States.[7] However, despite its inherent duplicity, many West Indian immigrants accepted the idea that racial conditions in their homelands were better than those in America. This acceptance was due partially to the effectiveness of ideological indoctrination and partially to the reality that American racism was, in fact, more brutal than that in the West Indies. The longevity of the viewpoint downplaying race and a somewhat extreme manifestation of West Indian social distancing from African Americans is evident in the following excerpt from a 1991 article by a columnist for the *Daily Gleaner*:

> If anybody doubts that the majority of Americans are racist, just watch the interaction between a group of white Americans and any sophisticated black Jamaican. They flock to him like bees to honey . . . incontrovertible evidence that the last place they would expect to find sophistication is in a black man. I say black "Jamaican" because . . . I can't remember meeting a sophisticated black American who wasn't a scamp. As soon as I hear an American accent using educated speech coming from a black, I begin to worry that this is a person who will give me a six for a nine.

The columnist blamed African Americans for "lowering" the standards of Jamaican culture and, in general, expressed disdain for American culture.

For instance, commenting on allegations that black and white speech patterns are drifting further apart, the columnist averred that:

> this is disastrous when one considers that the level of white American English was never very high in the first place. White Americans can't spell, they speak broken English, and they have no cultural values beyond Hollywood and Coca-Cola. The only thing worse than a white American is a black one; but if we have to imitate them, even the average white barbarian would have offered a somewhat better example of education and economic power.

The columnist concluded by arguing that blacks are too thin skinned; that "the issue of color is really pointless because in a thousand years the whole world will be brown"; and that money and education are the real keys to success in any society.[8]

Although not as extreme, similar sentiments exist among some present-day West Indian immigrants. For instance, in an article comparing West Indian and African-American levels of achievement, journalist James Traub has shown that some West Indians seek to differentiate themselves by holding rather negative stereotypes of African-Americans' ambition and work attitudes.[9] Similarly, Kessner and Caroli, in their discussion of post-1965 immigrants to this country, give the example of the Jamaican student at an ivy league university who made strenuous efforts—for instance, through exaggerating her accent—to underline the differences between herself and African-American students.[10] And Mary Waters, writing on the role of lineage in African-Americans' self-concept, posits that West Indians, "voice some of the worst stereotypes and negative perceptions of American blacks imaginable. American blacks are seen by the immigrants . . . as lazy, unambitious, uneducated, unfriendly, welfare-dependent and lacking in family values."[11]

Some of the Jamaicans I interviewed echoed similar sentiments, but this was most true of immigrants who had lived in the country only a few years. Those who had lived in America many years tempered their criticism of African Americans markedly. Indeed, they expressed disapproval of anti-African-American sentiments among West Indians. Instead, they tended to view all blacks as experiencing similar problems of racial discrimination and the problems of African Americans as resulting primarily from this factor, rather than some internal cause. These Jamaicans' stronger empathy with African Americans resulted, primarily, from many more experiences of discrimination than was the case for more recently arrived immigrants. Moreover, upwardly mobile Jamaican respondents also tended to express greater empathy, probably because they felt more keenly the contradictions between their socioeconomic status and their treatment as blacks.[12]

West Indians' desire to distance themselves from some African Americans revolves primarily around the issues of work, achievement, and culture. The first two are particularly important, since they are central to West Indians' sense of identity in this country. These immigrants perceive themselves as sober, hard-working individuals who possess definite goals and are willing to sacrifice to achieve these. The specific claims made by the Jamaicans I interviewed were that West Indians, in general, are more competent, more reliable, put in greater effort in their work, have "right" priorities, and, therefore, are likely to achieve material and educational success. In contrast, some view lower status African Americans (and Puerto Ricans) as exhibiting traits that are the opposite of all of these. Moreover, they sometimes linked these traits to the existence of criminal behavior which, in their view, lowers the image of all black people. In this respect, it should be noted that the Jamaicans saw a convergence between the behavior of some younger recent immigrants and some young African Americans. For instance, Ivan, a retired lineman, related, disparagingly, the story of a young immigrant acquaintance of his. The boy, having become involved in the selling of drugs, had been shot and paralyzed by a rival gang. Even so, he still continued to sell drugs from his wheelchair. The mother, in desperation, had turned to Ivan for help but he saw no hope for the boy, writing him off as part of a lost generation with very different morals from those of previous generations of West Indian immigrants.

Ivan expressed equally strong criticism of some African Americans. This emerged, for instance, in his strong stand against welfare, which he viewed as a scam perpetrated by lazy individuals:

> [Black Americans] believe that America owes them something from slavery. So since America owes them something they are looking, still, for a lump sum; for America to pay them off for what happened. . . . We [West Indians] all come here [to the West Indies] as slaves but we were taught to work for a living. We have nothing named welfare in Jamaica. If you don't work, you don't eat. . . . Welfare is for the handicapped. Welfare is for a child. . . . And when I say "handicapped" [I mean that] you lose your sight and so; and still, you have Braille—you can do something. But welfare is to assist you until you can come off your legs. . . . But nobody sit down, haughty and strong and accepting money: I don't believe in that. . . . A lot of that is going on.

Sentiments such as these reflect a distaste for what many West Indians see as the antithesis of their thrust as immigrants. The fear is that blacks, in general, are being stigmatized as lazy, and, therefore, immigrants have to put as much distance as possible between themselves and welfare. Ashley, a thirty-nine-year-old bus driver exemplified this. He had readily embraced America, arguing that the consequences of migrating had been unambiguously positive. A driver for the public transportation system in Kingston, he left Jamaica because of a subjective sense that, economically, he was not progressing quickly enough. He gained entrance to the United States through the relative preference categories in the immigration law and, once here, gravitated to the occupation he had followed in Jamaica.

> America is a very good place, very prosperous. . . . I try to tell my kids that they are in a country that they can get whatever they want. As long as they want to be somebody, they can. But I see where the black American, they born right here, grow right here and they . . . don't try to put themself in no form of . . . position [to be] somebody. . . . Mostly, with American youngsters they only want to have a car and that's it. They don't really . . . want a proper job. . . . They don't really check for [want] success.

He continued:

> I see where West Indians have a chance of getting a job over the black American because . . . these employers—mostly the whites—see where we . . . are better workers. . . . If . . . both of us should go in for a job—one as a American and [the other] a West Indian: . . . the West Indian will have a better chance over the American. . . . I work at about three other garages [since being in America] and I see the same problems at all of the places I've been: The American, if you got them five days for this week, you can take a bet, next week they [are] going to . . . work three or four days. . . . That's a problem with most of them. Puerto Ricans, forget about them. It's very rare you'll get them to work for a complete week. I [am] talking about what I saw.

Summarizing his argument: Ashley believed that opportunities for success exist in the United States, but that at least some African Americans are not enjoying this success because of inconsistent work habits. This is exacerbated by a focus on "wrong" priorities (e.g., wanting to buy cars, instead of securing stable employment), especially among the young. In contrast, West Indians enjoy success because not only do they seize opportunities and work hard, but white employers also prefer them over African Americans.[13]

Below, I present a sampling of similar views. A colleague of Ashley, Bernard, in America six years, stated:

> This is my opinion of [black] Americans in general: They sit down and they watch you. They don't like you because you will make progress. . . . On my job I have half-a-dozen (black) ex-marines. Now, You believe if I was born and I grow up here I would be driving a bus today? No! If I had gone in[to] the army, I would have made sure while I was there [that] I learn a skill that can profit me when I get out.[14]

Frank, a recent immigrant (five years), opined:

> I would say . . . that they are lazy and we from the West Indies work very hard. . . . They will work two weeks or three weeks; they get money, they just stop: They don't want to come to work. When that money finish now, they'll come back to work.

Ellis, a mason, resident in the country four years, stated:

> Well, these guys, they [do not] want to work. They work Monday up to
> Thursday. They get paid Thursday . . . [and] they don't show up until
> Monday. That means the boss is losing production.

While these sentiments seem to predominate among recent immigrants,
by no means is this always the case. In chapter 3 we met Bogle, the small
business man who took a strong stance against race thinking. His opinions
with respect to African Americans were equally adamant. He related the following to illustrate how he had formed his views:

> When I became service manager for a company . . . this [African-American]
> guy showed great potential. . . . M——— was really a first class tape recorder
> mechanic. But always over the weekend—and I could never understand it—
> he would always pawn out his tools to some pawnbroker shop . . . Mondays
> when I [would] call him and say: "Why are you not in?" He [would say]:
> "Boss, I need $40 or $60 because my tools in a pawnbroker's shop. . . .
> And . . . in my entire life of having employed between 80 and 130 people
> . . . in Jamaica and a couple here . . . they have never yet, no matter how
> things are tight, pawned out their tools which they make a living by. . . . A
> Jamaican becomes very sensitive to his tools. He will not even leave it in a
> . . . customer's home overnight, thinking that he may get a call at 4:00 am
> or 6:00 am in the morning. . . . That really disturbs me and I really say:
> "You [black] guys not going anyplace."

Southern Exceptionalism

In stating these unflattering views, the Jamaicans often issued a significant
qualification: They tended to distinguish, generally—and somewhat stereo-
typically—between northern and southern blacks.[15] This is part of a broader
tendency, among West Indians, to distinguish between the "North" and the
"South" in America. Where they ascribe unfavorable characteristics (both
geographic and moral) to the former, they imbue the latter with the opposite characteristics. For many, the North—typified by the core region of settlement in the New York City Metropolitan area—is a hostile environment.
It is cold, fast-paced, too large, and people are atomized. At minimum, this
lack of a sense of community expresses itself in a pervasive incivility and, at
its extreme, as violent crime. While they are aware, and wary, of the South's
history of brutal discrimination against blacks, they still tend to view the region as more attractive than the North. To begin with, it is warm—a very
attractive fact to a tropical people struggling to adjust to a cold climate.
Moreover, they perceive the region, as a whole, as being more easygoing
and—most important—possessing a deeper sense of community. In other
words: they tend to perceive the South as being more similar to the West
Indies than is the North.

These perceptions matter because they form the basis for action. Miami has long boasted the second highest concentration of West Indians in the United States. However, increasingly, West Indians are starting to fan out—especially as they become upwardly mobile—from their main concentration in New York City. That city's surrounding suburbs receive much of the outflow, but southern cities such as Richmond, Atlanta, and Houston are also proving popular.[16] But even among those who do not migrate, a general sense exists that people from the South possess traits that are reminiscent of West Indians. They view southerners as being hard working, ambitious, and polite; their children as being obedient to adults; and southern women as being more willing to perform household chores traditionally associated with females. In many ways the debate in this country over "traditional values" very much resonates with West Indian immigrants. Many of these immigrants perceive northerners as less likely to adhere to such values. A case in point was Andre, a thirty-four-year-old college student, who recounted his experiences while working a summer job as a construction worker. He stated that tensions existed on the worksite because the white workers held preconceptions about their black colleagues, while the latter fulfilled many of these stereotypes by performing inconsistent and shoddy work. The exception to this rule, he claimed, was an African-American friend from the South whose parents had instilled him with "traditional" values of hard work. In fact, the possession of these values was the reason why the two had become friendly, because Andre viewed this African American's attitudes as being similar to those exhibited by West Indians.

Turning to women, we find an overlap between the view that in the labor market and the home, women should adhere to more traditional roles; and that southern women more frequently match this ideal than those from the North. This view is very much a male point of view, since Jamaican women both embody and deny the ideal espoused by Jamaican men. Household chores such as cooking , cleaning, and washing have traditionally fallen on the former but Jamaican women have also had a long tradition of independence. This is reflected in the long-standing debate as to whether West Indian families are essentially matrifocal, with men being somewhat peripheral figures.[17] Less debatable is the fact that, in Jamaica, women have long dominated the selling of farm produce and dry goods ("higglering) in urban areas. As the economy entered a period of turmoil in the 1970s and 1980s, many of these women, hitherto content to act as outlets for such products, took more direct control over their sources of supply. Thus, they would travel to such places as Haiti and Miami, buy in-demand commodities (e.g., shoes) at relatively low prices, and sell these in Jamaica at a profit. Even fairly well-off women, realizing the profits to be made in this trade, became involved.[18] Political scientist Carl Stone has made the claim that some lower status women were able to advance to the middle class on the basis of profits made from the expansion of the higg-lering trade.[19]

Jamaican men, aware of this tradition of independence, expect their wives to both work outside the home and keep house.[20] Conversely, the men often express contradictory stereotypes of black women from the North: either that they are too willing to embrace nontraditional roles outside the home at the expense of housekeeping, or that they are unwilling to work at all. Simon, a married forty-year-old accountant, put it this way:

> The American female . . . think[s] more masculine than anything else. . . . They figure that there is no limit to what they can do. They don't limit themselves to basic things. I mean, they will go out there and do any-thing. . . . Even in terms of work; they will do from construction to any-thing. They think they are equal with men. . . . They should really limit themselves.

These sentiments, combined with a concern that marriage would lead to cul-tural conflicts, made the Jamaican men I interviewed leery of such relation-ships (see Table 4.1). Only two of these men were married to American women, and one of these respondents emphasized that it was because his wife had become very West Indian in her outlook. Leroy, a retired carpen-ter, put it quite bluntly when he stated:

> American women make good girlfriends but they never seem to make good wives. . . . When you do marry . . . an American woman there is a little . . . doubt . . . around it. And when you marry one of your own—which I can be wrong—you feel a little more safe. And the reason why I say that is that the average American, the things that they will do . . . would affect me if I [had] to encounter [them]; because I didn't come to America just to

TABLE 4.1 Male Jamaican Respondents' Views on Dating and Marrying African-American Women, by Length of Residence (percentage distribution)

| | Attitudes | | | |
| | Dating | | Marriage | |
Years of Residence	Favorable	Unfavorable	Favorable	Unfavorable
Less than 5 years	57	43	35	65
6–10 years	82	18	41	59
More than 10 years	84	16	42	58

Source: Interviews conducted with Jamaicans.

N = 64.

come to America. . . . I come here to make a livelihood; and I don't believe in spending money wherein I could save it. . . . Money should be spent . . . wisely. . . . So I marry a Jamaican. I feel a little [more] secure that way. . . . If I . . . marry an American . . . I [would] probably hit her and blame myself.

However, the Jamaicans perceived southern women differently. Notice the opinion of Rupert, a contractor who had married an American woman:

> Traditionally, one looks forward to the wife preparing the husband's meal and not really running to the corner store to buy a box of chicken legs and say[ing] that that's dinner. . . . Maybe as time goes by I might accept this but I don't think that's something good for me to accept. . . . They [southern women] will replace a missing button from your shirt and they know how to do it. A New Yorker, instead of replacing the button might buy you a new shirt. There's nothing wrong with buying a shirt and there's nothing wrong with replacing a button but it depends on how you look at it. A young lady who lives in New York . . . becomes more involved in commercialized items. Ladies, for example, that used to prepare their meals by hand and take great pains to prepare meals . . . now believe—because they live in the city—in going out to restaurants to eat . . . and [are] satisfied with McDonald's and Kentucky [Fried Chicken].

Similarly, Leon, an accountant, opined:

> Dating is fine if you don't intend to get married; but dating with the intention of going on: . . . I am not very open when it comes to that. . . . I don't want to say point blank [that] I wouldn't marry an American woman, but it would be a very difficult decision to make; except if she's from the South because, as I said earlier, our cultural backgrounds seem to be similar. But viewing some American girls from up North, here, I don't know if it's a good idea. . . . The way Jamaican men are brought up, I think it's very difficult for American women to accept that kind of man. Maybe he's not, but he thinks he's the leader of his house. . . . He thinks . . . people should hear what he says. . . . Now the average American woman is more liberated than the average West Indian woman; so I don't see her generally accepting that kind of person. So I think that should be problems from day one.

■ THE PULL OF RACE

West Indians who seek to distance themselves from African Americans face the formidable problem of how to consistently distinguish themselves from a population, whom they resemble phenotypically, in a society that regards this phenotype as being overwhelmingly important. Or to put the question another way: how do West Indians establish that they are different from

African Americans, when they resemble African Americans, and the society regards black skin as being a very significant marker for a wide range of imputed—often negative—traits? Phrased in terms of the social construction of ethnicity, it is known that, in the United States, individuals of African ancestry enjoy little leeway for departing from the definition of themselves as "blacks." Thus, in attempting to carve out an alternative identity (as "West Indians"), West Indian immigrants find themselves working uphill against centuries of American history. It would be safe to say that, so far, West Indians have not convincingly demonstrated to the larger society that, in all respects, they differ from African Americans; in certain spheres, they may be able to make the case for this difference but in others the society perceives little difference between the two groups. For instance, in an office situation in which West Indians interact intensely with whites on a long-term basis, the latter *may* come to perceive cultural differences between West Indians and African Americans. However, it is an open question whether such an understanding will result in consistently better treatment than is accorded to African Americans. Moreover, as was argued in the previous chapter, in public places whites perceive and treat African Americans and West Indians the same. Thus, though some West Indians may wish to distance themselves from African Americans, the reality is that society often discriminates against both groups as "blacks."

This reality inevitably causes West Indians—especially long-term residents and those who have experienced discrimination at work and in school—to coalesce with African Americans around racially tinged issues. Thornton, a thirty-four-year-old college instructor, illustrates how some West Indians begin to construct a panblack, rather than a more exclusive, West Indian identity:

> From the point of view of the wider society, there is no evidence in my mind that there is any major distinction that is made between external [and] internal blacks. . . . I feel [that] much of that is in our mind. And I tend to want to think that . . . we should view ourselves as a continuum—between ourselves and Americans. . . . There have been so many issues that have forced me to identify; classic cases . . . like the Howard Beach case. I have heard so many cases about people on the job . . . [who] . . . have been denied promotional opportunities: West Indians and [American] blacks. . . . We won't attain much by forming ourselves in a special group for special treatment. And I don't want to be a part of that movement. . . . I'd rather move one mile with all of us moving together.

Some respondents put the matter more bluntly. For instance, Al, a fifty-three-year-old engineer, angry at racial discrimination on his job stated:

> I have nothing against Haitians; I have nothing against black Americans. . . .
> If you're a nigger, you're a nigger, regardless of whether you are from

Timbuktu. . . . There isn't the unity that one would like to see. . . . Blacks have to appreciate blacks, no matter where they are from. Just look at it the way I look at it: That you're the same.

The following excerpt illustrates how some West Indians take social class into consideration in creating a panblack identity. Leon, the accountant, stated:

> Both at my current workplace and the former, I met American blacks from different levels in the spectrum: Those that are undereducated and simply clerical [as well as] professionals. I think the average clerical type, not too educated, is very antagonistic towards West Indians because they feel that people from the West Indies come here, and take their jobs away. But the professionals that I deal with, if they feel that way they don't bring it up front. They don't seem to be threatened.

He attributed this difference in attitude to education, arguing that African-American professionals feel very secure in their abilities, where those with less education do not. Thus, he continued:

> those [African-Americans] that I have worked with who are professionals work just as hard as West Indians. . . . But the ones on the lower end, those who I mentioned earlier, they don't work! They don't like work! So again, I think it has to do with the level of education. Probably that's the very reason why they are uneducated: They don't work in school either. But those that have managed to come through the school system and become professionals work very hard. I have a couple of people at work. One in particular . . . is from the South. She's a very hard worker and she's not the only one. In my previous workplace my supervisor was a black American.

Arthur, a thirty-eight-year-old job placement counselor, explained how racial discrimination in the educational system had helped him create a panblack identity. Already a nine-year resident of the United States at the time of the interview, he admitted that when he had first arrived in America he had viewed African Americans very negatively. However, his experiences at the small southern Christian college which he had attended had completely changed his viewpoint. One of only three Jamaican students attending the college, he found the whites with whom he interacted perplexed that these immigrant students did not conform to stereotypes of blacks. Meanwhile, according to Arthur, many of the black students seemed to conform to racist stereotypes:

> Everything I ever heard about the blacks was negative and they had a few blacks on campus . . . who really fit the stereotype of what . . . they [the whites] tend to regard American blacks as. . . . These blacks . . . there were probably about six of them . . . did very poorly in their work. . . . The way they spoke, the way they presented themselves: It was just typical of what whites tend to say about black Americans.

The Jamaicans' anomalous situation led to conflict with both African-American and white students. The former resented the grudging acceptance given to the Jamaicans by whites and warned that the Jamaicans only seemed to be accepted because they were a "novelty." Once that effect wore thin, whites would apply to the Jamaicans the same negative stereotypes and avoidance behaviors that characterized their relationship with the African Americans. Indeed, the Jamaicans had not escaped the racial tension existing between the whites and blacks on the college campus, since they found themselves subject to a range of racial slights, ranging from the subtle to the very blunt. On the former end of the spectrum, the Jamaicans found themselves being referred to, by the white students, as "oreos." Arthur interpreted this as his white classmates' attempt to quell the "cognitive dissonance" which resulted from seeing blacks who outperformed them. The "oreo" label said, essentially, that though the Jamaicans possessed the physical features of individuals defined as "black," they performed well because they thought and acted "white." Similar slights occurred in the area of extracurricular activities. For instance, Arthur found that though whites allowed him to socialize with them, they subjected him to crude jokes ridiculing the stereotyped physical features of blacks. And socializing became even more strained because, unlike the African-American students, he dated white female students. This, and the fact that he deliberately sought out the most attractive white women, led to increasing hostility from white male students who let it be known that, regardless of his "novelty," he had overstepped the bounds of racial etiquette. But Arthur replied that he saw himself as being equal or better than the white students and let them know it. As he stated: "I took it as a personal challenge to perform well enough, in school, to eradicate the stereotyping and actually . . . use my performance as leverage against some of the taunts that they [the whites] would use."

This response applied as much to his professors as it did to classmates, since several of the former expressed thinly disguised racist sentiments. For instance, one professor, implying that Arthur did not know his place, repeatedly accused him of regarding himself as being better than the African-Americans students. His reply that he not only thought but was, in actuality, academically better than these students was greeted by anger from the professor. Most blatant of all was the incident in which college administrators denied him a job, for which he was highly qualified, because of his race. His name had been brought to the attention of the administrators by a white friend who knew of his years of experience in the job that had been advertised. However, after it had become known that he was black the interview was suddenly canceled. Over time, Arthur's experiences at college made him much more sympathetic to blacks, in general. Though the African-American students at the college had directed a modicum of hostility toward the

Jamaicans, ultimately this paled in comparison to the hostility directed toward both groups by whites. Despite appearances to the contrary, the Jamaicans and African Americans bore more similarities to each other than either group did to the whites. As he stated:

> I am a lot more tolerant now, than I would have been before. I am tolerant more now because I have been exposed to a wider cross-section of American blacks; and, therefore, I know that . . . although you have a lot of American blacks who seem to be going nowhere . . . there are also those who are going places. . . . But also, I have a more sympathetic attitude towards those who settle at the bottom, who seem to lack motivation, who seem not to be going anywhere because I have become more aware of the forces that are involved; that shape them and make them the way they are.

One of the clearest indicators that West Indians have started to construct a panblack identity is criticism of coethnics for taking anti-African-American stances. David, a twenty-eight-year-old accountant, stated:

> I wouldn't say [that I have] a lot of black American friends but I am beginning to find out that I tolerate black Americans more than I do Jamaicans nowadays. . . . There is a certain arrogance that Jamaicans have that . . . is not warranted . . . and I find it very disturbing. . . . You see it in a million ways. . . . You can hear it in the way that Jamaicans typically refer to black Americans. They generally have nothing good to say. Whatever they say is generally derogatory. . . . It's this false sense of pride. . . . I don't know what the cause is, but there's this sense that I am Jamaican. I am hot. I am better than black Americans. I think it's wrong and I think it's ridiculous. . . . It doesn't do Jamaicans any good and it doesn't do black Americans any good.

Similarly, Nelson, a high level manager at a New York State agency, issued strong criticism of coethnics for not appreciating the situation of African Americans. He contrasted the situation of West Indians and African Americans in the South, where he went to college:

> Most West Indians' . . . evaluation of black Americans . . . is not quite right . . . because they do not understand what the black American has been through in the last thirty years. . . . When I came here I . . . was in the South and . . . saw what was happening. . . . Here I was coming from the West Indies and the Englishman said to me . . . : "Listen, if you go to school and study, you can be like me; you can have this position in this job." And . . . whether it was true or not, I believed that; that if I made good in school, I could achieve. But here . . . they were saying to the American black: Your skin is black and you can only get this far but you cannot go any further. In other words, you are being held at a certain level. . . . And they grow up in that environment thinking . . . : "Don't care what I do, I'm condemned to this level, so why try?"

Explaining the deleterious effects of racial discrimination on southern blacks, he continued:

> My wife is a southerner, and when I came here . . . her father was making about $7 per week. . . . He was still sharecropping and . . . at the end of the year, instead of owning something, they would owe the master of the sharecroppers that [amount]. So the man was completely emasculated; he couldn't support his family. . . . It was completely different than what we experienced in Jamaica; though Jamaica was very, very poor . . . we were filled with hope and aspirations.

Although being a foreigner sometimes blunted the impact of racism, he recognized it, intrinsically, as being directed against all blacks and, therefore, expressed deep skepticism toward the idea that West Indians enjoy special immunity. He related how, in the 1950s in the small southern town in which he had attended college, many whites reacted to him initially on the basis of skin color. Only later when, perhaps, they recognized his accent did some give him the benefit of the doubt. However, viewing the initial response as indicative of their true feelings, he discounted the effects of accent. Criticizing coethnics who rely on such factors as speech to distinguish themselves from African Americans, Nelson stated:

> Some of us . . . say we are different . . . but the truth is this: . . . in a mob action . . . they [will] lynch you before you have a chance to speak. So don't fool yourself, you are judged basically on this [pointing to his skin]. . . . So I don't let that get me carried away; say, well, I am West Indian, I am treated differently. That's nonsensical!

One reason for this skepticism was that he continued to experience deleterious racial episodes. For instance, shortly before I interviewed him, he related how an anonymous survey of his subordinates, that sought to evaluate his performance, had revealed surprising racial animus. The results of this survey disturbed him, because he had assumed that his subordinates had held goodwill toward him. The results shattered this illusion and left him struggling with feelings of anger and frustration: decades after encountering similar sentiments in the South, he found that they also existed among his coworkers in a city with a reputation for tolerance.

Political Responses

The panblack identity exhibited by some West Indians manifests itself in a number of ways. As shown before, criticism of the police for appearing to go beyond reasonable doubt and targeting blacks, in general, is one example. Also, some West Indians criticize the media for overplaying the black as criminal motif, while neglecting more positive stories. As one respondent argued:

[W]LIB[21] gives me home[22] news and gives me news that they [the white media] refuse from reporting. They give you sensational news about blacks on the TV, but things like this, where the police [are] brutalizing people: You don't hear about these things. . . . Things like these is only when you listen to [W]LIB that you hear these things. . . . There are so many Jamaicans going around thinking that they are different! And the police, the system don't see it that way. They may tell you that you are different but you are being treated the same way. . . . This [pointing at his skin] is what they [the police] look on. They don't ask you if you come from Africa, Trinidad, or Barbados . . . when they are out there conking you in the head.

Politically, panblack sentiments also manifest themselves in solid support in cases where the advancement of particular candidates will be of high symbolic value. Only slight reflection is needed to realize that with respect to political issues, complex forces are at work. To begin with, some of the issues that animate West Indians do not fall neatly along a liberal–conservative continuum. For instance, West Indians, like other immigrants, are concerned about growing antiimmigrant sentiments in the country. But it is not immediately apparent which established political organization would champion their cause since anti- and proimmigrant sentiments cut across ideological lines. In light of this, West Indians can be expected to pursue their own interests, and the growing size of the community is allowing the expression of more overt ethnic politics. Kasinitz's discussion of the 1985 attempt to rally the community behind the election of former New York City mayor Ed Koch, at a time when he was becoming increasingly unpopular with blacks, is a good example of ethnic politics in operation. Moreover, with their rather conservative attitudes on a variety of issues—from welfare to crime—West Indians would seem to be prime candidates for recruitment into various conservative causes. Colin Powell's call for more blacks to join the Republican Party could fall on receptive ears within the West Indian community.

There are, however, forces forestalling such an outcome. The most important of these is that West Indians are operating under cross-pressures. They may be conservative on certain social issues, but claims to their allegiance must contend with the fact that, as blacks, they suffer discrimination. Here, the Republican Party's reputation of being less than friendly to blacks is tellingly important, since West Indians, like most African Americans, tend not to perceive support for this party's candidates to be in their interest. The overwhelming view is that Democrats are more likely to possess an understanding of the racial and economic issues besetting the community.[23] In fact, 70 percent of the Jamaicans I interviewed identified themselves as supporters of various Democratic Party candidates.

In light of this, David Dinkins's campaign to become the first African-American mayor of New York City and Jesse Jackson's bid for the presidency in 1988 were viewed by the Jamaicans I interviewed as being of very high practical and symbolic importance. Although many were careful to note that these candidates would be good for Americans, as a whole, there was no mistaking the pride involved in seeing such historic firsts. Thus, in highly West Indianized Crown Heights, Dinkins won over 90 percent of the vote;[24] and Jesse Jackson came in for praise from many of the Jamaicans. Neil, a social worker, summed up the sentiment of many West Indians on Jackson, in the following way:

> I saw Jesse's candidacy as a sort of revolution in that . . . no other black man has gone that far. Not even Martin Luther King went that far. King was still a messenger. . . . Jackson was more than a messenger. . . . I would have voted for Jackson . . . on several grounds. . . . He spoke to a broad cross-section of the people. A lot of people have . . . doubts about him, but one of the things that would have made me vote for Jackson . . . is . . . simple . . . group solidarity: A black man [running] for office . . . and the issues he dealt with were the issues I deal with personally. . . . Jesse tested the integrity of the American democratic system as set down by the flipping founding fathers, and the damn system was found wanting because of the racist attitudes of many people! I am not saying that because him black, him must win, but . . . black people are the litmus test of the system.

All this is not to suggest that West Indians' political attitudes are monolithic or static. Since Colin Powell is a coethnic and the embodiment of the success for which West Indians strive, they would tend to regard, with favor, his stance on various issues. One gauge of this is that while Powell was considering whether or not to make a bid for the presidency, the North American edition of the *Daily Gleaner* carried an ongoing series entitled "The Powell Watch." As was the case with the rest of the country, the underlying question posed by the series was whether or not Powell would and, more importantly, should run for president. His Jamaican roots, hard-working immigrant parents, and rags-to-riches success story were frequently mentioned, and, overall, there was universal agreement that he was the role model par excellence for West Indians. While the existence of a few dissenting voices within the community was noted (chiefly over Powell's role in the Panama Canal invasion), the series reported that West Indians were pleased to see the overwhelming support which he was being shown throughout the country. On the other hand, many were not sure that he should actually make a bid for the presidency, since, as they saw it, the country was not ready for a black president. Echoing a fear expressed by some of my respondents with respect to Jackson's previous bids for the presidency, the West Indians sampled by the *Gleaner* felt that attempts would be made on Powell's life by racist individuals. Thus, the overall tone of the series was one of pride mixed with caution. Nevertheless, it would be reasonable to suggest that Powell remains a force to be reckoned with and that his desire to pull more blacks into the Republican Party adds a potent factor to the conflicting mix of elements motivating the political behavior of West Indians.

■ ROLE MODELING

An important aspect of the construction of ethnic identity is that the process is dynamic. West Indians who view a panblack identity as being most salient where racial issues are concerned can, in other circumstances, view a narrower ethnic identity as being more relevant. One important reason for noting this dynamism in the creation of identity is that even those West Indians who empathize strongly with African Americans have not lost their sense of "West Indianness." Though they may criticize the social system for making the lives of blacks—especially African Americans—difficult, many still hold to the view that the norms and values that typify West Indians can help sidestep obstacles. This is not to pretend that the obstacles do not exist but, rather, to ask what pragmatic steps can be taken to get around them. Thus, as part of their panblack identity, some West Indians advance the notion that the norms and values typifying West Indians can act as a guide for some African Americans. These West Indians view such a policy as being a logical extension of concern for African Americans—especially those who are experiencing persistent poverty and other social ills.[25]

This "role modeling" idea is, of course, controversial because it recalls the attitudes of superiority that some West Indians have historically demonstrated toward African Americans. The latter, understandably, resent such attitudes, since, whatever the motive, they inevitably seem paternalistic. To some African Americans, role modeling appears to be yet another instance of foreigners offering unsolicited advice on how native-born blacks should live their lives. Roger Waldinger, for instance, in his analysis of ethnic niches in New York City, has given examples of how some African-American contractors react negatively to the suggestion that West Indian contractors are better than they are. Moreover, role modeling downplays (largely unconsciously) the fact that most of the benefits enjoyed today by blacks have resulted from the sacrifices made by African Americans in their long drive to establish basic civil rights. This movement has, obviously, facilitated the advance of both native- and foreign-born blacks in the United States. Additionally, the later Black Power movement also impacted politics in the West Indies, since it heightened consciousness of race among young blacks in the region, caused civil unrest, and led some governments to increase restrictions on their populations.[26] Another important point missed by the role modeling idea is the reality that, on a cultural level, cross-fertilization is constantly occurring—especially among the younger generation—between African Americans and West Indians. For instance, the impact of reggae music on the early development of rap music is well known; and the dreadlocks hairstyle which is now ubiquitous among blacks in the United States derives from Rastafarianism.[27] However, not as well known is the fact that American blues and soul music influenced the development of reggae music, itself.[28]

Because of the various levels of interaction between West Indians and African Americans, it seems appropriate to treat the role modeling idea with a degree of skepticism—especially since it can easily slide into ethnocentrism. If the idea has any merit, this lies in its pointing to the important role played in achievement by pragmatic behaviors—e.g., focusing study on fields with a high potential for economic gain—and intangibles such as self-confidence. However, whether the experience of West Indians, specifically, can be applied to the situation of African Americans is problematic. One obvious reason for this stems from the different histories of the two groups and, as well, social structures in which they typically operate. Another factor making the West Indian\African American comparison problematic is that traditionally, West Indians, like other immigrants, have been self-selected and, therefore, are not necessarily representative, in all respects, of the stay-at-home West Indian population. It is well known that, typically, immigrants are more highly motivated than native-born peoples, regardless of ancestry. One implication of this is that immigrant West Indians may, also, be even more highly motivated than those West Indians who do not migrate.[29]

Bearing in mind these qualifications, role modeling, when examined, can be seen as being, in some ways, a merger between social distancing and panblack sentiments. It says, essentially, that from a socioeconomic perspective, West Indians are performing better than African Americans and, therefore, are distant from them. However, the idea also contains the paternalistic aspect which seeks, by emulating West Indians, to "improve" the performance of those African Americans who are believed to be performing badly. This latter aspect may be seen as being an extension of panblack sentiments among West Indians.

A number of the examples discussed previously illustrate this melding of social distancing and panblack sentiments. One instance would be Nelson, the high level manager, who though very problack, advocated that the lot of African Americans would be improved if they emphasized strong families and education instead of traditional civil rights strategies such as marching. My interview with Jack, a twenty-eight-year-old college student, evoked some of the more intangible aspects of role modeling. In a wide-ranging discussion, he tried to explain some of the differences between himself and his African-American friends:

> The major difference that we have is how we speak. I do not like street jargon and all my American friends tend to use it. Things like, "where's he at," and "I ain't know" and things like that. They'll get around me and

they'll say it and I will immediately correct them. . . . Still we are not angry
with each other. . . . I'll become very proper[30] in my English speaking and
they'll just laugh about it . . . because I'll understand what they are saying
and they'll understand what I am saying.

Explaining why he viewed using "proper" English as very important, he continued:

I think when you speak properly . . . it's a sign of proper upbringing; [of]
being very cultured. It's a sign of sophistication. . . . There's a time and a
place for everything. Naturally, if I am out with my friends, I might not be
as proper as I would be in the corporate office . . . [but] it's very important to be proper in the way that we speak and the way we behave!

While his friends did not necessarily behave badly, he found it disconcert-
ing that they sometimes drew attention to themselves in public. Thus, he
criticized them for,

being loud; talking loudly on the subway or in the street. Things like that
bother me. For example, one major thing that I tell all my friends: If you
see me on the street and you are not close enough to say hello, do not
shout-out my name across the street. I will not answer you!

For Jack, speaking properly was a matter of politeness, but more, an indicator of styles of dress and behavior. His argument was that "bad" English
goes hand-in-hand with sloppy dress and rude behavior—things that would
reduce the likelihood of his friends obtaining prestigious jobs.

Another college student, Andre, expressed role modeling ideas even
more explicitly. Explaining why he would prefer to live in a neighborhood
with mostly West Indians, rather than one with mostly African Americans,
he stated:

I invited one black American young lady who I tend to fancy more so than
the other black American young ladies in church. And when she came into
my house she said: "Wow, this house is beautiful. This house is well kept!"
. . . But of course there is a difference in this house, because it is kept by
West Indians! . . . I am having an influence upon her; as . . . against when
I am in [an African-American] neighborhood when it's . . . harder for me
to mold my children to think a certain way [because] their peer groups
around them have a totally different behavior pattern from what I am trying to inject into them in my home.

In other words, he believed that operating primarily in a West Indian
environment would enable him to mold his children around values that are
cherished by West Indians. Moreover, he believed that in such a context, he
could exert a significant and effective influence on African-American friends
whom he would invite into the environment from time to time.

My interview with Tommy, a twenty-nine-year-old used car salesman,
illustrates the economic rationale underlying role modeling:

For the most part, foreign blacks are the ones that set a more positive example for blacks here because the American blacks, as far as the foreign blacks are concerned, let themselves down and let us down. They think [that] America owes them a living because their foreparents were slaves and it's not so. . . . Everybody else in the country is going to progress but them because they still are slaves to something that happened 200 years ago. And the slavery is mainly in their minds. . . . In America, for the most part, everybody else is wrapped-up in their own life. You think they are wasting their time thinking about you? Not at all! All America owes you, basically, is an opportunity to work for that which you want in your life. And it affords that to everyone who lives here, day-in and day-out. But [if] you choose not to take advantage of that opportunity, then whose fault is that?

An increase in the rate of home ownership (an attribute often associated with West Indians) was one often-mentioned goal of role modeling. Byron, a fifty-six-year-old security guard, illustrates this:

Certain Americans seem to have a fuse against West Indians. They [are] claiming that the West Indian come here and [take] their jobs. They [West Indians] try to be big; they drive big cars; they buy houses and we don't. . . . I have talked to them by telling them to own their own, just the same as I do. . . . You are paying rent . . . and that same $500 rent could be a monthly payment on a house. Then you would be paying yourself. . . . In times to come . . . you cannot keep the house . . . you sell that house. All that money that you put in as . . . rent comes to you. You move with somebody; you try to give them insight of what they can do. . . . Lots of them take it; lots don't because they feel that they want to . . . have fun.

Byron, upset that some African Americans criticized West Indians for being too successful, too quickly (he owned several houses in different states), had taken it upon himself to show some of his African-American friends how to achieve the same. But, he complained, not everyone would take his advice. The ones who did not possessed "distorted" priorities, since they placed having "fun" over achievement.

Taken together, the examples of role modeling presented above illustrate some of the reasons why the concept is problematic. Though, in some instances—e.g., Byron—it seems to present pragmatic steps for bringing about material progress; in others—e.g., Jack—it veers much more clearly toward ethnocentrism. In fact, this ethnocentrism is a basic component of role modeling, being present (though not as obvious) even in relatively positive appeals such as those made by Byron. Ultimately, this ethnocentrism, along with the many qualifications within which role modeling must be couched, render the concept unworkable. Though it seeks to bridge the gap between West Indians' contradictory responses to African Americans, in reality it seems more likely to lead to tension between the two groups.

■ CONCLUSION

The attitudes that some West Indians display toward African Americans tend to excite comment because, from some perspectives, they seem peculiar. This is especially true if observers take a monolithic view of the black community. From that perspective some of the statements made by West Indians with respect to African Americans seem surprising, sensationalistic, and, at times, even supportive of stereotypes that have long been promulgated by society. However, these apparently anti-African-American sentiments constitute only one part of a complex dynamic. They never stand in isolation but, rather, make sense only when placed within the context of the contradictory forces which shape the identity of foreign blacks.

In the United States, individuals of African ancestry, unlike those of European ancestry, find their identity options to be constrained. Generally speaking, they are "black." In an increasingly heterogeneous society, such constraints are becoming increasingly problematic. They are also problematic because the society imbues "blackness" with negative characteristics. West Indians, while not strangers to negative characterizations of "blackness," nevertheless find American assumptions regarding African ancestry to be unusually oppressive. Their history has allowed for a somewhat wider range of identity possibilities. Most important, from their perspective, African ancestry does not imply the negative behavioral and social consequences which American society often seems to assume.

The problem which West Indians face is how to make this case against historically entrenched assumptions. Ideally, many West Indians would like to establish an identity as "West Indians," which combines pride in African ancestry, a focus on achievement, and conservative social values. Perhaps the most important impetus for the construction of this identity is the belief that whites view them positively. The darker side of the attempt to construct a West Indian identity is its tendency to invoke anti-African-American stereotypes as part of a process of social distancing. However, over time West Indians find that they bear no special immunity from antiblack sentiments. They are just as likely as African Americans to face racial discrimination. Upwardly mobile West Indians, especially, find such discrimination troublesome. Thus, on racially tinged issues— e.g., media representations of blacks— some West Indians gradually develop a panblack identity. Instead of ethnic separatism emphasizing their West Indianness, they highlight the commonalties which they share with African Americans. As much of the literature on West Indians has pointed out, this interplay between distancing from, and identification with, African Americans is one of the chief characteristics of these immigrants.

However, the complexities do not end there, since some West Indians take panblack sentiments a step further and advocate that some African

Americans, in order to achieve success, should emulate West Indian values and behaviors. This view does not seek to negate the structural reality of racial discrimination. Rather, it seeks to present pragmatic strategies for going around this barrier. This role modeling may be viewed as a synthesis of social distancing and panblack identification. Ultimately, though, role modeling needs to be treated with skepticism, since it bears a heavy load of qualifications.

Notes

1. Herbert Gans, "Symbolic Ethnicity: The Future of Ethnic Groups and Cultures in America," *Ethnic and Racial Studies*, Vol. 2, No. 1 (January 1979): 1–20; Richard Alba, "Italian Americans: A Century of Ethnic Change," in *Origins and Destinies*, ed. Silvia Pedraza and Ruben G. Rumbaut (Belmont: Wadsworth Publishing Company, 1996), pp. 172–181.
2. Stanley Lieberson, "A New Ethnic Group in the United States," in *Majority and Minority*, ed. Norman Yetman (Boston: Allyn and Bacon, 1991): 444–457.
3. See, for example, Joel Williamson, *New People: Miscegenation and Mulattoes in the United States* (New York: New York University Press, 1980); F. James Davis, *Who Is Black?: One Nation's Definition* (University Park: University of Pennsylvania Press, 1992); Maria P. P. Root, "The Multiracial Experience: Racial Borders as a Significant Frontier in Race Relations," in *The Multiracial Experience*, ed. Maria P. P. Root (Thousand Oaks: SAGE Publications, 1996), pp. xiii–xxviii.
4. Philip Kasinitz, *Caribbean New York* (Ithaca: Cornell University Press, 1992).
5. Gilbert Osofsky, *Harlem: The Making of a Ghetto* (New York: Harper and Row, 1966), pp. 131–135.
6. Keith S. Henry, "Caribbean Migrants in New York: The Passage from Political Quiescence to Radicalism," *Afro-Americans in New York Life and History*, Vol. II, No. 2. (1978): 29–41.
7. Ken Post, *Arise Ye Starvelings: The Jamaican Labour Rebellion of 1938 and Its Aftermath* (The Hague: Martinus Nijhoff, 1978).
8. Dawn Rich, "The Deculturation of Jamaica" (*The Daily Gleaner*, April 7, 1991). For a similar view of other West Indians, vis-à-vis Jamaicans, by the same writer, see "Getting the Best from the Best" (*The Weekly Gleaner*, May 15–21, 1997): 7.
9. James Traub, "You Can Get It if You Really Want It," *Harpers* (1982), pp. 27–31.
10. Thomas Kessner and Betty Boyd Caroli, *Today's Immigrants: Their Stories* (New York: Oxford University Press, 1982).
11. Mary Waters, "The Role of Lineage in Identity Formation Among Black Americans," *Qualitative Sociology*, Vol. 14, No. 1 (1991): 69.
12. The mismatch between social class and racial discrimination seems particularly important because of (1) the anger which it generates, (2) its potential for con-

vincing West Indians encountering it that race is of enduring significance, and (3) the resulting tendency to adopt panblack attitudes. However, this mismatch is only one possible explanation for why upwardly mobile West Indians might be more pro–African American. It is also likely that their higher educational levels have given them greater insight into the issue of race in the United States. Also, some of these respondents were long-term residents of the United States and, as noted before, this factor has exposed them to more episodes of discrimination.

13. Ashley's claims are controversial, since the existing data both support and undermine his argument. Some writers have shown that employers prefer immigrants—including West Indians—over native-born blacks. This preference stems from a perception that immigrants work harder and are more consistent and pliable than are African Americans. It also reflects racial discrimination, since it generalizes negative work attitudes toward all African Americans but, especially, to those from poor areas. See, for instance, William J. Wilson, "The American Underclass: Inner-city Ghettos and the Norms of Citizenship," The Godkin Lecture, delivered at John F. Kennedy School of Government, Harvard University (April 26, 1990); "Work," *New York Times Magazine* (August 18, 1996), pp. 26–52; Philip Kasinitz and Jan Rosenberg, "Why Enterprise Zones Will Not Work," *City Journal* (Autumn 1993): 63–69; Jonathan Kaufman, "Immigrants' Business Often Refuse to Hire Blacks in Inner City" (*Wall Street Journal*, June 6, 1995): A1; Roger Waldinger, *Still the Promised City?* (Cambridge: Harvard University Press, 1996). On the other hand, analysis comparing the economic fortunes of West Indians and African Americans has suggested that labor market discrimination in favor of West Indians does not take place. Susan Model has gone further, arguing that, "by 1980 any advantage that some Caribbean subgroups enjoyed over native-born blacks in the past has disappeared." See Suzanne Model, "Caribbean Immigrants: A Black Success Story?" *International Migration Review*, Volume 25 (Summer 1991): 273. See, also, Model, "West Indian Prosperity: Fact or Fiction?" *Social Problem*, Vol. 42, No. 4 (November 1995): 535–562; Nassu Daneshvary and R. Keith Schwer, "Black Immigrants in the U.S. Labor Market: An Earnings Analysis," *The Review of Black Political Economy* (June 29, 1994): 77–98; Mattijs Kalmijn, "The Socioeconomic Assimilation of Caribbean American Blacks," *Social Forces*, Vol. 74, No. 3 (March 1996): 911–930.

14. These sentiments reflect the fact that West Indian immigrants perceive the existence of a distinct status hierarchy where occupations are concerned. For instance, one respondent related how, upon migrating, he had taken a job as a used car salesman. In his estimate this represented a demotion from his occupation previous to migrating (policeman). Because of this perception, while a used car salesman, he spent a great deal of time worrying that he would encounter friends and be faced with justifying holding this particular job.

15. The Jamaicans' responses on this issue tended toward stereotyping and ethnocentrism.

16. See, for instance, Karen DeWitt, "Immigrants Look Outside New York for Better Life" (*New York Times*, September 4, 1990): B3; Gary Pierre-Pierre, "Heading to Florida, Nearer the Homeland" (*New York Times*, July 13, 1993): B3; Sarah

Vaughan, "Atlanta the Popular 'New Home' for Jamaicans" (*The Weekly Gleaner*, February 27–March 5, 1997): 20.

17. For example, see R.T. Smith, "The Family in the Caribbean," in *Caribbean Studies: A Symposium*, ed. Vera Rubin (Kingston: ISER, 1957), pp. 67–75.

18. The writer is acquainted with individuals, possessed of advanced degrees, who regularly visit Miami or New York for the purpose of buying in-demand commodities to be sold in Jamaica at a profit.

19. Stone, "Race and Economic Power in Jamaica," *Caribbean Review*, Vol. XVI (Spring 1988): 10–34.

20. Nancy Foner "Sex Roles and Sensibilities: Jamaican Women in New York and London," in *International Migration: The Female Experience*, ed. Rita James Simon and Caroline B. Brettel (Totawa: Rowman and Allanheld, 1986), pp. 133–151.

21. The premier black-oriented news radio station in New York City.

22. That is, news about the West Indies.

23. However, this was sometimes tempered by a view that Democrats tend to take black support for granted. Those who claimed to be Republicans gave this as one of their primary reasons for doing so. See, also, Deborah Sontag, "The Tired, the Poor, the Laundry" (*New York Times*, July 14, 1992): A11.

24. See the (*New York Times* (November 8, 1989): B8; (November 9, 1989): B10; *New York Newsday* (November 8, 1989): 29.

25. One is, here, referring to the controversial notion of the "underclass."

26. See, for instance, Eric Williams, *From Columbus to Castro* (New York: Vintage Books, 1970); Ivaar Oxaal, *Race and Revolutionary Consciousness: An Existential Report on the 1970 Black Power Revolt in Trinidad* (London: Schenkman Publishing Company, Inc., 1971); Selwyn D. Ryan, *Race and Nationalism in Trinidad and Tobago* (Toronto: University of Toronto Press, 1972); Rupert Lewis, "Black Nationalism in Jamaica in Recent Years," in *Essays on Power and Change in Jamaica*, ed. Carl Stone and Aggrey Brown (Kingston: Jamaica Publishing House, 1977), pp. 65–71; Obika Gray, *Radicalism and Social Change in Jamaica, 1960–1972* (Knoxville: University of Tennessee Press, 1991).

27. See, for instance, Lena Williams, "In Looks, a Sense of Racial Unity" (*New York Times*, May 9, 1990): C1; Anita M. Samuels, "Just Locks" (*New York Times*, January 23, 1994): C1.

28. Sebastian Clarke, *Jah Music* (London: Heinemann Educational Books, Ltd., 1981); Timothy White, *Catch a Fire* (London: Corgi Books, 1983).

29. See, for instance, Kathryn Tidrick, "Need for Achievement, Social Class, and Intention to Emigrate in Jamaican Students," *Social and Economic Studies*, Vol. 20, No. 1 (March 1971): 52–60.

30. Most West Indians speak a combination of standard English and patois, with the relative emphasis placed on either depending on social class and context (i.e., formal versus informal gatherings). Standard English, because of its association with higher education, is viewed as the ideal, while patois is often associated with the poor and uneducated. In reality, these sharp distinctions are blurred, since educated West Indians often slip into speaking patois in informal situations (e.g., in the home). Journalistic accounts indicate that, in recent years, larger numbers of immigrant children have been having trouble bridging the gap be-

tween standard English and patois. This has led to calls, in some quarters, for special education classes for these children. See Deborah Sontag, "Caribbean Pupils' English Seem Barrier, not Bridge" (*New York Times*, November 28, 1992): A1; J. A. Irish and E. B. Baisden, "Carib Students Face Crisis in NYC Public Schools," *Caribbean Life* (June 1991): 3.

C H A P T E R
5

Identity in a Changing Society

There can be little doubt that conceptions of race and ethnicity in America, always problematic, are poised to become even more so in the immediate future. Census Bureau estimates of population growth imply significant changes in the relative proportions of the various groups that compose the American population. Immigration and differential fertility rates are the driving forces behind these changes. Table 5.1 illustrates for five groups, the population shifts that could occur over the next fifty years. Clearly, minority groups—especially Hispanics and Asians—are on the rise, while the white population is declining. On a smaller scale, in cities, these population shifts are already evident. Several of the larger cities that have traditionally acted as magnets for immigrants have become "majority minority" cities, in the sense that, combined, their minority populations exceed their white populations. In the city of Los Angeles, for instance, Hispanics account for 40 percent, Asians approximately 10 percent, and blacks, 14 percent of the population. Similarly, census data show that blacks, Hispanics, and Asians account for approximately 60 percent of New York City's population; and the impact of the Hispanic population on Miami is well known.[1] These population changes portend not only a shift in relative proportions away from whites to various minority groups but also a shift among these groups. Thus, the census projects that by early in the next century, Hispanics will have surpassed blacks to become the largest minority group in the country (see Table 5.1).[2] This is already the case in Los Angeles and Miami, and other cities also demonstrate these relative shifts among minority groups. For instance, at 29 percent, the Asian population of San Francisco is almost three times the size of the black population. Significant population shifts are also occurring in smaller cities and, in fact, may show up even more clearly because of their smaller size. Notable examples would include the rapid growth of the Hmong population in Wausau, Wisconsin, and of the Asian population, in general, in the suburbs of Washington, D.C.[3]

Overall, these changes make the population more heterogeneous,

TABLE 5.1 Population Projections, 2000–2050, by Percentage of Population

	White	Black	N.Am	Asian	Hispanic
Low[a]					
2000	82.2	12.8	0.9	4.1	10.9
2010	80.7	13.3	0.9	5.0	12.5
2020	79.4	13.7	1.0	5.9	14.2
2030	78.0	14.1	1.0	6.9	16.1
2040	76.5	14.4	1.1	8.0	18.1
2050	75.0	14.7	1.2	9.1	20.2
Mid[b]					
2000	81.9	12.8	0.8	4.4	11.3
2010	80.0	13.4	0.8	5.7	13.5
2020	78.2	13.9	0.8	7.0	15.7
2030	76.4	14.5	0.9	8.1	17.9
2040	74.6	15.1	0.9	9.3	20.2
2050	72.8	15.7	1.0	10.3	22.5
High[c]					
2000	81.7	12.8	0.8	4.7	11.6
2010	79.4	13.4	0.9	6.3	14.2
2020	77.4	13.9	0.9	7.8	16.8
2030	75.7	14.4	0.9	9.1	19.4
2040	74.0	14.8	0.9	10.2	22.0
2050	72.5	15.3	1.0	11.3	24.6

Source: Statistical Abstract of the United States, 1995, Table 18; Original Source, Bureau of the Census.

[a]Lowest Series: net immigration = 350,000.
[b]Middle Series: net immigration = 880,000.
[c]Highest Series: net immigration = 1,370,000.

thereby aggravating the difficulties inherent in demarcating racial and ethnic identity. One good indicator of these difficulties is the inconsistencies present in census categories. These categories mix together categories that are defined using genetic criteria such as ancestry and skin color (i.e., "blacks") and categories that are defined on the basis of culture (e.g., "Hispanics"). Particular nationalities (e.g., Mexicans and Asian Indians) have been shifted between various categories, and categories, themselves, always subject to political pressure, have fluctuated. Hence, over the past 100 years, the number of racial and ethnic categories in the census have fluctuated from five to sixteen.[4] The debate over whether to add a "mixed-race" category to the 2000 census illustrates that the process of categorizing individuals is highly political and ongoing.[5]

■ WEST INDIANS' IDENTITY OPTIONS

Shifts in the composition of the overall population cannot help but affect subpopulations and blacks are no exception. In areas which have seen a large influx of immigrant blacks, such immigrants constitute a growing portion of the black population. New York City, of course, is the primary example of this growth, since, in that city, foreign blacks—chiefly West Indians—make up 25 percent of the black population. The figure is even higher in individual boroughs. For instance, census data indicate that approximately 32 percent of Brooklyn's black population is foreign-born. More problematic than these facts is the question of whether foreign-born blacks, simply by virtue of possessing African ancestry, are part of the larger "black community." As has been shown for West Indians, the issue of identity is difficult. To summarize: most of these immigrants are of African ancestry and hail from societies in which such individuals find themselves to be a majority of the population. Unlike the United States, these societies do not possess a rule of hypodescent assigning individuals into neat compartments of "black" and "white." Instead, racial categories have been blurred. To complicate matters, though West Indian societies have denigrated African ancestry, such attitudes have not been all-encompassing. Achievement—notably higher education and having a prestigious occupation—has long been as—if not more—important in determining the individual West Indian's place in the social hierarchy. The postindependence period of West Indian history (since 1962) has strengthened these tendencies. Yet, it remains true that a correlation exists—especially on the extremes—between wealth and poverty, on the one hand, and lightness and darkness of skin on the other. Some commentators have suggested that because of this correlation, West Indian societies have developed ideologies which posit the nonimportance of ancestry and exalted, instead, neutral ideals of nationhood. Out of all these contradictions have emerged a mindset among many West Indians which downplays ascription and emphasizes achievement. The self-selectivity of the immigrant experience only acts to further this tendency.

In the United States, West Indians' orientation toward achievement becomes an issue, because stereotypes of individuals of African ancestry often imply—erroneously—a contradiction between achievement and such ancestry. There is also the important fact that cultural differences exist between West Indians and African Americans. For West Indians, these issues make "blackness" a problem. The fact that blackness does not mean the same thing in the West Indies and the United States faces West Indians with the crucial question of identity. Two key points become important here: (1) American society exerts tremendous pressure on all individuals of African ancestry to submit to stereotyped views of "blackness"; and (2) West Indians wish to carve out a separate and distinct identity to counteract antiblack stereotypes and to further their goals of achievement. The question which has always faced West Indians and which will become increasingly pressing is which path they will take. At least three possible options exist. They could be forced by societal pressures to identify as "black" (i.e., in the sense of the term which involves the traditional unflattering stereotypes). They could attempt to establish a distinct identity as "West Indians"; or, third, they could continue their traditional pattern of identifying with African Americans on some issues but distancing from them (i.e., emphasizing their "West Indianness") on others. In fact, posing the issue of identity in the form of such seemingly clear-cut options oversimplifies matters, since West Indians will likely exhibit all of these patterns.[6]

The theory of the social construction of identity helps illustrate why a complex pattern of identity formation, rather than discrete identity options, should be the norm for West Indians. The theory posits that *both* external and internal forces are important in the process of identity formation. This interaction necessarily complicates issues of identity construction. In this process, external agencies seek to impose particular definitions of situations on individuals but these individuals do not automatically acquiesce to such attempts. Instead, they seek to establish their own definitions of situations. For instance, as shown previously, racial discrimination against West Indians in public places can be interpreted as an attempt to impose, on them, widely held stereotypes about blacks, in general. The intended message of such discrimination is that blacks are troublemakers, criminals, or otherwise morally culpable. With respect to residential discrimination, the intended goal is to curtail these assumed failings by excluding blacks from particular areas. On the other hand, West Indians and African Americans reject these stereotypes, regarding them as being unwarranted generalizations. From their perspective, blacks do not differ, inherently, from other groups in their potential for good or evil. The identity construction process for blacks involves, in given situations, a negotiation between these external and internal perspectives on reality.[7] This is not to imply, however, an equal struggle between the two perspectives. Often, discriminators possess greater power than their intended targets to impose particular identities.

These facts bear particular relevance to the desire exhibited by West Indians to carve out a distinct identity apart from the stereotyped "black" identity. Since social construction theory predicts the likelihood of greater power by outsiders to define identity, it is likely that West Indians will encounter great difficulty in their quest. The empirical evidence presented in chapter 3 shows that this is in fact the case, especially in public places. In such situations West Indians—especially males—are often assumed to have criminal intentions and they can do little to counteract such perceptions. Since, in this sense, they share the fate of many African Americans, it could be said that they are forced by the society to become "black." And, as noted previously, over time, this sense of shared fate pushes some West Indians to embrace a panblack identity.

Opting for a "West Indian" Identity

Yet, West Indians' attachment to their own cultures and anger at having stereotypes foisted on them should also push some to continue the carving out of a distinct identity. Those who are so inclined could find themselves aided by the growth in the size of the West Indian population. In some areas—again, preeminently New York City—this population is now large enough to allow West Indians, if they wish, to spend significant portions of their time interacting primarily with coethnics. An example, from my research, of this inward orientation was Drake, a thirty-eight-year-old immigrant, who explained how he had constructed his whole world such that it primarily involved just this sort of interaction. He had married an African-American woman but, consistent with the stereotypes that were discussed in the last chapter, argued that the marriage worked well because she had become more West Indian than African American. After work—especially on weekends—he headed for the homes of West Indian friends or to clubs frequented by West Indians. At these haunts, activities revolved around playing dominoes, cards, or—especially in his case—music. He played an instrument in a local reggae band and spent much time practicing with the other band members in their homes or in a local recording studio. Reviewing all of this he posed the rhetorical question: if he could enjoy most of the trappings of Jamaica in New York City, and since most of his close relatives and friends were living there, why did he need to go back to Jamaica? In fact he had not visited the island in twenty years. However, he had not completely assimilated into American life and very much saw himself as part of a West Indian, as opposed to an African-American or a white, community. This reflected itself in the fact that even after twenty years of residence he was still a permanent resident. Although Jamaicans can hold dual citizenship, his discussion of his life in America implied that he saw this legal status as preserving a link with Jamaica. He might not go back often but neither had he crossed the psychological and legal rubicon into citizenship. Thus, he reported being rather offended when, on his last trip out of the country, a customs officer advised him to become a citizen, since he had lived in the country for such a long time.

Until recent changes in the country's immigration laws, the issue of West Indian immigrants' legal status has been one of the clearest indicators of the determination of some to carve out a distinct West Indian identity. Although, as noted, many West Indians are eligible for dual citizenship, judging from my interviews with the Jamaicans, it would appear that many of them do not know this.[8] Instead, they assume that becoming American citizens means dropping their previous citizenship. The Jamaicans I interviewed did not view this positively. For instance, data on 1990 naturalization rates underscore this reluctance.[9] Although, at 38.3 percent, Jamaican immigrants' rate of naturalization did not differ significantly from the average for all immigrant groups (40.5 percent),[10] the length of time it had taken the Jamaicans whom I interviewed to naturalize indicates that they have been in no hurry to do so. Thirty-five percent of the Jamaicans who were eligible for citizenship had naturalized. However, they had taken an average of twelve years[11] to do so once they had waited the initial five years to become eligible. Thus, many had waited at least seventeen years to become citizens. Nine of the Jamaicans exceeded this average, with one individual residing in the country a total of thirty-eight years before naturalizing. Among noncitizens, the mean length of residence in the United States was seven years,[12] but 35 percent of the Jamaicans had lived here longer. At least nine individuals had resided in America more than twenty years.

The comments the Jamaicans made with respect to becoming citizens further underscored their reluctance, and often illustrated the link they made between seeking citizenship and seemingly acquiescing to pejorative views of blacks.[13] The responses of a thirty-four-year-old college student, Bryce, were typical. A junior accountant in a department of government in Jamaica, he left in 1979 because of widespread political violence and a feeling that he was not achieving economic success. Although academically successful, and in America for the express purpose of improving his economic situation, he was not happy. The cause was a pervasive sense of disillusionment that had been brought on by experiences of racial discrimination. This emerged at the very beginning of the interview when, unprompted, he announced that he intended to return to Jamaica. Asked how he viewed himself after ten years of residence in America, he replied:

> A Jamaican, first and foremost; a black person—and I have grown more and more conscious of that everyday: The society makes you do that—a struggling black person; one who aims to achieve something; take a little back from the people who took from us. . . . I didn't experience racism [in Jamaica] as I am experiencing it now. And the more I talk to these people in this part of the world, [the more] I feel that . . . it's something I can do without. . . . I want to go back to Jamaica because Jamaica is my home. I also want to go back to Jamaica because I know I will feel welcome there. . . . My wife applied for citizenship and I said to her . . . because we talk a lot about the pressures that the other groups lay on blacks: "You are so conscious of what is happening; it seems to me that . . . by wanting citizenship

you are actually telling them that I am willing to succumb to all the non-sense that you are giving me." I mean, it's her decision.

Other Jamaicans offered a similar point of view. Neil, a social worker, opined:

> Like a lot of Jamaicans I am not giving up my Jamaican citizenship. I might change my Jamaican citizenship if I was in Africa, but not America. I don't think I will become an American. . . . I like American people, but I don't intend to assimilate American culture. And there are a lot of Jamaicans who are like that who have not made an articulate, conscious decision like I have. . . . In terms of the objective state of their lives—having been here for the last thirty years—they have not assimilated.[14]

Mitchell, a financial consultant, stated:

> I would have to say I consider myself a black person—neither Jamaican nor American. I think my allegiance will always be to Jamaica because the sys-tem here is one that . . . even though I have become a citizen, I really don't feel a part of the system. Because, of course, being black, you . . . are re-ally a third class citizen. I became a citizen out of convenience.

Of course, some Jamaicans also took a positive view of citizenship, having concluded that being citizens would strengthen West Indians' political in-fluence. As one of these individuals put it:

> It doesn't make sense paying taxes here and you don't have a say in elect-ing your officials. I try to get as many West Indians as possible to become citizens that they can vote . . . that when the Jamaican government is being castigated in the media, that we can have a say; we can write to our con-gressperson and say: "Hey, we don't like this. It has got to stop."

The Anti-Terrorism and Effective Death Penalty Act, the Personal Responsibility and Work Opportunity Reconciliation Act (the Welfare Act), and the Illegal Immigration Reform and Immigrant Responsibility Act, all passed in 1996, have given procitizenship sentiments a strong boost. Indeed, these acts could reverse West Indians' traditional reluctance to become cit-izens, because of fear that the severe provisions in these acts could put an abrupt end to their quest for the "American dream." For instance, the Anti-Terrorism and Effective Death Penalty Act allows for the permanent de-portation of legal immigrants who have committed crimes, even if they have served sentences, have lived in the United States many years, and have fam-ily in the country. Most worrisome for immigrants is the retroactive nature of this act, the fact that it makes even minor crimes grounds for deporta-tion, and the hard line which the Immigration and Naturalization Service has adopted in enforcing it. Many immigrants first became aware of the act when, having gone away on vacation, they found themselves detained upon trying to reenter the country. A second example of the severity of the new legislation is that the Welfare Act now requires those sponsoring immigrants to have incomes equal to 125 percent of the poverty level. This requirement will tend to make the reunification of families more difficult; and in a third example of severity: the Illegal Immigration Reform and Immigrant Responsibility Act allows for bars on entry into the country, from three to ten years, depending on how long visiting aliens have overstayed their welcome.[15] The frequent stories appearing in the ethnic press denouncing these laws and calling on West Indians to protect themselves by becoming citizens is one measure of the concern that the new legislation has created.[16]

Continuing a Tradition: Distancing and Identification

The likelihood that West Indian immigrants will increasingly opt for citizenship over permanent resident status will probably not spell an end to their attempts to carve out, for themselves, a distinct identity. However, in the end it seems unlikely that they will be able to establish a firm identity that is completely separate from the African-American population. In all likelihood, most West Indian immigrants will continue their traditional pattern of distancing from African Americans in some social spheres but coalescing with them in others. The longevity of this pattern derives from the enduring cross-pressures that operate on West Indians, notably: to completely assimilate into the African-American population is to accept all of the negative stereotypes that the society heaps upon that population; but West Indians cannot completely extricate themselves from American society's presuppositions about, and tendency to lump together, individuals of African ancestry.

This is not to argue, however, that Americans' views of race will remain static. Population shifts appear to be having contradictory effects on the society. On the one hand, the population is undoubtedly becoming more diverse as larger numbers of immigrants seek to opt out of the society's well-worn "black"/"white" scheme for classifying races. Hispanics, for instance, are increasingly identifying themselves as "Other" when required to state identity. In the 1970 census, 93 percent of individuals of Hispanic origin identified themselves as "white," 5 percent as "black," and only 1 percent as "Other." The remaining 2 percent listed other specific choices. However, by 1980, the percentage identifying themselves as "white" had fallen to 56 percent and the percentage as "black" to 3 percent. In contrast, a full 40 percent placed themselves in the "Other" category.[17] Similarly, Rodriquez and Cordero-Guzman found in a 1989 study of Puerto Ricans that when posed with an open-ended question requesting identity, respondents offered eleven different categories. The majority (58 percent) saw themselves as belonging to an "Other" category. Similarly 56 percent placed themselves in such a category when forced to choose between "Black," "White," or "Other."[18]

While this is happening, other minorities—including some Hispanics—are, through intermarriage, reinforcing the notion of a racial dichotomy. In an analysis of intermarriage rates by decade, Farley has compared such marriages, by gender for several native-born groups. In the decade 1970 to 1980, 26 percent of Hispanic husbands married white wives and this increased to 33 percent in the following decade. Asians and Native Americans displayed even higher rates. In the case of the former, the 1970s saw approximately 40 percent of Asian husbands marrying white wives and this figure remained the same in the 1980s. In the 1970s, 43 percent of Native American husbands married white wives and this figure increased to 55 percent in the 1980s. Twenty-nine percent of Hispanic women in the 1970s and 39 percent in the 1980s married white husbands. The figures for Native American women were 50 percent in the 1970s and 57 percent in the 1980s. Asian women displayed the highest rates of all: 72 percent of Asian women married white husbands in the 1970s and 70 percent did so in the 1980s. While black/white rates of intermarriage are rising,[19] overall, they occur at much lower levels than is the case for other groups. For instance, in the 1970s, approximately 4 percent of black husbands married white wives. In the next decade, this figure increased to approximately 5 percent. The figures for black women were even lower: In the 1970s, 1 percent of black women married white husbands and this increased to 2 percent in the following decade.

These data imply that, in the future, a dichotomous racial classification will coexist with a diversifying of the society. However, that dichotomous system will be more accurately described as "black"/"nonblack," rather than "black"/"white."[20] In any case blacks seem likely to remain stigmatized in significant ways. A corollary to this is that all individuals of African ancestry will likely continue to experience strong pressure to coalesce. This, and West Indians' growing sense of ethnicity, should ensure the continuation of cross-pressures and contradictory West Indian behavior on questions of identity.

■ THE SECOND AND LATER GENERATIONS

The complex behaviors that West Indian immigrants demonstrate with respect to issues of identity show up just as clearly among second generation West Indians. As is the case with immigrants, the latter exhibit a spectrum of identities, ranging from a sense of oneness with African Americans to attempts to preserve an identity that is viewed as being distinctly West Indian.

However, as sociologist Mary Waters has pointed out, since they have been born in the United States, the key question faced by second generation West Indians is the extent to which this variation will continue to remain the case. Waters has argued that at least three identity options characterize these West Indians and that these stem from the West Indians' reactions to the issue of race, their social class, length of residence in the United States, social networks, and family structure. Focusing specifically on a sample of eighty-three adolescent second-generation West Indians, she shows that some of these West Indians have chosen a black American identity, others an ethnic identity which emphasizes their "West Indianness," while a third group identifies with an "immigrant" identity.[21]

The primary characteristic of second-generation West Indians who choose a black American identity is a sense of pessimism, stemming from the perception that racism is overpowering.[22] These West Indians argue that regardless of their efforts, they are unlikely to overcome the stereotypes foisted on those of African ancestry. Consequently, they tend to develop an adversarial stance toward society—especially whites. Perhaps the most important manifestation of this attitude is a tendency to define performing well in school as "acting white." The other primary characteristic of these West Indians is close identification with the culture of poor African Americans, with whom they routinely interact. Second-generation West Indians who choose an ethnic identity tend to display opposite characteristics from the first group. They perceive racism as being an important aspect of American society. However, they also believe that it can be overcome with study and hard work and that these behaviors characterize people of West Indian descent. Thus, they consciously cultivate traits that they perceive as being West Indian—for instance, exaggerating their accent; or, if they do not have one, attempting to learn one. A corollary to these attitudes and behaviors is a tendency to stereotype African Americans as overplaying race and not trying hard enough to boost themselves. Second-generation West Indians who exhibit an "immigrant" identity are so closely aligned with West Indian social networks that the question of whether they should be West Indian or African American does not even arise. Their orientation is so West Indian that they often express a desire to return there to live. However, unlike West Indian "ethnics," those with an "immigrant" identity tend to express neutral or positive attitudes toward African Americans. Waters implies that the key difference between these two groups of West Indians is that the "immigrant"-identified are very secure in their sense of "West Indianness" and do not feel threatened by African Americans. Not feeling a need to choose between being "black American" or "West Indian," they adopt a relaxed attitude toward the issue of identity.

As might be expected, these three identity options play out against a background of immigrant parents who stress the importance and desirability of West Indian norms and values. Indeed, a key point made by Waters is that the parents of second-generation West Indians all push the same message. The difference, with respect to their children, lies not in what they hear from their parents but, rather, in how they interpret this message. Here, other factors come into play. Children who choose a black identity tend to be poor, attend segregated, ill-equipped schools, and socialize with peers who share the same social circumstances. With the exception of teachers, they rarely interact with whites and when they do this interaction tends to occur in settings which reinforce, in their minds, the message that blacks are "bad." Hence, for these children of immigrants, such routine encounters as being followed in stores or having women protect their handbags upon the approach of these West Indians take on devastating impact. They tend to have little faith in the "American dream," reasoning that between their grim social circumstances and racial discrimination they are better off identifying with their African-American peers who seem to share the same fate.[23] This situation is often made worse by the fact that these children often come from single-parent families and, in many instances, rejoined the parent in the United States long after the parent had migrated. In effect, the attitudes of these children are one of the costs of the typical West Indian pattern of migration in which a parent or parents migrate and children are left with relatives.[24] Waters argues that this type of family structure is "weak" in the sense that though parents attempt to push their values onto their children, they cannot do so effectively because of the parents' work schedule and poor social networks. These realities result in a situation in which peers wield relatively more influence over children than do parents.[25]

Waters argues that middle class West Indian parents more effectively pass on their norms and values to their children than do their less well off counterparts. Among other things, this means much more optimism regarding the possibilities for attaining upward mobility in America. Not surprisingly, an important structural variable intertwines with these values: The children of these parents are often to be found attending better—e.g., magnet and private—schools. These parents—like poorer West Indians whose children disagree with their assessments—also pass on negative views regarding African Americans. A reflection of this, from the interviews I conducted, was the college student, Ron, whose parents had, in Jamaica, occupied high level positions in that island's civil service. After migrating to this country, they tried assiduously to inculcate, in him, what they considered to be "proper" norms and values. Thus, Ron reported, for instance, that his mother expressed anger if he used terms which she considered to be slang—e.g., "ain't." She insisted that Ron speak only standard English. Also, if he behaved in ways she considered "flashy"—e.g., dressing in particular fashions—she accused him of becoming "American."[26] Judging from Ron's account, his parents exercised a great deal of influence over him. Among other things, this meant that they pushed him to obtain as much education as he could and to focus on being upwardly mobile. It also meant that he tended to put a certain amount of distance between himself and the African-American students at his college.[27]

Dewey, a fifty-eight-year-old civil servant, typified the attitudes of parents such as Ron's. In my interview with him, he stressed the importance he placed on maintaining what he considered to be West Indian norms and values—i.e., education, hard work, and discipline. The result of holding these norms and values, he argued, was greater material success for West Indians; and as proof of this he offered up the very large house in the exclusive section of New York City in which he lived. Also, he stressed that several similar houses on his block were owned by West Indians. Dewey also pointed to his successful son (employed in financial services), noting that early-on, he had chided his son's high school teachers for praising the son when he got average grades. Dewey interpreted this as racist, in that the teachers held low expectations of the son because of his skin color.[28] Instead, he pushed his son to excel in his studies, and, for Dewey, a vital part of this process was a conscious stressing of the nonfunctionality of assimilating American culture. Or to put it another way, Dewey strove to inculcate, in his son, West Indian culture. As he stated:

> Once you assimilate you die . . . because all of the values that you were brought up with, you'll put it aside and what [will you] resort to: violence, anarchy, chaos, [and] thievery because this is what this country is made up of. . . . There are certain values that should not be compromised, for instance, the family. The family is the backbone of the society and when, in any society, the family structure deteriorates, you are going to find crime because the children are being born without any figurehead. . . . They just grow up with no manners, no etiquette. They never say "thanks" [or] "excuse me." They are not civil. They are like wild animals.[29]

Waters views the third identity option—the "immigrant" identity—as characterizing young people who are so West Indian-oriented that they evince little concern about American notions of what blacks should be. However, because American society places intense pressure on individuals of African ancestry to fit into a dichotomous "black"/"white" scheme, she also views this identity as being inherently unstable. As these individuals live in the United States for longer periods of time, they will tend to move to one of the other two identities. This behavior points to the fluidity of identity and raises the important question of how third and later generations of West Indian–descended children will identify. Past the third generation, it could be argued that making guesses becomes hazardous. However, the third generation is close enough to the second to suppose that some of the same processes influencing the latter should also influence the former.

With respect to the second generation, Waters has identified the reaction to race as the single most important factor determining identity. If the argument that societal perceptions of racial dichotomy—albeit modified—will continue into the future is valid, then race should remain as important to the third generation as it is to the second. Third-generation West Indian–descended individuals should feel as much, if not more, pressure to assimilate into the African-American population. However, it is not a foregone conclusion that a sense of West Indian ethnicity will disappear. Since many West Indians are convinced that there are aspects of their culture worth preserving, it is conceivable that even into the third generation, some West Indian–descended individuals may make the attempt to do so. This should be true as long as the perception of an economic advantage to identifying as "West Indians" exists. As has been shown in the case of the second generation, this perception probably means that the more affluent will exert greater effort to maintain a distinctive identity. The concept of transnational identity, advanced by writers such as Sutton and Basch, Schiller, and Blanc, becomes important here.[30] This concept posits that economic and social (and sometimes political)[31] bonds among West Indians remain strong across national boundaries because these individuals continuously interact. For instance, a Barbadian immigrant in Brooklyn quite likely, on a regular basis, remits a portion of his or her income to relatives on that island. Moreover, the New Yorker probably visits the island frequently and, in turn, quite likely receives frequent visits from relatives on the island. In fact, these transnational networks are sometimes even wider than this: the writer knows of Jamaicans who circulate between that island, the United States, and Britain. It is possible that such networks, with their emphasis on extended kin, could help to maintain West Indian ethnicity not only among the first and second generations but even among the third.

■ CONCLUSION

Racial and ethnic identity is becoming increasingly problematic as American society becomes more heterogeneous. This observation is also true of the black population in locations that have seen a large influx of foreign blacks, which, in practical terms, means West Indians. The presence of these immigrants has long provoked problems of identity. These problems have stemmed from West Indians' similar ancestry to African Americans, but origin in societies in which they form demographic and political majorities. These facts and the peculiar history of West Indians have combined with self-selectivity in immigration to cause West Indians to focus tightly on achievement. In the United States, this focus has become noteworthy because of antiblack stereotypes which posit a contradiction between African ancestry and achievement. These stereotypes also tend to lump together all people of African ancestry. West Indian immigrants face the choice of acquiescing to these social tendencies, disavowing them and establishing a distinct "West Indian" identity, or alternating between these two options. In practice, however, West Indian immigrants exhibit behaviors that straddle the range of identity options. Traditionally, the third option—that of alternating between social distancing from and identification with African Americans—has been the modal West Indian response to African Americans. Because of the unpalatable nature of acquiescing to antiblack stereotypes and structural constraints on establishing a completely autonomous West Indian identity, this third option is likely to remain West Indians' typical response to African Americans. Research on second-generation West Indians shows that this generation also faces what seems to be discrete identity options. However, the research also shows that identity is fluid and that one type of identity option can change into another. Hence the situation with identity is also complex for the second generation. Beyond this generation, the situation becomes more speculative. However, the third generation should face some of the same dynamics as the second; only with greater pressures to assimilation into the African-American population and the possibility—though less certain—of maintaining a vestige of West Indian identity.

Notes

1. See, for instance, Alejandro Portes and Alex Stepick, *City on the Edge* (Berkeley: University of California Press, 1993).
2. See, also, Felicity Barringer, "Census Shows Profound Change in Racial Makeup of the Nation," (*New York Times*, March 11, 1991): A1; "Demographic State of the Nation: 1997" (Washington, D.C.: U.S. Department of Commerce, March 1997).
3. On the Hmong, see Roy Beck, "The Ordeal of Immigration in Wausau," *The Atlantic Monthly* (April, 1994): 84–97; Sanford Ungar, *Fresh Blood* (Simon and Schuster, 1995).
4. See Sharon Lee, "U.S. Census Racial Classifications: 1890–1990," *Ethnic and Racial Studies,* Vol. 16, No. 1 (January, 1993): 75–94; Reynolds Farley, "Questions About Race, Spanish-Origin and Ancestry: Controversial Issues for the Statistical System." Paper presented at the "Beyond Black and White" Conference, Washington, D.C., February 12, 1996.
5. See, for instance, U.S. Census Bureau, "Results of the 1996 Race and Ethnic Targeted Test" (May 1997); Amitai Etzioni, "Let's Not Be Boxed In by Color" (*Washington Post,* June 8, 1997): C3; Joseph E. Lwery, "Counting by Race Adds Up to Progress" (*Washington Post,* June 8, 1997): C3.
6. See Mary Waters, "Ethnic and Racial Identities of Second-Generation Black Immigrants in New York City," *International Migration Review,* Vol. xxviii, No. 4 (1994): 795–820.

7. See, for instance, Joe Feagin and Melvin P. Sykes, *Living with Racism* (Boston: Beacon Press, 1994).

8. For instance, an article ("Target: 10,000 New Caribbean-American U.S. Citizens by December") in the June 16–22, 1995 (p. 21) issue of the *Jamaican Weekly Gleaner* described efforts being made by several West Indian organizations (e.g., the Caribbean Women's Health Association and the Caribbean American Family Services, Inc.) to increase naturalization and voting among West Indians. Speaking to these immigrants' fears of giving up their citizenship, the article noted that a necessary first step was to make West Indians aware of the existence of dual citizenship.

9. More recent naturalization data do not necessarily reflect traditional West Indian attitudes towards bcoming citizens. Instead, these data would tend to reflect the current fear, among West Indians, of restrictive new immigration legislation.

10. Calculated from the 1990 census, The foreign-born.

11. The mean was 11.59 years; median = 11.

12. The mean was 7.39; median = 5.

13. See Sarah Vaughan, "Taking the Vow of Citizenship" (*The Weekly Gleaner*, April 17–23, 1997): 19.

14. This overstates the case, somewhat, since a certain amount of assimilation is bound to occur with long years of residence in any country. What Neil meant was that many West Indian immigrants resist assimilation because they believe that the society intends for them, in this process, to embrace damaging stereotypes regarding blacks.

15. See Lena Williams, "Aimed at Terrorists, Law Hits Legal Immigrants" (*New York Times*, July 17, 1996): A1; INS, "Alien Eligibility for and Access to Public Benefits" (January 31, 1997); "Illegal Immigration Reform and Immigrant Responsibility Act of 1996: Summary" (March 30, 1997), "INS Details Major Provisions of New Immigration Law" (March 30, 1997); Illegal Immigration Reform and Immigrant Responsibility Act, sec. 237 (2) (1996).

16. The October 11–17, 1996 edition of *The Weekly Gleaner*, alone, contained four articles dealing with the new immigration legislation. Other issues of the paper have carried blaring headlines denouncing the legislation. For instance, the September 6–12, 1996 edition carried the following headline (in red block letters): "Trapped in the United States." Even before the new immigration legislation, activists in the community had begun to call for increased naturalization rates among West Indians as a way of boosting the political influence of the group as a whole. The June 16–22, 1995 *Jamaican Weekly Gleaner* article referred to above is an example of this. A second example comes from a June 30–July 6, 1995 (p. 19) article in the same paper entitled, "Caribbean Immigrants Defining Their Future." This blunt article argued that by targeting immigration, some American politicians were deliberately undermining the interests of West Indians. However, the community, itself, was largely to blame for its woes, since West Indians have "existed" rather than "lived" in the United States. They "raise their families, pay taxes and make no demands on the elected officials. Because they do not vote in sufficient numbers, they do not command attention." The article suggested that West Indians need to be forced out of their "comfort zones" to organize for greater political representation. See, also,

Lester Hinds, "New Laws Un-American," *The Weekly Gleaner* (April 10–16, 1997): 1; Vaughan, "Taking the Vow of Citizenship"; Garry Pierre-Pierre, "West Indians Adding Clout at Ballot Box" (*New York Times*, September 6, 1993): B1; "Citizens: Rev. Jesse Jackson Urges Caribbean-Americans to Become Citizens and Help Elect Politicians with Greater Interest in Region" (*New York Carib News*, September 18, 1990): 1.

17. Andrew Hacker, *U.S.: A Statistical Portrait of the American People* (New York: The Viking Press, 1983).

18. Clara Rodriquez and Hector Cordero-Guzman, "Placing Race in Context," *Ethnic and Racial Studies*, Vol. 15, No. 4 (1992): 523–541; see, also, Clara Rodriquez, "Challenging Racial Hegemony: Puerto Ricans in the United States," in *Race*, ed. Steven Gregory and Roger Sanjek (New Brunswick: Rutgers University Press, 1994).

19. See, for instance, Isabel Wilkerson, "Black-White Marriages Rise, but Couples Still Face Scorn" (*New York Times*, December 2, 1991): A1; Farley, "Questions About Race, Spanish-Origin and Ancestry: Controversial Issues for the Statistical System"; *Statistical Abstract of the United States: 1995* (Washington, D.C.: The Reference Press, Inc., 1995), Table 61.

20. See, for example, Charles Moskos and John Sibley Butler, *All That We Can Be* (New York: Basic Books, 1996), p. 139.

21. Mary Waters, "Ethnic and Racial Identities of Second-Generation Black Immigrants in New York City," *International Migration Review*, Vol. xxviii, No. 4 (1994): 795–820. Waters's sample consisted of eighty-three second-generation Anglophone and Haitian Americans, seventy-two first-generation immigrants, twenty-seven whites, and thirty African Americans. She drew the immigrants and the African Americans (unskilled workers) from a food service company in Manhattan and from among middle class school teachers. She drew the second-generation sample from four sites to reflect their social class: an inner-city public high school, an inner-city Catholic parochial school, from among a "street-based" sample of students who had dropped out of school, and from students attending magnet schools and colleges.

22. That is, antiblack prejudice and discrimination.

23. For a similar account see chapter 7 of Thomas Kessner and Betty Boyd Caroli's, *Today's Immigrants: Their Stories* (New York: Oxford University Press, 1982).

24. Recall the discussion of barrel children in chapter 2. The implication of Waters's argument is that the problems experienced by barrel children do not end when they leave the West Indies to join their parents. Instead, these problems of negative self-esteem can follow them and make for patterns of downward mobility in the United States.

25. Based on his many years of interaction with West Indians from many different social backgrounds, this writer would say that Waters's argument rings true.

26. As Waters notes, in doing this, these parents were following a pattern that has been played out among many generations of immigrants.

27. See, also, Kessner and Caroli, *Today's Immigrants: Their Stories.*

28. In accordance with Waters's discussion, Dewey, while very concerned with racial discrimination against blacks, tended to view this problem as one that could be sidestepped—though not necessarily eliminated—through hard work and education.

29. It should be pointed out that though Dewey's assessment of West Indian culture rings true, crime is a serious problem in some of these societies—for example, Jamaica.

30. Constance Sutton, "The Caribbeanization of New York City and the Emergence of a Transnational Socio-cultural System" in *Caribbean Life in New York City: Sociocultural Dimensions*, ed. Constance Sutton and Elsa M.Chaney (New York: Center for Migration Studies of New York, Inc., 1987), pp. 15–30; Linda Basch, Nina Glick Schiller, and Cristian S. Blanc. 1994, *Nations Unbound: Transnational Projects, Postcolonial Predicaments, and Deterritorialized Nation States* (Amsterdam: Gordon and Breach Publishers, 1994).

31. Caribbean immigrants in the United States have long interacted with and influenced politics in their home societies. For instance, Kasinitz has pointed out the Jamaica Progressive League, founded in 1936, served as a fund raiser for and overseas representative of Jamaica's People's National Party. More recently, the increase in the size of the Caribbean immigrant community in New York City has led a number of the city's leading politicians to court various nationalities in the community by traveling to the Caribbean. See Adam Nagourney, "The Route to City Hall? The Caribbean" (*New York Times*, December 4, 1996): B1; Philip Kasinitz, *Caribbean New York* (Ithaca: Cornell University Press, 1992).

REFERENCES

Abbott, George C. "Estimates of the Growth of the Population of the West Indies to 1975." *Social and Economic Studies*, Vol. 12, No. 3 (1963): 236–244.

Alba, Richard. "Italian-Americans: A Century of Ethnic Change." In *Origins and Destinies: Immigration, Race, and Ethnicity in America*, edited by Silvia Pedraza and Ruben Rumbaut. Belmont: Wadsworth, 1996.

Alba, Richards, Nancy A. Denton, Shu-yin J. Leung, and John R. Logan. "Neighborhood Change under Conditions of Mass Immigration: The New York City Region, 1970–1990." *International Migration Review*, Vol. 29 (Fall 1995): 625–656.

Allen, Theodore W. *The Invention of the White Race*. New York: Verso, 1995.

Anderson, Jervis. "Black and Blue." *The New Yorker* (April 29 and May 6, 1996): 62–65.

August, Thomas. "Jewish Assimilation and Plural Society in Jamaica." *Social and Economic Studies*, Vol. 36, No. 2 (1987): 109–122.

Austin, Diane J. *Urban Life in Kingston, Jamaica: The Culture and Class Ideology of Two Neighborhoods*. New York: Gordon and Breach, 1987.

Bakan, Abigail B., David Cox, and Colin Leys. *Imperial Power and Regional Trade*. Waterloo: Wilfrid Laurier University Press, 1993.

Baker, Russell. "He Filled a Vacuum" *The New York Times* (October 17, 1995): A25.

Barnett, Joan and Mark Ricketts. "Blacks in Multi-Racial Jamaica." *The Jamaica Record* (March 19, 1989): 1A.

Barrett, Leonard. *The Rastafarians*. Boston: Beacon Press, 1977.

Barringer, Felicity. "Census Shows Profound Change in Racial Makeup of the Nation." *The New York Times* (March 11, 1991): A1.

Barth, Fredrik. "Introduction." In *Ethnic Groups and Boundaries*, edited by Fredrik Barth. Boston: Little, Brown and Company, 1970.

Basch, Linda. "The Politics of Caribbeanization: Vincentians and Grenadians in New York." In *Caribbean Life in New York City: Sociocultural Dimensions*, edited by Constance Sutton and Elsa M.Chaney. New York: Center for Migration Studies of New York, Inc., 1987.

Basch, Linda, Nina Glick Schiller, and Cristian S. Blanc. *Nations Unbound: Transnational Projects, Postcolonial Predicaments, and Deterritorialized Nation States*. Amsterdam: Gordon and Breach Publishers, 1994.

Beck, Roy. "The Ordeal of Immigration in Wausau." *The Atlantic Monthly* (April, 1994): 84–97.

Beckford, George, and Michael Witter. *Small Garden, Bitter Weed*. London: ZED Books, 1980.

Berelson, Bernard R., Paul F. Lazarsfeld, and William N. McPhee. *Voting*. Chicago: The University of Chicago Press, 1954.

Bertram, Arnold. "The Light and the Dark." *The Jamaica Record* (March 19, 1989): 5A.

Best, Lloyd. "Size and Survival." In *Readings in the Political Economy of the Caribbean*, edited by Norman Girvan and Owen Jefferson. Kingston: ISER, 1977.

Best, Tony. "D.A. Denies Existence of List." *Carib News* (March 21, 1989): 3.

Black, Clinton V. *History of Jamaica*. London: Collins, 1971.

Blackwell, James E. *The Black Community: Diversity and Unity*. New York: HarperCollins Publishers, Inc., 1991.

Boas, Franz. *Anthropology and Modern Life*. New York: Dover Publications, Inc., 1986.

Bogue, Donald J. *The Population of the United States: Historical Trends and Future Projections*. New York: The Free Press, 1985.

Bonacich, Edna. "A Theory of Middleman Minorities." *American Sociological Review*, Vol. 38 (1973): 583–594.

Bonnett, Aubrey W. "The New Female West Indian Immigrant: Dilemmas of Coping in the Host Society." In *In Search of a Better Life: Perspectives on Migration from the Caribbean*, edited by Ransford Palmer. New York: Praeger, 1990.

Boyd, Derrick. "The Historical Materialistic-Symbolist Theory of Race Discrimination." *Social and Economic Studies*, Vol. 36, No. 2 (1987): 123–144.

———.*Economic Management, Income Distribution, and Poverty in Jamaica*. New York: Praeger, 1988.

Braithwaite, Lloyd. "Sociology and Demographic Research in the British Caribbean." *Social and Economic Studies*, Vol. 6, No. 4 : 523–571.

———. "Social Stratification and Cultural Pluralism." In *Social and Cultural Pluralism in the Caribbean*, edited by Vera Rubin. New York: Annals of New York Academy of Science, 1960.

———.*Social Stratification in Trinidad*. Kingston: ISER, 1975.

Brass, Paul. "Ethnic Groups and the State." In *Ethnic Groups and the State*, edited by Paul Brass. London: Croom Helm, 1985.

Brimelow, Peter. *Alien Nation*. New York: Random House, 1995.

Brodber, Erna. "Socio-cultural Change in Jamaica." In *Jamaica in Independence*, edited by Rex Nettleford. Kingston: Heineman Publishers (Caribbean) Ltd., 1989.

Broom, Leonard. "The Social Differentiation of Jamaica." *American Sociological Review*, Vol. 19, No. 2 (1954): 115–125.

Brown, Aggrey. *Color, Class, and Politics in Jamaica*. New Brunswick: Transaction Books, 1979.

Bryce-Laporte, Roy S. "Black Immigrants, the Experience of Invisibility and Inequality." *Journal of Black Studies* 3, No.1 (1972): 29–56.

———."The New Immigration: A Challenge to Our Sociological Imagination." In *Sourcebook on the New Immigration: Implications for the United States and International Community*, edited by Roy S. Bryce-Laporte. New Brunswick: Transaction Books, 1980.

———."Caribbean Migration to the United States: Some Tentative Conclusions." In *Caribbean Immigration to the United States*, edited by Roy S. Bryce-Laporte and Delores Mortimer. Washington, D.C.: Research Institute on Immigration and Ethnic Studies, Smithsonian Institution, 1983.

———."Introduction." In *Caribbean Immigration to the United States*, edited by Roy S. Bryce-Laporte and Delores Mortimer. Washington, D.C.: Research Institute on Immigration and Ethnic Studies, Smithsonian Institution, 1983.

———."New York City and the New Caribbean Immigration." In *Caribbean Life in New York City: Sociocultural Dimensions*, edited by Constance Sutton and Elsa M. Chaney. New York: Center for Migration Studies of New York, Inc., 1987.

Buchannan, Susan S. "The Haitians: The Cultural Meaning of Race and Ethnicity." In *New Immigrants in New York*, edited by Nancy Foner. New York: Columbia University Press, 1987.

Byron, Margaret. *Post-War Caribbean Migration to Britain: The Unfinished Cycle*. Aldershot: Avebury, 1994.

Campbell, Jenni. "US Demands J'cans Declare Complexion." *The Jamaican Weekly Gleaner* (March 15–21, 1996): 2.

"The Caribbean: Columbus's Islands." *The Economist* (August 6, 1988): 1–18.

Caribbean Research Center, "The Caribbean-American Labor Day Parade," *Focus*, Vol. 1, No. 3 (October, 1988): 1.

Cargill, Morris. "On Colonialism," *The Jamaica Weekly Gleaner* (April 28–May 4, 1995): 7.

Cockburn, Alexander. "Flimflam Meets Flamboyance." *The Nation*, Vol. 243, No. 11 (October 11, 1986): 334.

Chan, Sucheng. "European and Asian Immigration into the United States in Comparative Perspective." In *Immigration Reconsidered: History, Sociology and Politics*, edited by Virginia Yans-McLauglin. New York: Oxford University Press, 1990.

Chevannes, Barry. "Race and Culture in Jamaica." *World Marxist Review*, Vol. 31, No. 5 (1988): 138–144.

———. *Rastafari: Roots and Ideology*. Syracuse: Syracuse University Press, 1994.

Clarke, Colin. *Jamaica in Maps*. London: Hodder and Stoughton, Ltd., 1974

———. *Kingston, Jamaica: Urban Growth and Social Change*, 1692–1962. Berkeley: University of California Press, 1975.

———. "Introduction: Caribbean Decolonization—New States and Old Societies." In *Society and Politics in the Caribbean*, edited by Colin Clarke. Oxford: Macmillan, 1991.

Clarke, Sebastian. *Jah Music*. London: Heinemann Educational Books, Ltd., 1981.

Conway, Dennis, and Ulathan Bigby. "Where Caribbean Peoples Live in New York City." In *Caribbean Life in New York: Sociocultural Dimensions*, edited by Constance R. Sutton and Elsa M. Chaney. New York: Center for Migration Studies, 1987.

Coon, C. S., S. M. Garn, and J. B. Birdsell, *Races: A Study of the Problems of Race Formation in Man.* Springfield: Thomas, 1950.

Cooper, Carolyn. "'Only a Niggger Gal!': Race, Gender and the Politics of Education in Claude McKay's Banana Bottom." *Caribbean Quarterly,* Vol. 38, No. 1 (March 1992): 40–54.

———.*Noises in the Blood.* Durham: Duke University Press, 1995.

Cose, Ellis. *A Nation of Strangers: Prejudice, Politics and the Populating of America.* New York: William Morrow and Company, Inc., 1992.

———.*The Rage of a Privileged Class.* New York: HarperCollins, 1993.

Craig, Christine. "The Year in Review—Florida." *The Jamaican Weekly Gleaner (N.A)* (January 12–18, 1996): 20.

Craig, Susan. "Sociology as Montage." *Social and Economic Studies,* Vol.23, No.1 (1974): 127–139.

———."Sociological Theorizing in the English-Speaking Caribbean: A Review." In *Contemporary Caribbean: A Sociological Reader,* Vol. II., edited by Susan Craig. Maracas: The College Press, 1982.

Cross, Malcolm. "Cultural Pluralism and Sociological Theory: A Critique and Reevaluation." *Social and Economic Studies,* XVII (1968): 381–397.

Cruse, Harold. *The Crisis of the Negro Intellectual.* New York: William Morrow and Company, 1967.

Cundall, Frank, ed. *Lady Nugent's Journal.* London: The West India Committee, 1939.

Curtin, Philip. *Two Jamaicas: The Role of Ideas in a Tropical Colony, 1830–1865.* New York: Atheneum, 1970.

D'Souza, Dinesh. "Separation of Race and State." *The Wall Street Journal* (September 12, 1995): A26.

Daneshvary, Nassar, and R. Keith Schwer. "Black Immigrants in the U.S. Labor Market: An Earnings Analysis." *Review of Black Political Economy,* Vol. 22, No. 3 (Winter, 1994): 77–98.

Daniels, Roger. *Coming to America: A History of Immigration and Ethnicity in American Life.* New York: HarperCollins Publishers, 1990.

Davies, Omar and Michael Witter. "The Development of the Jamaican Economy since Independence." In *Jamaica in Independence,* edited by Rex Nettleford. Kingston: Heinemann Publishers (Caribbean), 1989.

Davis, F. James. *Who Is Black?: One Nation's Definition.* University Park: The University of Pennsylvania Press, 1991.

Davison, R. B. *West Indian Migrants: Social and Economic Facts of Migration from the West Indies.* New York: Oxford University Press, 1962.

Dean, Dennis. "The Conservative Government and the 1961 Commonwealth Immigration Act: The Inside Story." *Class and Race,* Vol. 35, No. 2 (October-December, 1993): 57–74.

Degler, Carl. "Slavery and the Genesis of American Race Prejudice." *Comparative Studies in Society and History,* Vol. II, No. 1 (October 1959): 49–56.

———.*Out of Our Past.* New York: Harper and Row, Publishers, 1984.

———.*In Search of Human Nature.* New York: Oxford University Press, 1991.

Denton, Nancy and Douglas Massey. "Trends in Residential Segregation of Blacks, Hispanics, and Asians, 1970–1980." *American Sociological Review,* Vol. 52 (1987): 802–825.

————."Racial Identity among Caribbean Hispanics: The Effect of Double Minority Segregation on Residential Status." *American Sociological Review*, Vol. 54, No. 5 (1989): 790–808.

————.*American Apartheid*. Cambridge: Harvard University Press, 1993.

Department of Statistics. *Kingston Metropolitan Area*. Kingston, 1977.

DeWitt, Karen. "Immigrants Look Outside New York for a Better Life." *The New York Times*, (September 4, 1990): B3.

Dobzhansky, Theodosius. *Evolution, Genetics, and Man*. New York: John Wiley & Sons, Inc., 1963.

Dookhan, Isaac. *A Pre-Emancipation History of the West Indies*. London: Collins, 1983.

————.*A Post-Emancipation History of the West Indies*. London: Collins, 1985.

Douglas, William and Merle English. "Bitter Memories for Hate Victims." *New York Newsday* (February 2, 1990): 8.

Dugger, Celia. "A Cultural Reluctance to Spare the Rod." *The New York Times* (February 29, 1996): B1.

Dunn, Richard S. *Sugar and Slaves: The Rise of the Planter Class in the English West Indies, 1624–1713*. New York: W.W. Norton and Company, 1972.

Ebanks, G., P. M. George, and C. E. Noble. "Emigration from Barbados, 1951–1970." *Social and Economic Studies*, Vol. 28, No. 2 (1979): 431–449.

Eddings, Jerelyn. "The Covert Color War." *U.S. News and World Report* (October 23, 1995): 40–44.

Eisner, Gisela. *Jamaica: 1830–1930*. Manchester: Manchester University Press, 1961.

Eller, Jack David and Reem M. Coughlan. "The Poverty of Primordialism: The Demystification of Ethnic Attachments." *Ethnic and Racial Studies*, Vol. 16, No. 2 (April 1993): 183–202.

EPICA Task Force. *Jamaica: Caribbean Challenge*. Washington, D.C.: EPICA Task Force, 1985.

Farley, Reynolds. "Questions About Race, Spanish-Origin and Ancestry: Controversial Issues for the Statistical System." Paper presented at the "Beyond Black and White" Conference, Washington, D.C., February 12, 1996.

Farley, Reynolds and Walter R. Allen. *The Color Line and the Quality of Life in America*. New York: Oxford University Press, 1987.

Farley, Reynolds and William H. Frey. "Changes in the Segregation of Whites from Blacks during the 1980s: Small Steps toward a More Integrated Society." *American Sociological Review*, Vol. 59 (February, 1994): 23–45.

Feagin, Joe. "The Continuing Significance of Race: Anti-black Discrimination in Public Places." *American Sociological Review*, Vol. 56, No. 1 (1992): 101–116.

Feagin, Joe and Melvin P. Sikes. *Living with Racism*. Boston: Beacon Press, 1994.

Fitzpatrick, Joseph P. *Puerto Rican Americans: The Meaning of Migration to the Mainland*. Englewood Cliffs, NJ: Prentice-Hall, Inc., 1971.

Fletcher, Michael A. and Hamil R. Harris. "Rift between Farrakhan, Jewish Leaders Resurfaces." *The Washington Post* (October 14, 1995): 1.

Foner, Nancy. *Status and Power in Rural Jamaica: A Study of Educational and Political Change*. New York: Teachers College Press, 1973.

————."The Meaning of Education to Jamaicans at Home and in London." In *Adaptation of Migrants from the Caribbean in European and American Metropolis*, edited by Humphrey E. Lamur and John D. Speckmann. Leiden: University of Amsterdam and the Royal Institute of Linguistics and Anthropology, 1975.

————.*Jamaica Farewell: Jamaican Migrants in London*. Berkeley: University of California Press, 1978.

————."Race and Color: Jamaican Migrants in London and New York." *International Migration Review* 19 (1985): 708–722.

————."Sex Roles and Sensibilities: Jamaican Women in New York and London." In *International Migration: The Female Experience*, edited by Rita James Simon and Caroline B. Brettel. Totawa: Rowman and Allanheld, 1986.

————."Introduction: New Immigrants and Changing Patterns in New York City." In *New Immigrants in New York*, edited by Nancy Foner. New York: Columbia University Press, 1987.

————."The Jamaicans: Race and Ethnicity among Migrants in New York City." In *New Immigrants in New York*, edited by Nancy Foner. New York: Columbia University Press, 1987.

Fordham, Signithia. "Racelessness as a Factor in Black Students' School Success: Pragmatic Strategy or Pyrrhic Victory?" *Harvard Educational Review*, Vol. 58, No. 1 (1988): 54–84.

Fordham, Signithia and John Ogbu. "Black Students' School Success: Coping with the 'Burden of Acting White.' " *The Urban Review*, Vol. 18, No. 3 (1986): 176–206.

Forsythe, Dennis. "Black Immigrants and the American Ethos: Theories and Observations." In *Caribbean Immigration to the United States*, edited by R. S. Bryce-Laporte and Delores Mortimer. Washington, D.C.: Research Institute on Immigration and Ethnic Studies, Smithsonian Institution, 1983.

————."West Indian Radicalism in America: An Assessment of Ideologies." In *Ethnicity in the Americas*, edited by Frances Henry. The Hague: Moutin Publishers, 1976.

————.Review of *Changing Jamaica. American Journal of Sociology*, Vol. 82, No. 2 (1977): 528–530.

Fraser, Peter D. "Nineteenth Century West Indian Migration to Britain." In *In Search of a Better Life: Perspectives on Migration from the Caribbean*, edited by Ransford W. Palmer. New York: Praeger, 1990.

Froude, James A. *The English in the West Indies*. New York: Charles Scribner's Sons, 1888.

Fugita, Stephen S. and David J. O'Brien. "Economics, Ideology, and Ethnicity: The Struggle between the United Farm Workers Union and the Nisei Farmers League." *Social Problems*, Vol. 5 (1977): 146–156.

Furnival, J. S. *Colonial Policy and Practice*. London: Cambridge University Press, 1948.

The Gallup Organization. "Black/White Relations in the United States." *The Gallup Poll Social Audit, Executive Summary* (June 10, 1997): 1–26.

Gans, Herbert. "Symbolic Ethnicity: The Future of Ethnic Groups and Cultures in America." *Ethnic and Racial Studies* (January, 1979): 1–20.

Garcia, John A. "Caribbean Migration to the Mainland: A Review of Adaptive Experiences." *Annals of the American Society of Political and Social Sciences*, 487 (1986): 114–125.

Gladwell, Malcolm. "Black Like Them." *The New Yorker* (April 29 and May 6, 1996): 74–81.

Glantz, Oscar. "Native Sons and Immigrants: Some Beliefs and Values of American Born and West Indian Blacks at Brooklyn College." *Ethnicity* 5 (1978): 189–202.

Glazer, Nathan. "Blacks and Ethnic Groups: The Difference, and the Political Difference It Makes." In *Key Issues in Afro-American Experience*, edited by Nathan I. Huggins, Martin Kilson, and Daniel M. Fox. New York: Harcourt Brace Jovanovich, 1971.

Glazer, Nathan and Daniel P. Moynihan. *Beyond the Melting Pot: The Negroes, Puerto Ricans, Jews, Italians, and Irish of New York City*. Cambridge: The MIT Press, 1970.

———. "Introduction." In *Ethnicity: Theory and Experience*, edited by Nathan Glazer and Daniel Patrick Moynihan. Cambridge. Harvard University Press, 1975.

Gordon, Derek. "Race, Class and Social Mobility in Jamaica." In *Garvey: His Work and Impact*, edited by Rupert Lewis and Patrick Bryan. Trenton: African World Press, 1991.

Gordon, Milton. "Assimilation in America: Theory and Reality." *Daedalus*, Volume 90, No. 2 (1961): 263–285.

Gordon, Monica. *The Selection of Migrant Categories from the Caribbean to the United States: The Jamaican Experience*. New York: Center for Latin American and Caribbean Studies, 1983.

———. "Dependents or Independent Workers?: The Status of Caribbean Immigrant Women in the United States." In *In Search of a Better Life: Perspectives on Migration from the Caribbean*, edited by Ransford Palmer. New York: Praeger, 1990.

Gossett, Thomas. *Race: The History of an Idea in America*. Dallas: SMU Press, 1975.

Gould, Stephen Jay. *The Mismeasure of Man*. New York: W. W. Norton and Company, 1981.

Gray, Obika. *Radicalism and Social Change in Jamaica, 1960–1972*. Knoxville: The University of Tennessee Press, 1991.

Greene, Eddie. "Jamaica." In *Latin America and Caribbean Contemporary Record*, Vol. VI, 1986–1987, edited by Abraham F. Lowenthal. New York: Holmes and Meier, 1989.

Grenier, Guillermo J. and Lisandro Perez. "Miami Spice: The Ethnic Cauldron Simmers." In *Origins and Destinies: Immigration, Race, and Ethnicity in America*, edited by Silvia Pedraza and Ruben G. Rumbaut. Belmont: Wadsworth Publishing Company, 1996.

Gunst, Laurie. "The Jamaican Posses Had Nothing to Lose," *New York Newsday* (March 6, 1995): A23.

Hacker, Andrew. *U.S.: A Statistical Portrait of the American People*. New York: The Viking Press, 1983.

———. *Two Nations: Black and White, Separate, Hostile, Unequal*. New York: Scribners, 1992.

Hall, Douglas. *Free Jamaica.* New Haven: Yale University Press, 1959.
———."The Apprenticeship System in Jamaican, 1834–1838." In *Apprenticeship and Emancipation.* Kingston: The Department of Extra-Mural Studies, 1970.
———."The Ex-Colonial Society in Jamaica." In *Patterns of Foreign Influence in the Caribbean*, edited by Emannuel DeKadt. London: Oxford University Press, 1972.
Handlin, Oscar. *The Uprooted.* New York: Grossett and Dunlap, 1951.
Headley, Bernard D. "Impressions of Mr. Seaga's Jamaica." *Freedomways.* (Summer, 1985): 95–100.
Heer, David. *Immigration in America's Future.* Boulder: Westview Press, 1996.
Henriques, Fernando. *Jamaica: Land of Wood and Water.* London: Macgibbon and Kee, 1957.
Henry, Balford. "Jamaican Priest Victim of New York Racism." *The Jamaican Weekly Gleaner* (August 4–10, 1995): 20.
Henry, Frances. "The West Indian Domestic Scheme in Canada." *Social and Economic Studies*, Vol. 17, No. 1 (1968): 83–91.
Henry, Keith S. "Caribbean Migrants in New York: The Passage from Political Quiescence to Radicalism." *Afro-Americans in New York Life and History.* Vol. II, No. 2 (1978): 29–41.
Heuman, Gad. *Between Black and White: Race, Politics, and the Free Coloreds in Jamaica, 1792–1865.* Westport: Greenwood Press, 1981.
Hinds, Lester. "New Laws Un-American." *The Weekly Gleaner* (April 10–16, 1997): 1.
Hoetink, H. *Caribbean Race Relations: A Study of Two Variants.* London: Oxford University Press, 1962.
Holzberg, Carol. *Minorities and Power in a Black Society.* Lanham: The North South Publishing Company, 1987.
Horowitz, Donald. *Ethnic Groups in Conflict.* Berkeley: University of California Press, 1985.
Horwitz, Tony. "The Face of Extremism Wears Many Guises—Most of Them Ordinary." *The Wall Street Journal* (April 28, 1995): A1.
Irish, J. A. and E. B. Baisden. "Caribbean Students Face Crisis in NYC Public Schools." *Caribbean Life* (June, 1991): 3.
Isaacs, Harold. "Basic Group Identity: The Idols of the Tribe." In *Ethnicity: Theory and Experience*, edited by Nathan Glazer and Daniel Patrick Moynihan. Cambridge: Harvard University Press, 1975.
Jaynes, Gerald D. and Robin Williams, ed. *A Common Destiny: Blacks and American Society.* Washington, D.C.: National Academy Press, 1989.
Jenkins, Richard. "Rethinking Ethnicity: Identity, Categorization and Power." *Ethnic and Racial Studies*, Vol. 17, No. 2 (April 1994): 197–223.
Johnson, Howard. "The Anti-Chinese Riots of 1918 in Jamaica." *Caribbean Quarterly*, Vol. 28, No. 3 (1982): 19–32.
Johnson, Kirk. "Black Workers Bear Big Burden as Jobs in Government Dwindle." *The New York Times* (February 2, 1997): A1.
Johnson, Violet. "Culture, Economic Stability, and Entrepreneurship: The Case of British West Indians in Boston." In *New Migrants in the Marketplace*, edited by Marilyn Halter. Amherst: The University of Massachusetts Press, 1995.

Jones, Charisse. "West Indian Parade Returns to Fill Streets of Brooklyn." *The New York Times* (September 1, 1996): B41.

Jones, Rhett S. "The End of Africanity? The Bi-Racial Assault on Blackness." *The Western Journal of Black Studies*, Vol. 18, No. 4 (1994): 201–210.

Jordan, Winthrop. *The White Man's Burden*. New York: Oxford University Press, 1974.

Kalmijn, Mattijs. "The Socioeconomic Assimilation of Caribbean Blacks." *Social Forces*, Vol. 74, No. 3 (March 1996): 911–930.

Karch, Cecilia A. "The Growth of the Corporate Economy in Barbados: Class/Race Factors, 1890–1977." In *Contemporary Caribbean: A Sociological Reader*, edited by Susan Craig. Maracas: Susan Craig, 1981.

Kasinitz, Philip. "From Ghetto Elite to Service Sector: A Comparison of the Role of Two Waves of West Indian Immigrants to New York City." *Ethnic Groups*, Vol. 7 (1988): 173–203.

———.*Caribbean New York: Black Immigrants and the Politics of Race*. Ithaca, New York: Cornell University Press, 1992.

Kasinitz, Philip and Judith Freidenberg-Herbstein. "The Puerto Rican Parade and West Indian Carnival: Public Celebrations in New York City." In *Caribbean Life in New York City: Sociocultural Dimensions*, edited by Constance Sutton and Elsa M. Chaney. New York: The Center for Migration Studies, 1987.

Kasinitz, Philip and Jan Rosenberg. "Why Enterprise Zones Will Not Work." *City Journal* (Autumn, 1993): 63–69.

Kaufman, Jonathan. "Help Unwanted: Immigrant's Businesses Often Refuse to Hire Blacks in Inner City." *The Wall Street Journal* (June 6, 1995): A1.

Kaufman, Michael. *Jamaica Under Manley: Dilemmas of Socialism and Democracy*. London: ZED Books, 1985.

———."Sitting in Limbo in Jamaica." *The Nation* (December 27/January 3, 1987): 734.

Keely, Charles B. "Immigration Policy." In *International Encyclopedia of Population*, Vol. 1, edited by John A. Ross. New York: The Free Press, 1982.

Kerbo, Harold. *Social Stratification and Inequality*. New York: The McGraw-Hill Companies, Inc., 1996.

Kerr, Madeline. *Personality and Conflict in Jamaica*. Liverpool: The University Press, 1952.

Kessner, Thomas and Betty Caroli. *Today's Immigrants: Their Stories*, New York: Oxford University Press, 1982.

King, James C. *The Biology of Race*. Berkeley: The University of California Press, 1981.

Kluegel, James P. "Trends in Whites' Explanation of Black-White Gap in SES." *American Sociological Review*, Vol. 55, No. 4 (August, 1990): 512–525.

Knight, Franklin. *The Caribbean: The Genesis of a Fragmented Nationalism*. New York: Oxford University Press, 1978.

Koch, Charles W. "Jamaican Blacks and Their Descendants in Costa Rica." *Social and Economic Studies*, Vol. 36, No. 3 (1977): 339–361.

Kohn, Howard. "Humiliation, Sunny Side Up." *The New York Times Magazine* (November 6, 1994): 42–80.

Kraly, Ellen Percy. "U.S. Immigration Policy and the Immigrant Populations of

New York." In *New Immigrants in New York,* edited by Nancy Foner. New York: Columbia University Press, 1987.

Kraut, Alan M. *Silent Travelers: Germs, Genes and the 'Immigrant Menace.'* Baltimore: Johns Hopkins Press, 1994.

Kristol, Irving. "The Negro Today Is Like the Immigrant of Yesterday." In *Nation of Nations: The Ethnic Experience and the Racial Crisis,* edited by Peter I. Rose. New York: Random House, 1972 [1966].

Kuper, Adam. *Changing Jamaica.* London: Routledge and Kegan Paul, 1976.

Kurlansky, Mark. *A Continent of Islands.* Reading: Addison-Wesley Publishing Company, 1992.

Labaton, Stephen. "Denny's Restaurants to Pay 54 Million in Race Bias Suits." *The New York Times* (May 25, 1994): A1.

Lacey, Terry. *Violence and Politics in Jamaica, 1960–1970.* Bristol: Manchester University Press, 1977.

Lee, Sharon. "U.S. Census Racial Classifications: 1890–1990." *Ethnic and Racial Studies,* Vol. 16, No. 1 (January, 1993): 75–94.

LeFranc, Elsie. "Higglering in Kingston: Entrepreneurs or Traditional Small Scale Operators?" *Caribbean Review,* Vol. XVI, No.1 (1988): 15–35.

Levi, Darrell E. *Michael Manley: The Making of a Leader.* Athens, Georgia: The University of Georgia Press, 1989.

Lewinson, Edwin R. *Black Politics in New York City.* New York: Twayne Publishers, Inc., 1974.

Lewis, Anthony. "Racist Chic—The Flood of Anti-black Books." *The New York Times* (October 13, 1995): A33.

Lewis, Gordon K. *Puerto Rico: Freedom and Power in the Caribbean.* New York: Monthly Review Press, 1963.

———.*The Growth of the Modern West Indies.* New York: Monthly Review Press, 1968.

———."The Contemporary Caribbean." In *Caribbean Contours,* edited by Sidney Mintz and Sally Price. Baltimore: Johns Hopkins University Press, 1985.

Lewis, Rupert. "Black Nationalism in Jamaica in Recent Years." In *Essays on Power and Change in Jamaica,* edited by Carl Stone and Aggrey Brown. Kingston: Jamaica Publishing House, 1977.

———."Blacks in the Corporate Economy." *The Jamaica Record* (March 19, 1989): 2A.

———."Garvey's Perspective on Jamaica." In *Garvey: His Work and Impact,* edited by Rupert Lewis and Patrick Bryan. Trenton: African World Press, 1991.

Lieberson, Stanley. "A New Ethnic Group in the United States." In *Majority and Minority: The Dynamics of Race and Ethnicity in American Life,* edited by Norman Yetman. Boston: Allyn and Bacon, 1991.

Lieberson, Stanley and Mary C. Waters. *From Many Strands.* New York: Russell Sage Foundation, 1990.

Light, Ivan. *Ethnic Enterprise in America.* Berkeley: University of California Press, 1972.

Lipset, Seymour Martin. *Political Man.* Baltimore: The Johns Hopkins Press, 1981.

Locke, Hubert G. *The Black Anti-Semitism Controversy: Protestant Views and Perspectives*. Selinsgrove: Susquehanna University Press, 1994.

Lopez, David. and Yen Espiritu. "Panethnicity in the United States: A Theoretical Framework." *Ethnic and Racial Studies*, Vol. 13, No. 2 (April 1990): 198–224.

Lowenthal, David. *West Indian Societies*. London: Oxford University Press, 1972.

Major, R.H., ed. *Christopher Columbus: Four Voyages to the New World*. New York: First Carol Publishing Group, 1992.

Manley, Michael. *Jamaica: Struggle in the Periphery*. London: Writers and Readers Cooperative Society, Ltd., 1982.

Marks, Jonathan. *Human Biodiversity: Genes, Race, and History*. New York: Aldine de Gruyter, 1995.

Marshall, Dawn. "A History of West Indian Migrations: Overseas Opportunities and 'Safety-Valve' Policies." In *The Caribbean Exodus*, edited by Barry B. Levine. New York: Praeger, 1987.

Martin, Mick and Marsha Porter. *Video Movie Guide, 1994*. New York: Ballantine Books, 1993.

Massing, Michael. "Crack's Destructive Sprint Across America." *New York Times Magazine* (October 1, 1989): 38–62.

Mau, James A. "The Threatening Masses: Myth or Reality?" In *Consequences of Class and Color: West Indian Perspectives*, edited by David Lowenthal and Lambros Comitas. New York: Anchor Books, 1973.

Maunder, W. F. "The New Jamaican Emigration." *Social and Economic Studies*, Vol. 4, No. 1 (1955): 38–61.

McKenzie, H. I. "The Plural Society Debate: Some Comments on a Recent Contribution." *Social and Economic Studies*, XV (March, 1966): 53–80.

Miles, Robert. *Racism*. London: Routledge, 1990.

Miller, Errol. "Education and Society in Jamaica." In *The Sociology of Education: A Caribbean Reader*, edited by Peter Figueroa and Ganga Persaud. London: Oxford University Press, 1976.

Milne, Tom., ed. *The Time-Out Film Guide*. London: Penguin Books, 1991.

Mintz, Sidney. "The Caribbean Region." *Daedalus*, Vol. 103, No. 2 (1974): 45–71.

Model, Suzanne. "Caribbean Immigrants: A Black Success Story?" *International Migration Review*, Vol. 25 (Summer,1991): 249–275.

———."The Ethnic Niche and the Structure of Opportunity: Immigrants and Minorities in New York City." In *The "Underclass" Debate: Views from History*, edited by Michael B. Katz. Princeton: Princeton University Press, 1993.

———."West Indian Prosperity: Fact or Fiction?" *Social Problems*, Vol. 42, No. 4 (November, 1995): 535–552.

Molnar, Stephen. *Human Variation: Races, Types, and Ethnic Groups*. Englewood-Cliffs: Prentice-Hall, 1992.

Monroe, Trevor, *The Politics of Constitutional Decolonization: Jamaica, 1944–62*. Kingston: Institute of Social and Economic Research, 1983.

———."The Left and Questions of Race in Jamaica." In *Garvey: His Work and Impact*, edited by Rupert Lewis and Patrick Bryan. Trenton: African World Press, 1991.

Montagu, Ashley. " 'Ethnic Group' and 'Race.' " *Psychiatry*, Vol. 8 (1945): 27–33.

Morse, Richard. "The Caribbean: Geopolitics and Geohistory." In *Caribbean Integration*, edited by S. Lewis and T. G. Matthews. Puerto Rico: Institute of Caribbean Studies, 1967.

Moses, Knolly. "The 'Barrel Children.' " *Newsweek* (February 19, 1996): 45.

Moskos, Charles C. and John Sibley Butler. *All That We Can Be*. New York: Basic Books, 1996.

Mufuka, K. Nyamayaro. "The Jamaican Experiment." *Current History*, Vol. 74, No. 434 (1978): 70–89.

Mydans, Seth. "Black Identity vs. Success and Seeming 'White.' " *The New York Times* (April, 1990): B9.

Nagel, Joane. "The Political Construction of Ethnicity." In *Competitive Ethnic Relations*, edited by Susan Olzark and Joane Nagel. Orlando: Academic Press, 1986.

———.*American Indian Ethnic Renewal: Red Power and the Resurgence of Identity and Culture*. New York: Oxford University Press, 1996.

Nagel, Joane and C. Matthew Snipp. "American Indian Social, Economic, Political and Cultural Strategies for Survival." *Ethnic and Racial Studies*, Vol. 16, No. 2 (April 1993): 203–235.

Nagourney, Adam. "The Route to City Hall? The Caribbean." *The New York Times* (December 4, 1996): B1.

Nelson, Jill. *Volunteer Slavery*. Chicago: The Noble Press, Inc., 1993.

Nettleford, Rex. *Identity, Race and Protest in Jamaica*. New York: William Morrow & Company, Inc., 1972

———.*Caribbean Cultural Identity: The Case of Jamaica*. Kingston: Institute of Jamaica, 1978.

———."This Matter of Melanin: Calling a Spade a Spade." *The Jamaica Record* (March 19, 1989): 4A.

Norris, Kathleen. *Jamaica, the Search for an Identity*. London: Oxford, 1962.

Nossiter, Adam. "A Jamaican Way Station in the Bronx." *The New York Times* (October 25, 1995): B1.

Oliver, Melvin N. and Thomas Shapiro. *Black Wealth/White Wealth: A New Perspective on Racial Inequality*. New York: Routledge, 1995.

Omi, Michael and Howard Winant. *Racial Formation in the United States from the 1960s to the 1980s*. New York: Routledge, 1990.

Osofsky, Gilbert. *Harlem: The Making of a Ghetto*. Harper and Row, 1966.

Ottley, Roy and William J. Weatherby. *The Negro in New York: An Informal Social History*. New York: Praeger Publishing, 1967.

Oxaal, Ivaar. *Race and Revolutionary Consciousness: An Existential Report on the 1970 Black Power Revolt in Trinidad*. London: Schenkman Publishing Company, Inc., 1971.

Palmer, Ransford. "Illegal Migration from the Caribbean." In *In Search of a Better Life: Perspectives on Migration from the Caribbean*, edited by Ransford Palmer. New York: Praeger, 1990.

———.*Pilgrims from the Sun: West Indian Migration to America*. New York: Twayne, 1995.

Papademetriou, Demetrios G. "Illegal Caribbean Migration to the United States and Caribbean Development." In *Migration and Development in the Caribbean*, edited by Robert Pastor. Boulder: Westview Press, 1985.

Pastor, Robert. "The Impact of U.S. Immigration Policy on Caribbean Emigration: Does It Matter?" In *The Caribbean Exodus*, edited by Barry B. Levine. New York: Praeger, 1988.

Patterson, Orlando, *The Sociology of Slavery*. London: Granada Publishing, 1973.

———."Toward a Future That Has No Past—Reflections on the Fate of Blacks in the Americas." *The Public Interest*, No. 27 (1972): 25–62.

———.*Ethnic Chauvinism: The Reactionary Impulse*. New York: Stein and Day, 1977.

———."Context and Choice in Ethnic Allegiance: A Theoretical Framework and Caribbean Case Study." In *Ethnicity: Theory and Experience*, edited by Nathan Glazer and Daniel Patrick Moynihan. Cambridge: Harvard University Press, 1995.

Payne, Anthony. "Jamaica's Approach to Independence." *Caribbean Review*, Vol. XVI, No. 1 (1988): 4–30.

———."Liberal Economics versus Electoral Politics." In *Modern Caribbean Politics*, edited by Anthony Payne and Paul Sutton. Baltimore: The Johns Hopkins University Press, 1993.

Pedraza, Silvia. "Cuba's Refugees: Manifold Migration." In *Origins and Destinies: Immigration, Race, and Ethnicity in America*, edited by Silvia Pedraza and Ruben Rumbaut. Belmont: Wadsworth Publishing Company, 1996.

Persaud, Ganga. "The Hidden Curriculum in Teacher Education and Schooling." In *The Sociology of Education: A Caribbean Reader*, edited by Peter Figueroa and Ganga Persaud. London: Oxford University Press, 1976.

Pettigrew, Thomas F. "Race and Class in the 1980s: An Interactive View." *Daedalus* 110 (1981): 233–255.

Phillips, Peter. "Jamaican Elites: 1938 to Present." In *Essays on Power and Change in Jamaica*, edited by Carl Stone and Aggrey Brown. Kingston: Jamaica Publishing House, 1977.

Pierre-Pierre, Garry. "Heading to Florida, Nearer the Homeland." *The New York Times* (July 13, 1993): B3.

———."West Indians Adding Clout at Ballot Box." *The New York Times* (September 6, 1993): B1.

Portes, Alejandro. *City on the Edge: The Transformation of Miami*. Berkeley: University of California Press, 1993.

Portes, Alejandro and Alex Stepick. "Unwelcome Immigrants: The Labor Market Experiences of 1980 (Mariel) Cuban and Haitian Refugees in South Florida." *American Sociological Review*, Vol. 50 (1985): 493–514.

Portes, Alejandro and Robert D. Manning. "The Immigrant Enclave: Theory and Empirical Examples." In *Competitive Ethnic Relations*, edited by Susan Olzak and Joane Nagel. Orlando: Academic Press, Inc., 1986.

Portes, Alejandro, Alex Stepick, and Cynthia Truelove. "Three Years Later: The Adaptation Process of 1980 (Mariel) Cuban and Haitian Refugees in South Florida." *Population Research and Policy Review* 5 (1986): 83–94.

Post, Ken. *Arise Ye Starvelings: The Jamaican Labour Rebellion of 1938 and Its Aftermath*. The Hague: Martinus Nijhoff, 1978.

Prescod-Roberts, Margaret, and Norma Steele. *Black Women: Bringing It All Back Home*. London: Falling Wall Press, 1980.

Purdy, Mathew. "Parade Shows Off West Indian Political Clout." *The New York Times* (September 7, 1994): A1.

Ransford, Edward H. *Race and Class in American Society: Black, Chicano, Anglo.* Cambridge: Schenkman Publishing Company, Inc., 1977.

Raphael, Lennox. "West Indians and Afro-Americans." *Freedomways* (Summer, 1964): 438–445.

Raveau, Francois. "An Outline of the Role of Color in Adaptation Phenomena." In *Color and Race*, edited by John Hope Franklin. Boston: Beacon Press, 1968.

Reid, Ira De A. *The Negro Immigrant.* New York: Columbia University Press, 1939.

Reid, Stanley. "An Introductory Approach to the Concentration of Power in the Jamaican Corporate Economy and Notes on Its Origin." In *Essays and Power and Change in Jamaica*, edited by Carl Stone and Aggrey Brown. Kingston: Jamaica Publishing House, 1977.

Rich, Dawn. "The De-culturation of Jamaica." *The Sunday Gleaner* (April 7, 1991).

———."Getting the Best from the Best." *The Weekly Gleaner* (May 15–21, 1997): 7.

Richardson, Bonham C. "Slavery to Freedom in the British Caribbean: Ecological Considerations." *Caribbean Geography*, Vol. 1, No. 3 (May, 1984): 164–175.

———.*Caribbean Migrants.* Knoxville: The University of Tennessee Press, 1983.

Richardson, Mary F. "Out of Many, One People—Aspiration or Reality? An Examination of the Attitudes to the Various Racial and Ethnic Groups within Jamaican Society." *Social and Economic Studies*, Vol. 32, No. 3 (1983): 143–167.

Richmond, Anthony H. and Aloma Mendoza. "Education and Qualifications of Caribbean Immigrants and Their Children in Britain and Canada." In *In Search of a Better Life: Perspectives on Migration from the Caribbean*, edited by Ransford Palmer. New York: Praeger, 1990.

Roberts, G. W. *The Population of Jamaica.* London: Cambridge University Press, 1957.

Roberts, G. W. and D.O. Mills. "Study of External Migration Affecting Jamaica, 1953–55." *Social and Economic Studies*, Vol. 7, No. 2 (1958): 1–350.

Roberts, Michael. "Jamaicans on DA's Drug List." *Carib News* (March 21, 1989): 3.

———."Jamaican Drug Gangs Targeted." *Carib News* (March 6, 1990): 4.

Roberts, Sam. "Blacks Reach a Milestone in Queens: Income Parity." *The New York Times* (1992): A1.

———.*Who We Are: A Portrait of America.* New York: Random House, 1993.

———."In Middle-Class Queens, Blacks Pass Whites in Household Income." *The New York Times* (June 6, 1994): A1.

Roberts, Steven. "An American Tale." *U.S. News and World Report* (August 21, 1995): 27–30.

Rodriquez, Clara E. "Challenging Racial Hegemony: Puerto Ricans in the United States." In *Race*, edited by Steven Gregory and Roger Sanjek. New Brunswick, N.J.: Rutgers University Press, 1994.

Rodriguez, Clara E. and Hector Cordero-Guzman. "Placing Race in Context." *Ethnic and Racial Studies*, Vol. 15, No. 4 (1992): 523–541.

Rohter, Larry. "The Real Caribbean: Paradise Stops at the Beach's Edge." *The New York Times* (February 16, 1997): Section 4, 1.

———."Death-Row Rule Sours Caribbean on Britain." *The New York Times* (July 7, 1997): A1.

Roof, Wade Clark. "The Ambiguities of 'Religious Preference' in Survey Research— A Methodological Note." *Public Opinion Quarterly* 44 (3) (1980): 403–407.

Root, Maria P. P. "The Multiracial Experience: Racial Borders as a Significant Frontier in Race Relations." In *The Multiracial Experience*, edited by Maria P. P. Root. Thousand Oaks: SAGE Publications, 1996.

Rose, Peter. *They and We*. New York: McGraw-Hill Publishing Company, 1990.

Ross, John A., ed. "Immigration Policy." In *International Encyclopedia of Population*, Vol. 1, New York: The Free Press, 1982.

Rubin, Vera. "Social and Cultural Pluralism by M.G. Smith." In *Social and Cultural Pluralism in the Caribbean*, edited by Vera Rubin. New York: Annals of the New York Academy of Sciences, 1960.

Rumbaut, Ruben G. "The Crucible Within: Ethnic Identity, Self-Esteem, and Segmented Assimilation among Children of Immigrants." In *The New Second Generation*, edited by Alejandro Portes. New York: Russell Sage Foundation, 1996.

Ryan, Selwyn D. *Race and Nationalism in Trinidad and Tobago*. Toronto: University of Toronto Press, 1972.

Schaefer, Richard T. *Racial and Ethnic Groups*. New York: HarperCollins, 1993.

Schermerhorn, Richard. *Comparative Ethnic Relations*. New York: Random House, 1970.

Schuman, Howard, and Charlotte Steeth. "The Complexity of Racial Attitudes in America." In *Origins and Destinies: Immigration, Race, and Ethnicity in America*, edited by Silvia Pedraza and Ruben Rumbaut. Belmont: Wadsworth, 1996.

Schuman, Howard, Charlotte Steeth, and Lawrence Bobo. *Racial Attitudes in America*. Cambridge: Harvard University Press, 1991.

Seaga, Edward. "Toward Resolving the Debt Crisis." *Caribbean Review*, Vol. XVI, No. 1 (1988): 1–30.

Segal, Ronald. *The Black Diaspora*. New York: Farrar, Straus, and Giroux, 1995.

Shenon, Philip. "Judge Denounces U.S. Visa Policies Based on Race or Looks." *The New York Times* (January 23, 1998): A1.

Sherlock, Philip. *Norman Manley: A Biography*. London: Macmillan, 1980.

Shipman, Pat. *The Evolution of Racism*. New York: Simon and Schuster, 1994.

Sigelman, Lee and Susan Welch. *Black Americans' Views of Racial Inequality: A Dream Deferred*. New York: Cambridge University Press, 1991.

Smith, M. G. "Social and Cultural Pluralism." In *Social and Cultural Pluralism in the Caribbean*, edited by Vera Rubin. New York: Annals of the New York Academy of Sciences, 1960.

———.*The Plural Society in the British West Indies*. Berkeley: The University of California Press, 1965.

Smith, R. T. "The Family in the Caribbean." In *Caribbean Studies: A Symposium*, edited by Vera Rubin. Kingston: ISER, 1957.

Smith, T. E. *Commonwealth Migration*. London: The Macmillan Press, 1981.

Sniderman, Paul M. and Thomas Piazza. *The Scar of Race.* Cambridge: Harvard University Press, 1993.

Sontag, Deborah. "Caribbean Pupils' English Seem Barrier, Not Bridge." *The New York Times* (November 28, 1992): A1.

Sowell, Thomas. *Ethnic America: A History.* New York: Basic Books, 1981.

——.*Markets and Minorities.* New York: Basic Books, 1981.

——.*The Economics and Politics of Race: An International Perspective.* New York: Quill, 1983.

Stafford, Susan Buchannan. "The Haitians: The Cultural Meaning of Race and Ethnicity." In *New Immigrants in New York,* edited by Nancy Foner. New York: Columbia University Press, 1987.

Staples, Brent. "The West Indian Reaganaut: Colin Powell's Caribbean Journey." *The New York Times* (1995): A24.

Statistical Institute of Jamaica. *Pocketbook of Statistics, 1989.* Kingston: The Statistical Institute of Jamaica, 1989.

Steinberg, Stephen. *The Ethnic Myth.* Boston: Beacon Press, 1989.

Stinchcombe, Arthur. "Freedom and Oppression of Slaves in the Eighteenth-Century Caribbean." *American Sociological Review,* Vol. 59 (December, 1994): 911–929.

Stone, Carl. *Class, Race and Political Behavior in Urban Jamaica.* Kingston: ISER, 1973.

——.*Understanding Third World Politics and Economics.* Kingston: Earle Publishers, 1980.

——.*The Political Opinions of the Jamaican People (1979–81).* Kingston: Blackett Publishers, 1982.

——."Race and Economic Power in Jamaica." *Caribbean Review,* Vol. XVI (Spring, 1988): 10–34.

——."Power, Policy, and Politics in Independent Jamaica." In *Jamaica in Independence,* edited by Rex Nettleford. Kingston: Heinemann, 1989.

——."Crime Trends in Jamaica." In *Carl Stone on Jamaican Politics and Society,* edited by Carl Stone. Kingston: The Gleaner Company, 1989.

——."The Black Self-Concept." In *Carl Stone on Jamaican Politics and Society,* edited by Carl Stone. Kingston: The Gleaner Company, 1989.

——."A Look at Minority Economic Power." In *Carl Stone on Jamaican Politics and Society,* edited by Carl Stone. Kingston: The Gleaner Company, 1989.

——."Completing Garvey's Work." In *Carl Stone on Jamaican Politics and Society,* edited by Carl Stone. Kingston: The Gleaner Company, 1989.

——.*Politics versus Economics: The 1989 Elections in Jamaica.* Kingston: Heinemann Publishers (Caribbean), 1989.

——."Race and Economic Power in Jamaica." In *Garvey: His Work and Impact,* edited by Rupert Lewis and Patrick Bryan. Trenton: African World Press, 1991.

Sutton, Constance. "The Caribbeanization of New York City and the Emergence of a Transnational Socio-cultural System." In *Caribbean Life in New York City: Sociocultural Dimensions,* edited by Constance Sutton and Elsa M. Chaney. New York: The Center for Migration Studies, 1987.

Sutton, Constance and Susan Makiesky-Barrow. "Migration and West Indian Racial and Ethnic Consciousness." In *Caribbean Life in New York City:*

Sociocultural Dimensions, edited by Constance Sutton and Elsa M. Chaney. New York: The Center for Migration Studies, 1987.

Takaki, Ronald. "Reflections on Racial Patterns in America." In *From Different Shores*, edited by Ronald Takaki. New York: Oxford University Press, 1987.

Thernstrom, Abigail. "Two Nations, Separate and Hostile?" *The New York Times* (October 12, 1995): A23.

Thomas, Clive Y. *The Poor and the Powerless: Economic Policy and Change in the Caribbean*. London: Latin American Bureau, 1988.

Thomas-Hope, Elizabeth. "Caribbean Diaspora—The Inheritance of Slavery: Migration from the Commonwealth Caribbean." In *The Caribbean in Europe*, edited by Colin Brock. London: Frank Cass and Company Limited, 1986.

Thompson, Mel E. "Forty-and-One Years On: An Overview of Afro-Caribbean Migration to the United Kingdom." In *In Search of a Better Life: Perspectives on Migration from the Caribbean*, edited by Ransford Palmer. New York: Praeger, 1990.

Tidrick, Kathryn. "Need for Achievement, Social Class, and Intention to Emigrate in Jamaican Students." *Social and Economic Studies*, Vol. 20, No. 1 (March 1971): 52–60.

Tracey, Lenworth. "Corporate Power Structure—The Stock Exchange." *The Jamaica Record* (March 19, 1989): 3A.

Traub, James. "You Can Get It if You Really Want It." *Harpers* (1982): 27–31.

Turner, Virginia. "Jamaicans Outraged!: New York Police Targeting West Indians." *The Weekly Gleaner* (January 24–30, 1997): 1.

Ueda, Reed. "West Indians." In *Harvard Encyclopedia of American Ethnic Groups*, edited by Stephan Thernstrom, Ann Orlov, and Oscar Handlin. Cambridge: Harvard University Press, 1980.

Ungar, Sanford J. *Fresh Blood: The New American Immigrants*. New York: Simon and Schuster, 1995.

United States Bureau of the Census. *Statistical Abstract of the United States: 1993*. Washington, D.C.: The Reference Press, Inc., 1993.

United States Bureau of the Census. *Statistical Abstract of the United States: 1994*. Washington, D.C.: The Reference Press, Inc., 1994.

United States Bureau of the Census. *Statistical Abstract of the United States: 1995*. Washington, D.C.: The Reference Press, Inc., 1995.

United States Bureau of the Census. *Demographic State of the Nation: 1997*. Washington, D.C.: U.S. Department of Commerce, 1997.

United States Bureau of the Census. "Results of the 1996 Race and Ethnic Targeted Test." Washington, D.C.: May, 1997.

van den Berghe, Pierre. *Race and Racism*. New York: John Wiley and Sons, Inc., 1965.

———."Race and Ethnicity: A Sociobiological Perspective." *Ethnic and Racial Studies*, Vol. 1, No. 4 (1978): 401–411.

———."Ethnicity and the Sociobiology Debate." In *Theories of Race and Ethnic Relations*, edited by John Rex and David Mason. New York: Cambridge University Press, 1988.

Vaughan, Sarah. "Taking the Vow of Citizenship." *The Weekly Gleaner* (April 17–23, 1997): 19.

———. "Atlanta the Popular 'New Home' for Jamaicans." *The Weekly Gleaner* (February 27–March 5, 1997): 20.

Verkuyten, W. De Jong, and C. N. Masson. "The Construction of Ethnic Categories: Discourses of Ethnicity in the Netherlands." *Ethnic and Racial Studies*, Vol. 18, No. 2 (April 1995): 251–276.

Vickerman, Milton. "The Response of West Indians towards African-Americans: Distancing and Identification." In *Research in Race and Ethnic Relations*, Vol. 7, edited by Rutledge Dennis. Greenwich: JAI Press (1994): 83–128.

Video Hound's Golden Movie Retriever. Detroit: Visible Ink Press, 1994.

Volsky, George. "Jamaican Drug Gangs Thriving in U.S. Cities." *The New York Times* (July 19, 1987): A17.

Wagley, Charles and Marvin Harris. *Minorities in the New World.* New York: Columbia University Press, 1958.

Waldinger, Roger. "Beyond Nostalgia: The Old Neighborhood Revisited." *New York Affairs*, Vol. 10, No. 1 (Winter, 1987):1–12.

———."Ethnic Business in the United States." In *Immigration, Multiculturalism and Economic Development*, edited by R. J. Holton. Flinders: Flinders University of South Australia, 1987.

———."Minorities and Immigrants—Struggle in the Job Markets." *Dissent* (Fall 1987): 519–522.

———."The 'Other Side' of Embeddedness: A Case-Study of the Interplay of Economy and Ethnicity." *Ethnic and Racial Studies*, Vol. 18, No. 3 (July, 1995): 555–580.

———."The Jobs Immigrants Take." *The New York Times* (March 11, 1996): A17 .

———.*Still the Promised City?: African-Americans and New Immigrants in Post Industrial New York.* Cambridge: Harvard University Press, 1996.

Walt, Vivienne. "Caught between Two Worlds: Immigrants Discover Success, Racism in the U.S." *New York Newsday* (April 15, 1988): 9–27.

Waters, Mary. *Ethnic Options.* Berkeley: The University of California Press, 1990.

———."The Role of Lineage in Identity Formation among Black Americans." *Qualitative Sociology*, Vol. 14, No. 1 (1991): 57–76.

———."Ethnic and Racial Identities of Second-Generation Black Immigrants in New York City." *International Migration Review*, Vol. xxviii, No. 4 (1994): 795–820.

———."Optional Ethnicities: For Whites Only?" In *Origins and Destinies: Immigration, Race, and Ethnicity in America*, edited by Silvia Pedraza and Ruben Rumbaut. Belmont: Wadsworth, 1996.

Watkins-Owens, Irma. *Blood Relations: Caribbean Immigrants and the Harlem Community, 1900–1930.* Bloomington: University of Indiana Press, 1996.

Waugh, Alec, ed. "The Black Republic." In *Love and the Caribbean.* New York: Farrar, Straus, and Cudahay, 1959.

Weinstein, Norman. "The Making of Jewmaicans," *Tikkun*, Vol. 3, No. 4 (July/August, 1988): 70.

West, Cornell. *Race Matters.* New York: Vintage, 1993

White, Timothy. *Catch a Fire.* London: Corgi Books, 1983.

Wilkerson, Isabel. "Black-White Marriages Rise, but Couples Still Face Scorn." *The New York Times* (December 2, 1991): A1.

Willcox, Walter F, ed. 1996. *International Migrations,* Vol. 1. New York: Gordon and Breach Science Publishers, 1996.

Williams, Eric. *The Negro in the Caribbean.* New York: Haskell House Publishers, Ltd., 1942.

————.*Capitalism and Slavery*. New York: Russell and Russell, 1961.

————.*From Columbus to Castro: The History of the Caribbean*. New York: Vintage Books, 1970.

Williams, Gregory Howard. *Life on the Color Line*. New York: Dutton, 1995.

Williams, Lena. "When Blacks Shop, Bias Often Accompanies Sale." *The New York Times* (April 30, 1991): A14 L.

————. "Aimed at Terrorists, Law Hits Legal Immigrants." *The New York Times* (July 17, 1996): A1.

Williamson, Joel. *New People: Miscegenation and Mulattoes in the United States*. New York: New York University Press, 1980.

Wilson, Kenneth L. and W. Allen Martin. "Ethnic Enclaves: A Comparison of the Cuban and Black Economies in Miami." *The American Journal of Sociology*, Vol. 88, No. 1 (1982): 135–160.

Wilson, William J. *The Declining Significance of Race*. Chicago: The University of Chicago Press, 1980.

————.*The Truly Disadvantaged: The Inner City, the Underclasss, and Public Policy*. Chicago: The University of Chicago Press, 1987.

————."The American Underclass: Inner-city Ghettos and the Norms of Citizenship." The Godkin Lecture, delivered at John F. Kennedy School of Government, Harvard University (April 26, 1990).

————."Work." *The New York Times Magazine* (August 18, 1996): 26–52.

Winant, Howard. *Racial Conditions*. Minneapolis: University of Minnesota Press, 1994.

Worsley, Peter. *The Three Worlds: Culture and World Development*. Chicago: The University of Chicago Press, 1984.

INDEX

Achievement, ix–x, 5, 73–77, 91–92, 117, 126, 139, 141–142, 156, 158, 167–168, 177–178; *see also* Merit
Adam (interview subject), 106, 112
Adventures of Buckaroo Banzai Across the 8th Dimension, The (film), 1, 14n1, 14n2
African Americans, 3, 4, 5, 13, 93, 115, 116, 119, 120, 137–163
  cultural differences between West Indians and, 167–168
  economic issues and, 66, 73, 74–75, 76, 78–79, 80–81
  education and, 149–151
  employment discrimination and, 161n13
  ethnic identity and, 6, 8
  identification with, 172–173, 178
  identity as, 168, 169, 173, 174
  marriage to, 116, 146–147, 169
  occupational distribution in, 72
  pull of race and, 147–155
  role modeling and, 103, 104, 155–158
  social distancing from, 110, 139–147, 156, 172–173, 178
  socioeconomic characteristics of, 122t
  southern exceptionalism and, 144–147
African ancestry, 5, 9, 13, 19n, 26, 30–32, 33, 40, 42, 43, 46n11, 57n101, 93, 98, 126, 138, 147, 159, 167, 168
African immigrants, 2t
Aggressive racism, 96, 97
Aggressive response, 96–97
Al (interview subject), 104, 148–149

Alba, Richard, 8, 137
Allen, Debbie, 129n19
Allen, Walter R., 77–78
American dream, 5, 175
Anansi (folk hero), 99
Andre (interview subject), 145, 157
Anglophone Caribbean, 10–11
Anglophone West Indies, 12, 78
Anguilla, 10, 60
Antigua, 60, 64t
Anti-immigrant sentiments, 153
Anti-Terrorism and Effective Death Penalty Act, 171–172
Arthur (interview subject), 149–151
Ashley (interview subject), 142–143
Asians, 1, 2, 42, 79
  ethnic identity and, 6
  growth in population, 165
  intermarriage in, 173
  population projections for, 166t
  socioeconomic characteristics of, 67t
Assertion, 96–97, 103–106
Assimilation, 8, 43, 125, 138, 171, 179n13
Atlanta, GA, 63, 106, 145
August, Thomas, 28
Austin, Diane, 34, 65
Avoidance, 103–104, 106–107

Bahamas, 10, 60, 64t
Bananas, 60, 61
Barbadian immigrants, 11, 61, 64t
Barbados, 60
Barrel children, 72, 87n38, 87n39, 180n23
Basch, Linda, 177
Belizian immigrants, 2, 10, 64t
Bensonhurst, NY, 107
Bernard (interview subject), 143

Beyond the Melting Pot (Glazer and Moynihan), 4, 74
Bias crimes, x, 101
Black Anti-Semitism Controversy (Locke), 125
Black Diaspora, 23
Black Diaspora, The (Segal), 29
"Black Immigrants, the Experience of Invisibility and Inequality" (Bryce-Laporte), 77
Black Manhattan (Johnson), 84n21
Blackness, x, 6, 9, 19n33, 26, 32, 42, 98, 138–139, 159, 167–168
Blackouts, 121; *see also* Denny's restaurant
Black Power movement, 26, 39, 155
Blacks; *see also* specific ethnic groups
   classification of, 172
   definitions of, 3, 13
   ethnic identity and, 8–9
   foreign born, 2, 15n8
   free, 28
   identity as, 168, 174, 175
   in Jamaica, 24–26, 27, 30
   population projections for, 166t
   rate of intermarriage in women, 173
   social and economic characteristics of, 67t
Blanc, Cristian, 177
Bob (interview subject), 108
Bogle (interview subject), 113–114, 144
Bonacich, Edna, 74
Boston, MA, 65
Brazil, 34, 35t
British, 99; *see also* United Kingdom
   in Jamaica, 27, 28, 32, 33
   West Indian identification with, 100, 139–140
British Guyana, 10
British West Indians immigrants, 67t
Brooklyn, NY, 3, 10, 167
Brooklyn College, 75
Browns, 30; *see also* Coloreds
Bryce (interview subject), 170
Bryce-Laporte, Roy, 4, 5, 6, 77, 79, 91
Bush, George, 114
Bustamante, Alexander, 49n43, 99
Bustamante Industrial Trade Union, 49n43, 50n43
Byron (interview subject), 158

Cambria Heights, NY, 3
Canada, 61
Capital punishment, 17n20; *see also* Conservatism; Law and order orientation
Caribbean, 10–11, 60, 61; *see also* West Indies
Caribbean Basin Initiative, 10
CARICOM, 11
CARIFTA, 11
Caroli, Betty, 141
Central America, 1, 10, 60, 61–62; *see also* Caribbean; West Indies
Chevannes, Barry, 24, 130n25
Chinese immigrants, 8, 25t, 29, 33, 42, 63
Civil Rights movement, 8
Civil service (and upward mobility in Jamaica), 33, 65
Clara's Heart (film), 1
Class. *See* Middle class; Social class
Class, Race, and Political Behaviour in Urban Jamaica, 49n40
Classic model of race relations, 27–29
Cliff (interview subject), 105
Cochran, Johnnie, 125
College education, 67t, 79; *see also* Education
Color-blind society, ix-x, 113
Coloreds, 3, 27–28, 30–31
Columbus, Christopher, 27
Common Destiny, A: Blacks and American Society (Jaynes and Williams), 121
Confrontation, 96, 97, 98–102, 103
Connecticut, 63
Conservativism, 5, 17n20, 92, 131n34, 132n43, 153
Construction industry, 72, 80
Cool Runnings (film), 1
Cooper, Carolyn, 15n4, 44
Coping strategies (for racial discrimination), 96–112; *see also* Assertion; Confrontation; Pragmatism; Resignation
Cordero-Guzman, Hector, 172
Cose, Ellis, 124
Costa Rica, 60–61, 71
Craig, Susan, 48n32
Crime, 110, 180n28; *see also* Conservatism; Police bias, 101

Cross-pressures, 4–5
Crown Heights, NY, 3, 131n33, 154
Cuba, 10, 61
Cultural pluralism, 29–31, 44, 48n32
Culture, 3, 4
    economics and, 77–78, 80
    identity and, 167–168
    social distancing and, 141–142
Curtin, Philip, 37, 46n16

Daily Gleaner, 23–24, 54n69,
    140–141, 154
David (interview subject), 151
De Jong, W., 7
Democratic Party, 153
Demographics, in Jamaica, 35–36
Denny's restaurant, 121
Deportation, 171–172
Dewey (interview subject), 108,
    111–112, 176
Dinkins, David, 153–154
Distancing. *See* Social distancing
District Attorney's drug list, 99,
    130n24
Domestic work, 66, 71–72, 87n42
Dominica, 64t
Dominican Republic, 10, 60, 63
Drake (interview subject), 169
Dreadlocks, 156; *see also* Rastafarianism
Drug posses, 99, 109, 129–130n23, n30
Drug trade, 34, 99, 142
Dual citizenship, 169, 170; *see also*
    Naturalization
Du Bois, W. E. B., 93
Dunn, Richard, 46n9
Dutch people, 7

Earnings. *See* Income
Economics, 59–89; *see also* Income;
    Poverty
    ethnic niches and, 66–72
    ethnic niches and racial issues in,
        72–81
    stereotypes in, 63–65
Economics and Politics of Race, The
    (Sowell), 74
Economist survey, 65
Education, ix, 65, 104, 141, 149–151,
    175
    of British West Indian and Asian
        immigrants, 57, 67t

college, 67t, 79
    ethnic niches and, 79
    high school, 67t
    in Jamaica, 38–39, 44
Ellis (interview subject), 144
El Salvador, 10, 61
Elton (interview subject), 95–96
Emergent ethnic groups, 7–8
Employment discrimination, 104–106,
    148–149, 161n13; *see also* Labor
    force participation; Occupational
    distribution
Entrepreneurship. *See* Self-employment
Espiritu, Yen, 11
Ethnic America (Sowell), 74
Ethnic identity, 6–9, 16n13
    social construction of, 7, 9–12,
        97–98, 148, 168
    symbolic, 8, 138
Ethnicity (Glazer and Moynihan), 74
Ethnic Myth, The (Steinberg), 77
Ethnic niches, 66–72, 155
    racial issues and, 72–81
Ethnic separatism. *See* Separatism
Ethnocentrism, 77, 139, 156, 158,
    161n15; *see also* Social
    distancing
Europeans, 2, 27, 30, 137–138

Falwell, Jerry, 114
Family Income Index, 74
Farley, Reynolds, 77–78, 173
Farrakhan, Louis, 125–126, 135n63,
    135n66
Fauntleroy, Walter, 125, 135n63
Feagin, Joe, 96, 98, 123, 124,
    128n13
Female-headed families, 74; *see also*
    Single-parent families
Fighting, 100–101
Filipino immigrants, 63, 67t
Films, 1, 14–15n3, 99
Flatbush, NY, 2, 10
Florida, 63, 106
Foner, Nancy, 34, 38, 48–49n39, 91,
    93
Forsythe, Dennis, 73, 74
Frank (interview subject), 143
Free blacks, 28
French, 60
French Guyana, 10

Gallup Poll on Black/White Relations, 122–123
Gangs, 142
Gans, Herbert, 8, 137
Garvey, Marcus, 32, 93
Genetics, 7
Gladwell, Malcolm, 113
Glantz, Oscar, 75
Glazer, Nathan, 4, 65, 73, 74
Gordon (interview subject), 105
Gordon, Derek, 33
Gravesend, NY, 107
Great Depression, 32, 61, 62
Grenada, 64t
Griffith, Michael, 130n27
Growth of the Modern West Indies, The (Lewis), 99
Gunst, Laurie, 129n23
Guyana, 8, 10, 60
Guyanese immigrants, 2, 12, 63
  economics and, 66
  percentage distribution of workers per family, 71t
  socioeconomic characteristics of, 67t by year, 64t

Haile Selassie, 54n69
Haiti, 36, 60
Haitian immigrants, 11, 12, 61, 64t, 71t
Harlem, NY, 3, 4, 63, 65, 139, 140
Harry (interview subject), 94–95, 98
Hart-Cellar Immigration Act, 62, 66
Hate groups, 41
Health care field, 66, 72, 79, 87n42
Heer, David, 63
Henriques, Ferdinand, 31
Henry, Keith, 140
Herrenvolk, 40
High school education, 67t
Hispanics, 42, 172
  ethnic identity and, 6
  growth in population, 165
  intermarriage in, 173
  population projections for, 166t
Historic Preservation Association, 41
Hmong population, 165
Home ownership, 66, 87n45, 158
Hooks, Benjamin, 125, 135n63
House slaves, 28
Houston, TX, 145
Howard Beach, NY, 101, 107, 130n27

Hypodescent, rule of, 138; *see also* One-drop rule

Identification with African Americans, 39, 116–120, 147–155, 168–169, 172–174, 178
Identity, 165–181
  African-American, 168, 169, 173, 174
  black, 168, 174, 175
  ethnic. *See* Ethnic identity
  immigrant, 174, 176
  options for, 167–173
  in second generation, 173–177, 178
  in third generation, 177, 178
  transnational, 177
  West Indian, 168–172, 173, 174, 175, 177, 178
Ideology, 37–39, 114
Illegal Immigration Reform and Immigrant Responsibility Act, 171, 172
Immigrant identity, 174, 176
Immigration
  to Caribbean and Central America, 59–61
  to the United States, 61–63, 64t
  Sex distribution, 66, 71, 86n33
Immigration Act of 1965, 12
Immigration and Naturalization Service, 171–172
Immigration legislation, 62, 66, 84n17, 171–172, 179–180n15
Income; *see also* Poverty
  distribution by country, 35t
  distribution in Jamaica, 34, 35t
  mean, 78
  median family, 4, 67t, 79, 124
India, 35t
Indians, 25t, 33, 67t
Informal/formal continuum (of identity construction), 98
Intermarriage, 8–9, 11, 42, 173
Ivan (interview subject), 80, 142

Jack (interview subject), 156–157, 158
Jackson, Jesse, 125, 135n63, 153–154
Jamaica, 10–11, 23–56
  Chinese immigrants in, 8, 25t, 29, 33, 42
  comparision of race in United States and, 40–43, 51n54

cultural pluralism in, 29–31, 44
downplaying race (ideology), 37–39, 54n69; (demographics), 35–36
explaining change in, 29–35
income distribution in, 34, 35t
independence achieved by, 33
national motto of, 37
race relations in (classic model), 27–29
racial and ethnic composition of population, 25t
racial consciousness in, 35–39
Jamaica Labour Party (JLP), 33, 34, 49–50n43
Jamaican immigrants, 2, 12, 63, 93–94
avoidance of white neighborhoods by, 107
becoming "black" after migrating, 24–26, 93
citizenship and, 169–171
in Costa Rica, 60–61
dating and marriage to African-American women, 146t
drug trade and, 99
economic issues and, 65
employment discrimination and, 76–77, 80–82, 96, 104–105, 108, 117–120
generational differences, 110, 142, 162–163n30
occupational distrubition in female, 68–69t
occupational distrubition in male, 70t
percentage distribution of workers per family, 71t
police and, 109–111
racial consciousness and, 113, 114
skin color and, 24
social distancing and, 141–142
socioeconomic characteristics of, 67t
by year, 64t
Jamaica Progressive League, 181n30
James (interview subject), 95, 102
Jaynes, Gerald, 121
Jenkins, Richard, 97–98
Jerry (interview subject), 115–117, 124
Jews, 28–29, 32, 42, 131n33
Jim Crow system, 4, 41, 99–100
Joel (interview subject), 95, 102
Joey Breaker (film), 1

Johnson, James Weldon, 74, 84n21
Johnson, Violet, 65, 73
Jonathan (interview subject), 76–77

Kalmijn, Mattjis, 78
Kasinitz, Philip, 3, 62, 91, 138, 153
Kerner Commission, 124
Kessner, Thomas, 141
King, Coretta Scott, 125
King, Martin Luther, Jr., 23
Kingston, Jamaica, 28, 41
Kinship, 7
Koch, Ed, 153
Ku Klux Klan, 41
Kuper, Adam, 27, 29, 31–32, 34, 38, 48n39, 65
Kurlansky, Mark, 23

Labeling, 7
Labor Day parade, 3, 11, 15n9
Labor force participation, 67t, 75, 78; *see also* Employment discrimination; Occupational distribution
Labor unions, 49n43, 50n43
Latin America, 2
Law (and upward mobility in Jamaica), 65
Law and order orientation, 38, 98, 109, 114; *see also* Conservatism; Police
Leon (interview subject), 107–108, 147, 149
Leroy (interview subject), 146–147
Lewis, Gordon, 10, 93, 99
Lieberson, Stanley, 138
Live-in domestic work, 71–72, 86n36
Living with Racism (Feagin and Sikes), 98
Locke, Hubert, 125
Lopez, David, 11
Los Angeles, CA, 165
Lowenthal, David, 30

McCarran-Walter Act, 62, 84n17
Majority groups, 52–53n61
Majority minority cities, 165
Malveaux, Julianne, 129n19
Manley, Michael, 33, 39, 50n43, 131n34
Manley, Norman, 49n43

Mark (interview subject), 100–101
Marked for Death (film), 1, 15n4, 99
Marriage
   to African Americans, 116, 146–147,
     169
   inter, 8–9, 11, 42, 173
Married to the Mob (film), 1
Maryland, 106
Massachusetts, 63
Masson, C. N., 7
Mean income, 78
Media, 99, 152–153
Median family income, 4, 67t, 79, 124
Medicine (and upward mobility in
     Jamaica), 65
Melting pot concept, 6
Men, occupational distribution in, 70t,
     72
Merit, x, 5, 9, 13, 38, 104–105, 114,
     117; *see also* Achievement
Mexico, 60
Miami, FL, 63, 106, 145, 165
Mid-Atlantic states, 63
Middle class, 32, 33, 65–66
Million-Man March, 135n66
Mills, D. O., 86n33
Minority groups, 52–53n61
Mitchell (interview subject), 114–115,
     171
Mixed-race category, 25t, 166–167
Model, Suzanne, 78
Modern Problems (film), 1
Montserrat, 64t
Moses, Knolly, 72
Moynihan, Daniel P., 4, 65, 73, 74
Mufuka, Nyamayaro, 23
Multiple job-holding, 71–72

Nagel, Joane, 7
Nationalism, 137
National Origins system, 62
National Worker's Union, 50n43
Nation of Islam, 124–126
Native Americans, 7, 42, 166t, 173
Naturalization
   rate among West Indian Immigrants,
     170
   recent erosion of resistance,
     171–172, 179n14, 15
   traditional resistance to, 170–171

Negro Immigrant, The (Reid), 3–4, 139
Neil (interview subject), 104, 115,
     154, 171
Nelson (interview subject), 109–110,
     151–152, 156
Nelson, Jill, 124
Neo-Nazi organizations, 41
Nettleford, Rex, 34
Nevis, 60
New England, 63
New Jersey, 63
New York City, 2–3, 10, 63, 107, 145,
     155, 165, 167, 169
   economy of, 66
   interviews in, 13–14
   labor force participation in, 75
   percentage foreign born in, 15n8
   percentage West Indians in, 2, 12,
     15n8
   tradition of immigration in, 61
New York Newsday, 75
New York Times, 75
Nonracialism, ideology of, 37–39
North Bronx, NY, 3
Northern African Americans, 144–145,
     146
Nugent, Maria, 36
Nursing, 66, 68t, 79, 89n69

Occupational distribution, 4; *see also*
     Employment discrimination;
     Labor force participation
   in men, 70t, 72
   in women, 68–69t, 71–72, 79,
     87n42
Oil fields, 61
One-drop rule, 19n33, 138; *see also*
     Hypodescent
Oppositional identity, 19n40
Oreos, 150
Osofsky, Gilbert, 65, 140
Other category (in the classification of
     race), 25t, 172, 173

Palmer, Ransford, 72, 79
Panama, 10, 60, 71
Panama Canal, 60, 61
Panama Canal invasion, 154
Panethnicity, 11, 151, 152–153, 156,
     169
Passive racism, 96, 97

Passive response, 97
Paternalism, 155, 156; *see also* Role
    modeling
Patterson, Orlando, 8, 42
People's National Party (PNP), 33, 34,
    49–50n43, 52n57, 115, 181n30
People's Political Party, 39
Personal Responsibility and Work
    Opportunity Reconciliation Act
    (Welfare Act), 171, 172
Pete (interview subject), 99–100
Pettigrew, Thomas, 120–121
Philadelphia, PA, 63
Piazza, Thomas, 123–124
Plantation system, 27, 32, 36
*Plural Society in the British West Indies,
    The* (Smith), 29
Police, 4, 123
    coping strategies and, 94–95, 97
    pragmatic approach to, 109–112
Politics, 152–155, 181n30
    in Jamaica, 33, 34, 39, 44–45,
        49–50n43
    panethnicity and, 152–153
Post, Ken, 54n69, 140
Poverty; *see also* Income
    in British West Indian and Asian
        immigrants, 67t
    in Jamaica, 37, 38, 39
Powell, Colin, 75, 125, 153, 154–155
Pragmatism, 96t, 97, 109–112
Predator II (film), 1, 99
Primordialist theory, 6–7, 18n26
Public places (discrimination in), 41,
    94–98, 106–107, 128n13,
    128n18, n19, 123, 126, 148,
    168–169; *see also* Racial
    discrimination
Puerto Ricans, 72, 142, 172–173
Puerto Rico, 10, 60
Pullman Coach Company, 99

Queens, NY, 3, 75
Quotas (immigration), 62

Race
    defined, 16n13
    in Jamaica, 23–57
    racial consciousness, 97
    in Jamaica, 35–39
    religion and ideology in, 114

in the United States, 97, 112–120,
    126
Racial discrimination, 92
    coping strategies and. *See* Coping
        strategies
    economics of, 76, 80, 81
    employment, 104–106, 148–149,
        161n13
    in Jamaica, 41–42, 43
    perceptions of, 122
    residential, 4, 132–134n48, 168
    social class and, 6, 43, 76–77, 92,
        120–126, 160–161n12
Racial pride, 9, 43, 139, 154, 159
Railways, 60–61
Ralph (interview subject), 95, 106
Ransford, Edward, 128n13
Raphael, Lennox, 77, 91
Rap music, 156
Rastafarianism, 9, 32, 39, 57n101,
    54n69, 131n34, 156; *see also,
    Adventures of Buckaroo Banzai*
Reagan administration, 10
Reggae music, 45, 155–156
Reid, Ira De A., 3–4, 63, 91, 92–93,
    99, 139
Religion, 114
Republican Party, 153, 155
Residential discrimination, 4,
    132–134n48, 168
Resignation, 96t, 97, 106–109
Resurgent ethnic groups, 7–8
Reunification of families, 62, 172
Richardson, Mary, 43, 57n101
Richmond, VA, 63, 106, 145
Roberts, G. W., 61, 86n33
Roberts, Sam, 75
Roberts, Steven, 75
Rodriquez, Clara E., 172
Role modeling, 4, 103, 104, 155–158
Ron (interview subject), 175–176
Rumbaut, 57n102
Rupert (interview subject), 111, 147

St. Albans, NY, 3
St. Croix, 60
St. Kitts, 60, 64t
St. Lucia, 60, 64t
St. Vincent, 64t
Salience of race, 92–96

San Francisco, CA, 165
Santo Domingo, 10
Scar of Race, The (Piazza and
    Sniderman), 123
Schiller, Nina, 177
Seasonal migration, 60
Second generation, 173–177, 178
Secret Service agents (Denny's
    incident), 121
Segal, Ronald, 23, 29
Self-employment, 4, 33, 65, 66, 67t, 105
Self-help, 122
Separatism, 134–135n61, 139; *see also*
    Farrakhan, Louis
Sequential migration, 72
Service sector, 72
Sigelman, Lee, 122, 123, 125
Sikes, Melvin P., 96, 98, 123, 124,
    128n13
Silver Spring, MD, 106
Simon (interview subject), 146
Simpson, O. J., 124
Single-parent families, 175; *see also*
    Female-headed families
Skin color
    in Jamaica, 26, 27–28, 32, 34,
        49n39
    as question for immigrants, 24
    social class and, 26, 32
    in the United States, 93
Slavery, 73
    in the Caribbean, 60
    in Jamaica, 28, 30, 32, 36, 37, 40,
        41, 43–44, 46–47n18, 55n84
    in the United States, 40
Smith, M. G., 29, 30–31, 65
Sniderman, Paul M., 123–124
Snipp, C. Matthew, 7
Social categorization, 98
Social class, 120–121, 160–161n12; *see*
    also Socioeconomic status
    in Jamaica, 26, 31–32, 34
    interaction with race, 120–125
Social construction of ethnic identity,
    7, 9–12, 97–98, 148, 168
Social distancing, 110, 139–147
    identification and, 172–173, 178
    role modeling and, 156
Socialism, 39, 49n43
Socioeconomic status, 67t, 120–121,
    122t; *see also* Social class

South America, 1, 10
Southern exceptionalism, 144–147
Southern League, 41
Sowell, Thomas, 4, 73, 74–75
Sponsorship, 71
Stafford, Susan Buchannan, 12
Stan (interview subject), 111
Standard English, 38, 157,
    162–163n30, 175
Stanley (interview subject), 117–120
Steinberg, Stephen, 77
Stereotypes, 91, 138–139, 168, 174,
    177–178; *see also* Social
    distancing
    of African Americans, 139–147
    in educational system, 149
    of West Indians, 14n3, 15n4, 63–65,
        73–74, 84n19, 99, 130n24, n25
Stinchcombe, Arthur, 47n18
Stone, Carl, 27, 29, 32–35, 39, 48n32,
    49n40, 99, 145–146
Sugar cane industry, 27
Suicide, 72
Suriname, 10
Sutton, Constance, 177
Syrians, 29, 32, 42

Taiwanese immigrants, 63, 66, 67t
Teaching (and upward mobility in
    Jamaica), 65
Thelma and Louise (film), 1
Thernstrom, Abigail, 124
Third generation, 177, 178
Thomas, Clarence, 125
Thomas-Hope, Elizabeth, 60, 61
Thornton (interview subject), 148
Tobago, 2
Tommy (interview subject), 157–158
Trading Places (film), 1
Tradition of immigration, 59–63
Transnational identity, 87n37, 177,
    180n29–30
Traub, James, 75, 141
Trinidad, 3, 10–11, 35t, 60
Trinidadian immigrants, 2, 12
    economics and, 65, 66
    percentage distribution of workers
        per family, 71t
    socioeconomic characteristics of, 67t
    by year, 64t

United Kingdom, 35t, 61, 63; *see also* British

United States, 91–135
  apprehending the salience of race in, 92–96
  comparision of race in Jamaica and, 40–43, 51n54
  generalizing the West Indian experience in, 120–126
  income distribution in, 35t
  racial consciousness in, 112–120, 126
  racial encounters and coping strategies in, 96–112

Unskilled workers, 3–4

Upward mobility, 4, 5, 6, 65, 92, 120
  in Jamaica, 26, 28, 29, 33, 34, 38–39, 43, 44
  racial consciousness and, 43, 113

U.S. News and World Report, 75

van den Berghe, Pierre, 7

Venezuela, 61

Verkuyten, M., 7

Waldinger, Roger, 66, 72, 79, 80, 155

Washington, D. C., 63, 165

Waters, Mary, 8, 91, 138, 141, 173–174, 175, 176, 177, 180n20

Watkins-Owen, Irma, 65

Wausau, WI, 165

Welch, Susan, 122, 123, 125

Welfare, 92, 127–128n4, 142, 153

Welfare Act (Personal Responsibility and Work Opportunity Reconciliation Act), 171, 172

West Indian identity, 9, 168–172, 173, 174, 175, 177, 178

West Indians
  distancing from African Americans, 139–147, 159, 168, 172–176
  ethnic identity formation in the U.S., 9–12

  formation of panblack identity, 139, 147–155, 159–160, 168–169, 172–174

"West Indians and Afro-Americans" (Raphael), 77

West Indies
  Anglophone, 10–12, 78
  defined, 10

Whiteness, 28, 32, 42–43, 48–49n39

Whites
  avoiding neighborhoods of, 107–108
  decline in population, 165
  definitions of, 8, 138
  educational system and, 149–151
  ethnic identity and, 6, 8–9
  identification as, 172
  in Jamaica, 25t, 27, 28, 30, 32, 36, 41–43
  occupational distribution in, 79
  population projections for, 166t
  refusal to do business with blacks, 80
  socioeconomic characteristics of, 67t, 122t

Whore (film), 1

Williams, Lena, 129n19

Williams, Robin, 121

Wisconsin, 165

Women
  economic issues and, 78
  as heads of families, 74
  independence of, 145–146
  Jamaican, 145–147
  occupational distribution in, 68–69t, 71–72, 79, 87n42
  rate of intermarriage in, 173
  southern, 145–147

World War II, 61

Yankelovich Partners survey, 122–123, 125

"You Can Get It If You Really Want It" (Traub), 75

Young, Andrew, 125, 135n63